For Marigan Robertson
Best Wishes from
all three authors
Ernest Wilson
6/7/90

# ARCHITECTURE

# ARCHITECTURE
# Fundamental Issues

Forrest Wilson
with
Ron Keenberg
and
William Loerke

VNR VAN NOSTRAND REINHOLD
New York

Printed in the United States of America
Design by East End Graphic Arts
Drawings by Forrest Wilson

Van Nostrand Reinhold
115 Fifth Avenue
New York, New York 10003

Van Nostrand Reinhold International Company Limited
11 New Fetter Lane
London EC4P 4EE, England

Van Nostrand Reinhold
480 La Trobe Street
Melbourne, Victoria 3000, Australia

Nelson Canada
1120 Birchmount Road
Scarborough, Ontario M1K 5G4, Canada

16   15   14   13   12   11   10   9   8   7   6   5   4   3   2   1

**Library of Congress Cataloging-in-Publication Data**

Wilson, Forrest, 1918-
    Architecture : fundamental issues / Forrest Wilson with
Ron Keenberg and William Loerke.
        p.   cm.
    ISBN 0-442-23948-3
    1. Architectural practice—Canada—Case studies.
2. Architectural services marketing—Canada—Case
    studies.   I. Keenberg, Ron.   II. Loerke, William C.   III. Title.
    NA1996.W517      1990
    720′.68—dc20                                    89-29395
                                                    CIP

# Contents

# Preface

# Either/or—No Both/and—Yes

For the past two centuries agricultural and manufacturing technologies drove economic growth in the affluent nations of the world. Today large, capital intensive service industries take their place.

Service industries account for 71 percent or $2,996 billion of the U.S. gross national product and 75 percent of all jobs, reported the *Scientific American* in December 1987. The profession and practice of architecture is vitally affected by this transformation.

"Anything sold in trade that could not be dropped on your foot," is defined as *service* says the London *Economist*. This includes all economic activities whose outcome is not a physical product, is consumed at the time produced, or provides added value, convenience, amusement, comfort, or health.

Electronic communication stimulates innovation in retailing, wholesale trade, engineering and architectural design, finance, communication, and entertainment. In affluent societies a nation's wealth is measured as often by the level of its services, arts, education, health, and social services as by its abundance of physical goods.

Investment in complex technology for "information workers" has risen rapidly since the mid-1960s. It is now greater, worker for worker, than the investment in basic industrial production. Large service companies buy technology and play a crucial role in the creation and diffusion of new technologies. For example, Citicorp helped develop and introduce the first automated teller machines. Federal Express Corporation researched and financed major innovation in package-sorting, handling, and tracking equipment.

These technologies precipitate major changes in services and employment. They also demand architectural accommodation. Building form is altered and new building types emerge. The automated drive through teller station is pure service without architectural amenities. It takes the place of banks housed in imitations of classic Greek Temples. Gasoline service station patrons now pump their own gas. The attendant consults a remote digital readout and sells junk food from the booth between sales. The design of service stations has changed and is not much different in form or function than the drive through bank teller station.

Industrial and commercial firms precisely schedule and immediately tranship products to eliminate inventories. Electronic processing makes warehouses unnecessary.

Computer and communications technologies rapidly integrate the world's financial centers into a single marketplace. The flow of money from country to country is now independent of the movement of goods or trade.

World trade in goods and services amounts to between $3 and $4 trillion per year. Financial transactions handled by a single intermediary, the Clearing House for International Payments, totaled $105

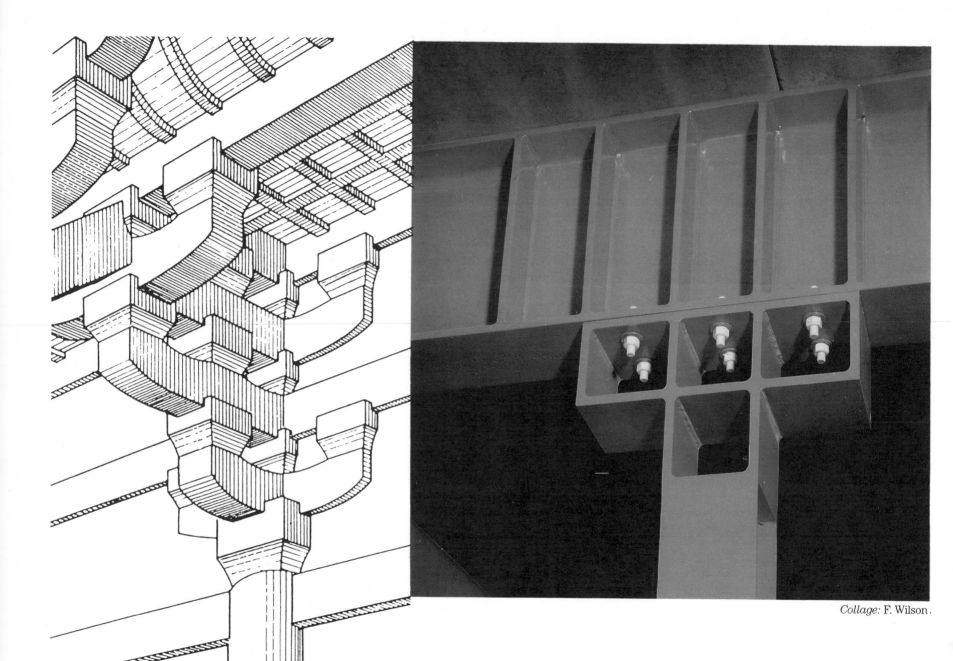

*Collage:* F. Wilson.

trillion in 1986, and transactions in early 1987 proceeded at a rate of $200 trillion per year (*Scientific American*, 12/87). These vast sums flow toward the highest available real interest rates, safer stable economic or political conditions. The finances necessary to build great buildings is no longer connected to an accumulation of goods or to trade success. Architects have new clients. It was predicted not long ago that the world's tallest building would be built in Hong Kong, which has no major heavy manufacturing facilities or agriculture.

As variations in the cost of capital among nations decrease, countries with higher labor and materials costs are undersold by foreign manufacturers. Building materials are international commodities, as are architectural services. Architects and building organizations compete in foreign countries to sell their services and fight off foreign competition in their own country.

All of this has taken place in a remarkably short period of time. The practice of architecture and the demands placed upon buildings have changed dramatically. What building ideas are appropriate for this new condition?

Architecture is not excepted from the general upheaval. The change appears to be as fundamental as the conversion of Romanesque building to Gothic by the abbé Suger in the 11th Century, Gothic to Renaissance building that Alberti attempted to design in the 15th Century, or the social changes designed by modern architects at the beginning of this century. Architecture must once again find fitting ideas to express aesthetic, social, economic and technical change.

This book is an examination of an architectural response to today's conditions and what can be learned from architectural solutions of the past. A decade of work by a Canadian architectural firm is used as a case study. It typifies a comprehensive search for a synthesis of human clarity, warmth and understanding in aesthetic, economic, technical solutions amid the rapid, often chaotic, transitions of the past 20 years.

*Collage:* F. Wilson.

*Collage:* F. Wilson.

The Canadian experience is close enough to that in the U.S. to understand but far enough removed for perspective. As an added bonus, the Canadian climate is extremely demanding and building problems are magnified. U.S. and Canadian architects alike can learn a great deal from Canadian research and building.

This is not a book about architectural heroes or architectural styles. Architectural design is examined as a synthesis. Aesthetic preference is but one of its elements. Technical and economic decisions are considered important generators of architectural ideas. Aesthetic decisions are tempered by client demands, and disciplined by material, technical, and economic restraints as well as human warmth, clarity, and understanding. Architecture is defined in this book as the reward of skillfully synthesizing building and human problems.

This book is a pioneering effort to "tie it all together." We have mixed past and present, design, economics, and technology. Our reason for doing this is the belief that ideas today can no longer be presented in neat packages of *either/or* alternatives but instead must synthesize all *both/and.*

# Chapter 1

# The Origins of Design

The permanent element in humankind, said Herbert Read, is aesthetic sensibility. It is the interpretation humans give to the forms of art that is variable. Forms corresponding to immediate feelings are said to be expressive but the same forms may have different expressive value for different people at different times. Therefore, Read concluded, "I do not think we can say that Primitive art is a lower form of beauty than Greek art; although it may represent a lower kind of civilization, it may express an equal or even a finer instinct for form..."[1]

The architecture of any age is an expression of people doing the best they can to solve the problems of their time with the tools they have at hand.

The formal expressions of today's architecture have different expressive value than those of Greek art or even Modern art at the beginning of this century. They are not necessarily a lower form of art even though they have a strangeness about them. They may, in fact as Read says, express an equal or even a finer instinct for form.

## BASICS

We avoid the discussion of styles, movements, "isms," fads. The issue of style in architecture is postponed to a later chapter. We compare selected contemporary works with masterpieces of past architecture and avoid trivia to address contemporary architecture on a fundamental level.

Building demands skill and creative imagination. Sometimes the result is memorable architecture, sometimes not. Our interest is in the modern application of the principles of building from which architecture may emerge. All great architecture in all cultures and at all times has followed basic patterns, although the patterns may be followed and great architecture not result.

The modern buildings we have selected for examples are constructed of today's industrial materials, using contemporary manufacturing and labor skills and are designed for today's building market. The work of a single firm is used to demonstrate our thesis and is compared to past and present buildings. Many of the projects were published and some given design awards. This is not of major interest in our discussions for, as George Nelson once wisely remarked, a bad design might have done as well.

## History

Technology and design have always been as intimately related as the eye and hand of a skilled worker. In some architectures we are more immediately aware of technological skills; in others, of striking and creative design. But the relation is so entwined in all architectures that close examination leaves us doubtful the two can be separated.

Egyptian architecture exhibits granite blocks up to 100 tons in weight. We admire the builder's skill in extracting them from the quarry, transporting them to the site, and maneuvering them into position with virtually no tolerance for error. We also admire the severe abstraction of their forms and envy the confidence with which they established the eternal permanence of their structures.

1

Opaque and transparent control grid panels on the facade of the Provincial Center, Flin Flon Manitoba. *Photo:* F. Wilson.

Control Grid

Arch at Uxmal, Yucatan. *Photo:* F. Wilson.

Erechtheion: North porch, Northeast corner, detail of columns capital and Ionic entablature. *Photo:* National Gallery, Washington, D.C.

Northwest Recreational Center, Regina, Canada.
*Photo:* IKOY.

U.S. Pavilion at Expo 67, Montreal, Canada; Buckminster
Fuller, Designer. *Photo:* Expo 67 Corp.

Egyptian technology and design stems immediately and directly from their view of the cosmos, of the gods and the Pharaoh. It would probably make no sense to an Egyptian master builder to try to distinguish between technology and design. This is a modern distinction not applicable to ancient Egypt.

The more graceful and subtle forms of Greek architecture quickly impress us with their gift for sophisticated design, both in the overall proportioning of a structure and in the articulation of its critical parts. The Greek sense of form in architecture, the servant of geometry, demanded a perfected, finished object, "unmarred" by personal idiosyncrasies. The process, or technology, which led to this goal, was naturally obliterated in the act of achieving it.

Yet skill and esthetic aim worked hand and glove, and the fact that they rarely wrote about technological matters (except for treatises on siege machines) should not blind us to their technological achievements, obscured though they may be behind the finished forms of their architecture.

The Roman revolution in architecture, certainly one of the most significant and pregnant in the history of the craft, radically changed the footprint of structures and inverting the ratio of building mass to building void that had dominated architectural design until their time. The potential diagonal thrusts of vaults and domes were brought vertical in a monolithic mass of brick and pozzolan cement (not matched in strength until hydraulic cements of the last century) articulated into massive piers and walls and heavily packed above the spring points of the vaults.

Both in their ruins (Roman Imperial Baths and in the one completely preserved structure, the Pantheon), Roman technology is immediately impres-

Nuclear Reactor, Rehovot, Israel; Philip Johnson, Architect.

sive. Vaults spanning 80 feet were stabilized at least at the height of their radius. The dome of the Pantheon spans 142 feet 6 inches and holds steady after 1860 years despite frequent heavy flooding and severe earthquakes.

To appreciate Roman design, we must people their baths with 2,000 bathers, freely moving under lofty vaults through a clear ground plan, unimpeded by substantial walls and piers. Technology and design are one in the service of a rising population, an imperial budget, and an emperor's recognition of what made a city. The great triple bay central room of these baths survived as an isolated, public structure at Rome in the Basilica of Maxentius. A third portion survived to inspire the nave of St. Peter's and numerous other progeny. The most recent was Pennsylvania Station in New York City, torn down in 1965.

Technology and design achieved perhaps the perfect marriage in the Gothic cathedral. Master builders in the 12th and 13th Centuries created a high rise structure carried by uniform piers set on the corners of a bay system, which ignored the distinction between interior and exterior. In short, they destroyed the wall. They linked piers with pointed arches, slender ribs, and flying buttresses angled to catch the principal vectors of force generated by stone vaults and a steeply pitched, lead-covered roof.

Like the Roman achievement, the Gothic creation of dramatic spaces was the product of skill, creative geometry, and a communal desire to create a hall fit for an otherworldly king. Every aspect of the building was infused with its ultimate esthetic aim—to deny gravity.

*(Top, left)* Chefren Temple, Pillared Hall, 4th Dynasty, 2400 B.C. *Photo:* National Gallery.

*(Left)* Greek Architecture. *Photo:* Loerke.

Notre Dame of Paris, choir and apse, 1160–1200 A.D. *Photo:* National Gallery.

Notre Dame of Paris, North flank choir, double flyers
(buttresses spanning 2 aisles) late 13th Century. *Photo:*
National Gallery.

Notre Dame of Paris, apse exterior, 1160 to late 13th
Century. *Photo:* National Gallery.

## Modern Problems

Antonio Gaudi's great church of the Sagrada Familia, begun in 1884 in Barcelona, remains incomplete. It marks the end of technical intuition. Its place is now taken by complex theories of structural mechanics. The invention of methods to calculate and verify conditions of equilibrium extended the limits of design and technology for a century until intuition and complex theories of structural mechanics were bypassed by massive electronic number crunching.

The modern problem is to find in this new wealth of technical ability that which is linked to the technology and beauty of past architecture and how it can assist architects today.

Investigations now explore new forms and new materials used in response to new functional demands. Longer spans and taller buildings are easily achieved as mechanical and electrical systems create a new vocabulary of architectural expression in response to the new problems of a radically reorganizing society.

Architectural forms that respond to this challenge today are crude beginnings. They are like the timber post that grew to become the Doric column, the simple arch that became the great Roman vault and the crude pier that grew to the flying buttress. As they develop they will create an architectural language as aesthetically satisfying as the classic language based on entablature, capital, column, flying buttress, and pointed arch.

"Designers of the past were forced to rely on experience, close constant observation and proportioned by feeling," Pier Luigi Nervi said in his Harvard lectures in 1961–62 and "their work enriched structure with human warmth, clarity and understanding." The subject of this book is the develop-

Computer Center, University of Waterloo, Ontario, Canada. *Photo:* IKOY.

ment and blending of technology and beauty combined with human warmth, clarity, and understanding when structural intuition is simulated and hunches confirmed by software programs.

## REFERENCE

1. Read, Herbert, *The Meaning of Art,* p. 21. First published in 1931, reprinted by Pelican, Baltimore, 1949.

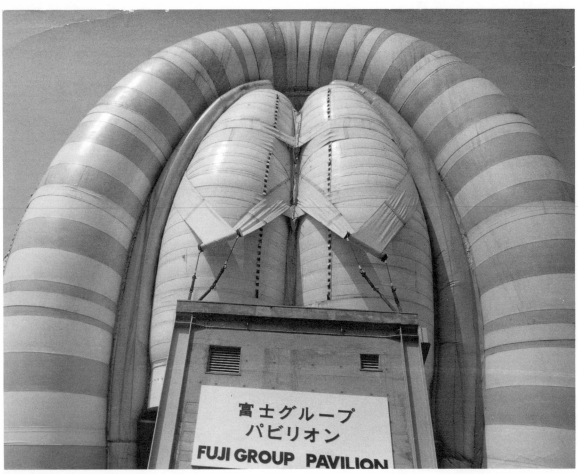

Fuji Group Pavilion, Expo 70, Osaka Japan. *Photo:* Expo 70.

# Chapter 2

# Terms

There are many interpretations of architecture. We therefore define our terms.

## A UTILITARIAN ART

Architecture, painting, and sculpture are called the "fine arts." They appeal to the eye as music does to the ear. But architecture is not judged by visual appeal alone. Buildings enclose space and are made of building materials. They are sited in the landscape and have mechanical, electrical, and communication systems. Buildings affect all of the human senses—sound, smell, touch, taste and vision.

Architects, like sculptors and painters, work with form, mass, and color, but they solve practical problems. Architecture is a functional art and no matter how beautiful the building may be, if the people inside are miserable, the building is a failure. Therefore, a building's utility forms part of our judgment of it.

*Photo:* F. Wilson.

*Photo:* F. Wilson.

## ARCHITECTURAL INSTINCT

Animals walk, jump, and swim shortly after birth. Children learn to do this slowly and with considerable effort. They taste, touch, feel, toddle over, and crawl under. Children are nature's most sophisticated universal testing machines.

Later as adults our response to the world is based on this deeply rooted knowledge gathered from childhood experiments. We know more than we can say about materials and structure, for a great deal of our knowledge of it was gathered before we could talk.

## BEAUTY IN ECONOMY

The relationship between economic efficiency and functional structure, proper proportions, spatial relationships, ornamental richness, and convivial materials are naturally pleasing.

## BUILDING CORRECTLY

The great engineer Pier Luigi Nervi claimed there were architectural constants and these can be identified. Structures, large or small, must be stable and lasting, and must satisfy the needs for which they were built. They should achieve maximum results with minimum means.

These conditions: stability, durability, function, and maximum results with minimum means are constants of all buildings from a mud hut in the Hindu Kush to Chartres cathedral. They can be summed in the phrase Nervi used, "building correctly."

Each technical solution employed in building correctly prompts a perceptual response and therefore adds or detracts from the beauty of the completed work.

## BUILDING EXPRESSION

Building stability can be achieved by exposed or hidden structures, said Nervi, and each approach stimulates a different perceptual reaction that influences the building's "expression."

Even though walls and roof are securely fastened, if they appear to be verging on collapse it is difficult to feel comfortable. Stability is essential for a feeling of well-being. Instability stimulates an anti-architectural sensation. Missing key stones, very thin beams or columns are anti-architectural expressions.

Selection of materials, their finishes and textures stimulate emotional response. There is a different feeling in the presence of stone, brick, wood, or paper walls (Japanese). The sensations of structure, materials, proportion, and craft skill are fused and can not be separated.

## CLARITY

The brush stroke of the painter and the chisel cuts of the sculpture are personal expressions. In contrast, the architect designs and others build. Builders contribute their abilities to the whole design. Connection of wood, stone, metal and their finishes are the architect's personal expressions like

the painter's brush stroke and the sculptor's chisel marks.

The underlying principle of building is organization, said Sean Rasmussen. But this does not say that architecture, because of its discipline lacks emotional sensitivity. The opposite is true. It can communicate intimate personal messages and because of its order and organization has universal appeal and great clarity.

Romanesque column, Catholic University, Washington, D.C. *Photo:* F. Wilson.

*(Left)* Maillart Bridge, Switzerland. *Photo:* John Pile.

# TECHNOLOGY AS FORM GIVER

"There is a connection between building technology and architectural expression," said Nervi and it is demonstrated in the development and refinement of fundamental building elements. What is now the stone column began as a simple unadorned timber. It describes its juncture with the architrave by an ornamental capital, expresses its load with a slight swelling of its shaft, and contains this load at bottom with a base of horizontal torus mouldings whose convex-concave profile effectively tie the base with a "rope." These cast deep shadows and transmit the full load lightly to the podium or stylobate.

The decorative cornice and window pediment began humbly, like the stone column. They were simply structural methods used to protect facades from water. Architraves, arches, corbels above openings, stone without acute angles and corners protected with bosses, all of the characteristic details of past architecture were born of technical necessity.

Practical solutions evolved aesthetic expressions and eventually appear on buildings as decorative ends in themselves. The birth, development and refinement of utilitarian architectural elements and their growth to purely decorative forms is an eloquent statement of the form giving power of technology.

Column capital, Computer Center, University of Waterloo. *Photo:* IKOY.

*(Left)* Student project, Pratt Institute. *Anonymous Photo,* 1963.

# SENSUAL ORDER

To understand a building one must discover how it was designed, for what purpose, and how it reflects the sensations of a specific time. Building space must be experienced, textures and colors felt and seen, the path of light through it observed. The great difference acoustics makes must be sensed. Strangely enough, the way we hear a space is the way we "see" it.

The way a building presents its function and structure to an observer may be described in a summary way as its attitude. In this definition, the term *function* must be taken in its broadest, most comprehensive meaning that is not only its physical function as gymnasium, post office, law court, apartment building, office building, bridge, or the like, but also its "psychological" function. This includes human exercise, speedy communication, government (impersonal, majestic) private enclosure, cheerful work space, etc. The term *structure* includes the total structure in all its aspects, physical elements, and manner of assembly. When the designer brings the total structure into close harmony with the broadest definition of its function he or she has created a building every part of which contributes to the telling of its own story. The building strikes an attitude which any one can read.

Architecture brings utility and sensual order through the building's attitude to human surroundings. The preferences in utility and sensual order differ with each age but the underlying principles of building remain constant whether the building is a marble Parthenon, a stone palazzo, or welded steel auto diesel shop.

Proud fire hydrant, Honolulu, Hawaii, 1979. *Photo: F. Wilson.*

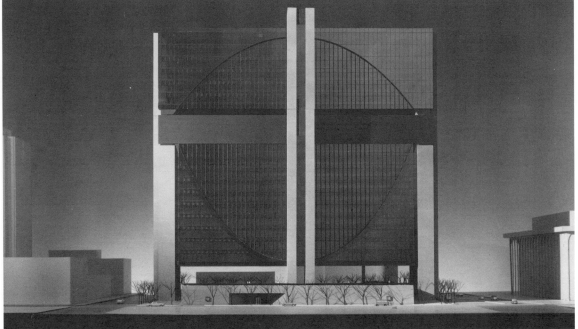

# TECHNOLOGY

There are two aspects of architecture:

- a structure obeying physical laws and

- a perceptual impression evoking subjective emotion.

Technology plays a more vital role in architecture than it does in the fine arts for it is dominated by laws independent of the designer's personality.

Architectural criticism is often limited to the critic's subjective emotions. Building schemes are praised for their beauty or condemned for lack of it even though they may be impossible to build. Such criticism may or may not be useful, but in either instance addresses only one aspect of architecture.

On the other hand, technically exact buildings may lack expression. All past buildings that are accepted as great and beautiful architecture today are also technically excellent. We must therefore conclude that, good technology and beauty are essential, but neither is enough, in itself, to assure good architecture.

*(Top left)* Model photo of Federal Reserve Bank, by Gunnar Birkerts.

*(Left)* Model photo with catenary arch and catenary cable.

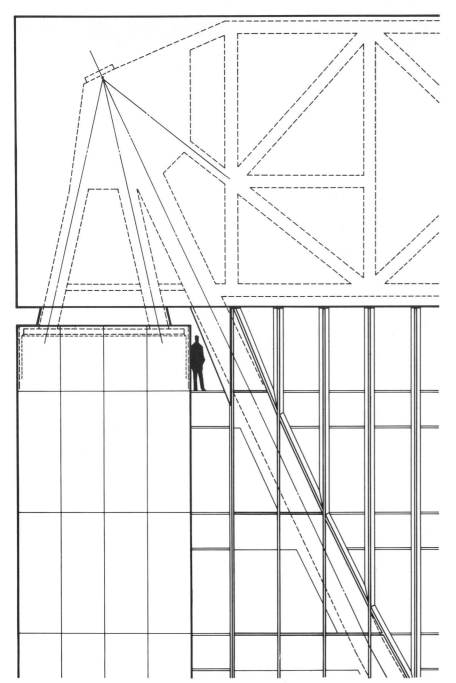

Red River Community College, Auto Diesel Repair
Shops, Winnipeg, Canada. *Photo:* IKOY.

(*Left*) Connection of catenary cable and truss of Federal
Reserve Bank by Gunnar Birkerts

Corbusier's Carpenter Center at Harvard University.

FBI Building, Washington, D.C. *Photo:* F. Wilson.

# Chapter 3

# Nine Buildings in Ten Years

## THE SHRINE
### The Origins of Design

### Vitruvius

Vitruvius a Roman architect wrote *The Ten Books of Architecture* about the time that Christ was born. They are the most familiar account we have of the art of building in the ancient world. Vitruvius began the first book as follows: "The men of old were born in woods, caves, and groves like wild beasts and lived on savage fare. The discovery of fire gave warmth, companionship, and speech." Humans were not obliged to walk with their faces to the ground, like bears, beavers and moose, he continued, and as a result became naturally gifted beyond other animals. "They used their hands and fingers to construct shelters of mud, twigs, stones, and caves in mountain sides."

"Since humans were imitative and teachable, they learned from each other. They are also naturally boastful so knowledge was quickly dispersed," which explains the beginnings of building science.

"As human building skill grew their brains were forced to keep pace. As building forced them to be smarter they moved to other arts and sciences, thus passing from barbarians to civilization, prompted by the builder's art."

Houses with foundations took the place of huts. They had walls of brick and stone and timber roofs with tiles. At this time, Vitruvius says, the rules of symmetry were defined and architecture was born.

To build in response to basic needs, adopting elemental materials into structural units, is to concentrate mind and hand, theory and skill to the solution of building problems. This conjunction of mind and hand lies at the origin not only of "primitive" building, but also of all good architecture.

Incidentally, we cannot say "he" when we talk of building and the foundations of civilization, for the great archaeologist Gordon Childe has offered convincing evidence that the first building designers were women.

## In the Beginning

In the beginning, shortly after people learned to walk on two feet and talk to and impress each other

and before they invented power saws, jackhammers, and all the machinery we now have to cut wood into boards and stone into blocks, builders believed that rocks and trees had souls.

Ancient builders worked building materials carefully. They begged the stone's forgiveness when they removed him from the ground and asked the tree's pardon for thinning her branches.

When builders built by hand corner stones were laid with ceremony, thresholds blessed, and the spirit of the building revered. Today trees and stones are curiosities walled into building atriums. Huge cranes lift entire building sections into place and concrete mixing trucks carry enough in one load to build foundations for twenty houses.

But it takes more than machines and materials to create architecture. No one can define exactly what that more is, except that architecture has a spirit that building may not.

Architecture combines external form and internal space, structure and material into one essence. The structure of the building can be calculated and the strength of the building materials tested, but the spirit of the building is sensed as the ancients sensed spirits in rocks and trees.

There is a building "attitude," given to it by its builders. The ability to create attitude does not come with an architectural diploma. Builders that never attended school at all may have it and those registered as architects all over the world may not. Once acquired it is not a permanent possession.

Architectural skill must be continually renewed. Every builder, learned or illiterate, intuitive or scientific, man or woman, from ancient times to our own must continually refine and nourish their sensibilities.

This is a brief description of a fishing camp, built by architects in the Canadian bush. They go to it to talk to trees, listen to rocks, and ponder the spirits of steel and concrete.

# The Shrine
## The Camp

The camp is 60 miles northeast of Flin Flon and Flin Flon is 700 miles north of Winnipeg. During the summer float planes land on the lake, and during the winter a trapper on a snowmobile may find it and stay overnight. Except for a few weeks between May and August when the architects fly in and out or when an occasional trapper happens by in the winter, the rocks, trees, moose, beaver, bear, pike, and pickerel go about their business undisturbed. The world is much the same as it was when the first people gathered around a fire and learned to talk to impress each other.

## The Cabin

The cabin is a plexiglass walled platform pegged to the igneous rock of the Canadian shield. The gabled north and south walls are solid. Both have narrow platform porches. The one at the entrance is for washing and looking at the lake. It has a rail to lean against, drink coffee, and study a strange rock on the opposite shore called the "great bird of the north." The south end platform is for casting, listening to loons and the northern silence, and looking at the lake.

Just inside the entrance door is a sink and pump that draws water through a long plastic pipe laid far out in the lake. This is where water for coffee, cooking, and dish washing comes from. A long table with ceramic tile top reaches from stove, sink, and pump and stops three feet short of a fire pit and smoke hood.

This is where the men settle, in a circle, early morning and late night, to talk. There are things that men talk about in firelight and that is what is done here as the art of talking and listening is remembered.

Late at night when stories have been told the men,

*Photo:* F. Wilson.

beer and whiskey drunk, cross over the log bridge to the bunkhouse and sleep in a row on the bunkhouse floor.

## Building the Cabin

The cabin was built in parts in Winnipeg and put together on the rock by the architects. It is finely engineered to be practically built. Roof trusses are nailed and glued rigid and firm. The columns are held taut by wires and turnbuckles at the ends, but there is a downward sag. Even stout steel eye bolts and braided steel cables can not restrain the movement of strong fir beams with a will to sag.

The size of each cabin piece was limited by the entrance doors and cabin size of an *Otter.* This is the largest float plane that flies into bush camps. The cabin was put together in four days by eight young

*Photo:* F. Wilson.

The sun's rays turn the cabin into a sweltering greenhouse for two or three hours each afternoon. It is cool in the early morning and late evening. That is what the fire is for. Woodsmen ritually broil their faces and freeze their backsides around camp fires as part of the mystique of the wild. This distinguishes the bush from the even temperatures of civilization, where controlled conditioning systems uniformly warm and cool backside and face in unison.

Bears have clawed the bunk house wall and parts of a moose jaw and skeleton are scattered on the cabin sill. They are from the skeleton of a young moose that fell into a narrow rock crevice and died there. The skeleton was left intact by the builders but visitors bring parts of it to the cabin and leave them there to contemplate them as Hamlet did the skull of Yorick.

## The Lesson

The bush, lake, rocks, scrub pine, white birch trunks, and two loons enter the house through the transparent walls and are reflected back. Bush camp and bush merge and image each other.

The bush is a wonderfully complex ordered chaos reflected in size and season. Size measures time. Trees grow larger and taller, die, fall, and rot. Trees have a hierarchy of size and difference. There is a trunk, large limbs, small limbs, twigs and leaves all arranged in an order. Leaves never become branches, nor branches limbs, nor limbs a trunk. There is an autonomy of forms on different levels that collected together become wholes.

Trunk to twig the tree is a movement system. The leaves take in sunlight and manufacture carbohydrates from carbon dioxide and water in the presence of chlorophyl which is transported downward through twig branch and trunk. The trunk sucks up water and the earths juices and distributes them upward through trunk, branch, and twig.

There are lessons in the lichen and how trees split

men who had drawn and built many huge buildings of concrete and steel but never built a cabin. Each had an assigned task. The ceramic tile was set by a man whose father was a tile setter. He asked him how to do it, was told, and did it.

The cabin is an "architectural statement" of sorts, and the bunkhouse on shore is "chainsaw gothic." It was built in a day and a half. An indian trapper named Moody built the bridge, two more trappers built the dock. There is an outhouse, with plexiglass sides and bear scratches on the door. It sits on the highest point of rock above the bunkhouse and was built in Winnipeg and shipped to the camp as a single unit.

Stove and refrigerator are powered by bottled gas. There are no electric lights. When the plane leaves there is no way or word out or in until it returns. Bathing is in the cold lake, or there is a simple black plastic bladder that can be filled with water and suspended in the sun and in the evening milked of lukewarm lake water for those brave and dirty enough to endure it.

*Photo:* F. Wilson.

the hard igneous rocks. Much can be learned by looking at the remarkable cantilevers of limbs and the exquisite pine needle to twig, twig to branch, branch to trunk. The folds of water grasses and stressed skin surfaces of mushroom fungus hold thousands of individual, unique lessons. The most important lesson builders can learn is that nature has no need to repeat itself. There is no Nature Graphic Standards.

The cabin is a place to remind builders who they are and what they do and the great importance of their craft. The cabin is a temporary infringement on the bush beyond. It is a place away from hockey games, and the terrible loneliness of crowds. It sits on the edge between lean and comfort.

Discomfort is natural. Comfort is paid for in effort. Warmth and security are man made. The building mediates between pain and security. It reminds those it protects that there is no assurance in the human contract that we will not be hungry or cold or fall prey to wolf or bear. The cabin says, I am a thin, man-made membrane between you and the great Canadian North. I am your life support system and if the builders have built with skill I may also be beautiful.

## Factual Information

*Construction time.* Sept. 19–23, 1975.

*Area.* 416 square feet.

*Cost.* $15,000 (U.S.), $36 a square foot. Most of the cost was in air transport of materials to the site. The structure was totally prefabricated; glued trusses of diagonally cut 4 × 8 plywood panels nailed to 2 × 2 frame. Sized to industrial sheet size, no waste.

*Structure.* Paired 2 × 8 columns, glued laminated truss roof, 2 × 8 joists floor, pinned to granite rock.

*Materials.* Walls, 4 × 8 plexiglas without frames; floor wood joist 3/4″ plywood sheet. Turnbuckles at end to stiffen wall structure, for the plexiglas has no rigidity.

*Mechanical.* Open fire pit, hand-operated pump, porch for pissing, coleman lanterns.

*Fitments.* Island counter, propane refrigerator, and range.

*Remarks.* All work performed by unskilled on-site labor consisting of 13 architects from the IKOY offices.

## IKOY OFFICES
## Building with Style

A building designed to meet the demands of a working architectural office expressing the design philosophy and method of building.

## An Ordering System

IKOY was formed in 1968. They described their philosophy in the Royal Architectural Institute of Canada 1986 Awards Program which awarded Governor General's Medals for Architecture to two of the firm's projects: "an architectural philosophy based in purpose, assemblage, transformation, economics and the intrinsic beauty of reality."

A building is a building—not a form, nor a function—but a purpose. Each building has a preceding functional program defining its purpose. That purpose will be modified before its completion and will continue to modify or even change during the next 100 to 500 years.

Therefore, performance is directly proportionate to the building's ability to change.

In order to deal with this complex problem through the action of building, a technique is used whereby the building is fragmented into six components of purpose:

1. Action syntactics
2. Structure
3. Mechanical
4. Electrical
5. Skin
6. Fitments (partitions and furnishings).

General and specific action syntactics, such as comprehension, enhanced amplification, transparency, assembly, and transformation and eco-

*Drawing:* F. Wilson .

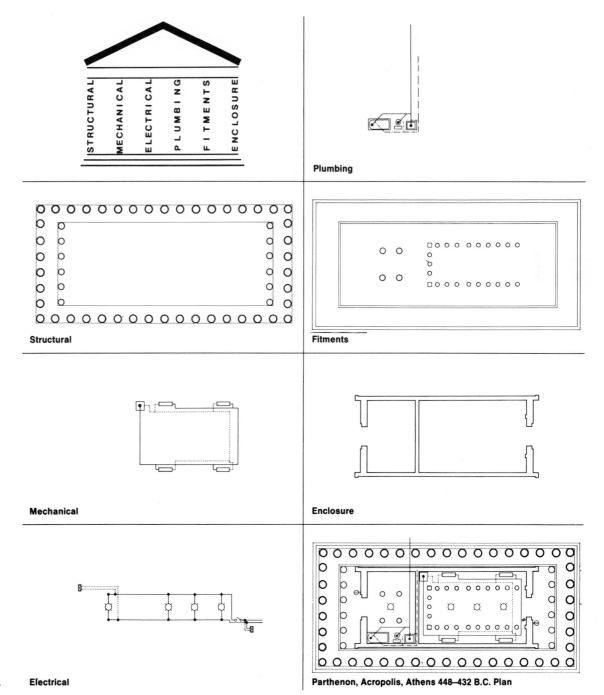

STRUCTURAL MECHANICAL ELECTRICAL PLUMBING FITMENTS ENCLOSURE

**Plumbing**

**Structural**

**Fitments**

**Mechanical**

**Enclosure**

**Electrical**

**Parthenon, Acropolis, Athens 448–432 B.C. Plan**

nomics are developed based on the functional program and the sites to guide the direction of development of the constructive components.

Each component is designed to express its purpose, visually telling its story and standing alone while interacting with the other components. It is the collective expression and synthesis of the singular components which generates the building's purpose and thus its form. All texture, scale, grain and space is generated by what is required without the use of decoration.

The same philosophy and techniques used for the Auto/Diesel Shop have been used for other competition winning buildings, Computer Research Centre, University of Waterloo; Recreation Center, Regina; Earth Sciences, University of Manitoba; and the courthouse Office Building in Flin Flon.

This idea for an architectural strategy or plan of action which they termed "action syntactics" was in its beginnings in 1978 when the firm designed its offices. It is not unlike the efforts of Vitruvius to find a strategy or an ordering system for making architectural decisions.

Western Greece, Olympia; Temple of Zeus, South flank.
*Photo:* Loerke.

## The Life Style

The working style of the office is that of a studio rather than a corporate office. The visitor enters a corporate office complex through a reception room. Behind the receptionist are the principals' offices and conference rooms. The great communal room in which architects and technicians toil to design buildings in corporate architectural offices is far to the rear behind the leading executive offices. It is reached down a long corridor, and the visitor has the impression that this remote space is secret, mysterious, and probably guarded by attack dogs.

Studios are the exact opposites of corporate offices. The visitor enters the working design space when they enter the building's entrance door. Clients step into the midst of the work being done. The office draftsmen and secretaries watch the partners working with the clients, the clients see their buildings designed.

Studios are cheaper to build than executive offices. The money saved here bought a 23-foot-high ceiling with a mezzanine. Meeting rooms for staff and partners are underneath the mezzanine. On top there are a steam room and locker room, showers, kitchen, billiard table, sit-down chairs, and a view looking over the river. Below the studio space, at ground level, there is a swimming pool reached by stairs down from the drafting room.

This was the tradeoff for soundproof partitions, heavy carpet, and expensive executive furniture. The amenities are not innocent gifts bestowed by a benign management. This is an arrangement that

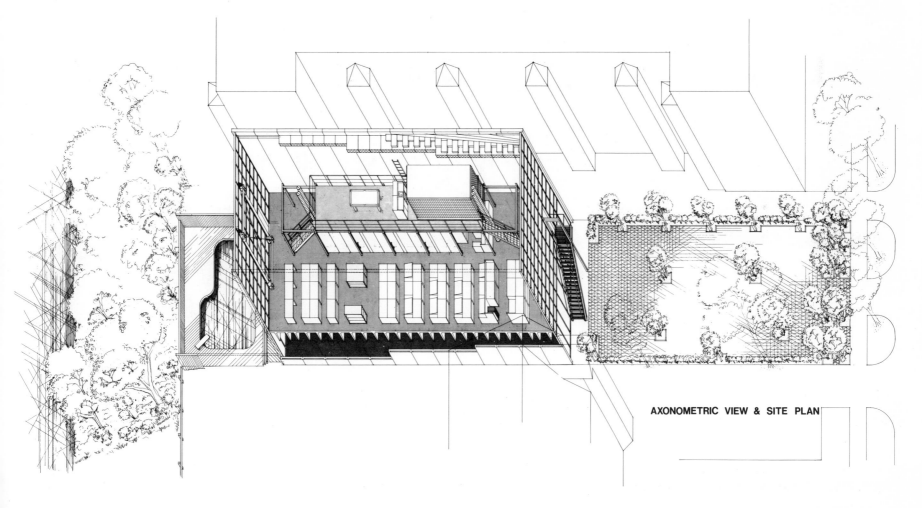

AXONOMETRIC VIEW & SITE PLAN

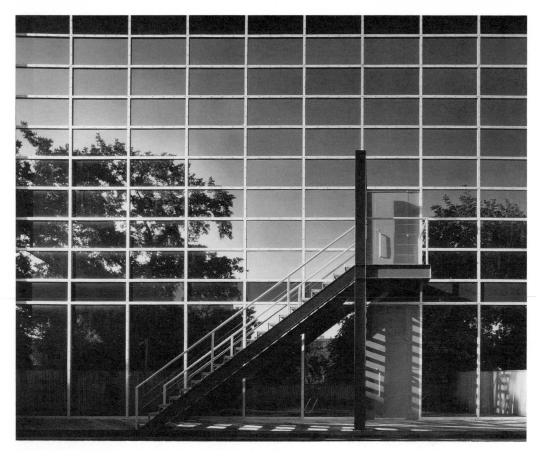

Front entrance, sitting and exercise. *Photo:* IKOY.

softens the reality that successful architects, from partners to draftsmen, work 60–80 hours a week. The building must be more than a building.

First the building must say *style*—life style. All architects work differently and all new members of the staff from secretary to designer must be trained. If a new member works for 3 or 4 years and resigns,

the cost of training a replacement is large. Pay is periodically increased but is never enough for wives, and husbands threaten divorce if their spouses spend most of their waking hours over a drafting board in the office.

The billiard table and swimming pool is to stop the costly loss of talent and time. The amenities are

for wives, husbands, kids, and special friends. On hot evenings, Saturday or Sundays when their loved ones are working, they can romp. Staff and partners occasionally join in. The pool table is the toy of 4 and 5 year olds during the winter. Balls are shot into pockets with cue stick or overhand toss. The exposed wind bracing of the structure is a "jungle

Mezzanine. *Photo:* IKOY.

gym." A comparatively stable staff have worked in the jungle gym studio, overtime and weekends for the past ten years while their entourage swam in the pool, steamed in the sauna, and racked up snooker scores by fair means or foul.

## Style—A Structural Flourish

The architects were their own clients. The building, they decided, would be built as they knew a building could be, with no-nonsense simplicity and speed. They sent a thousand invitations to the people in the surrounding community inviting them to attend an open house in 90 days. This was a dare to them-selves, for building a building in three months is unheard of in Winnipeg's harsh climate. The invitations were a "put up or shut up" community challenge with a no backout clause. Ninety days later the building opened for a party for 1200 guests.

The office building is "all dry" (no wet materials such as poured-in-place concrete, masonry, or plaster). The superstructure and bearing walls are pre-cast concrete slabs. The second floor is double Ts that can carry 250 lbs per square foot. The present structural steel mezzanine could be cut out and another one or almost anything else put in its place or any place on the floor. The roof spans 50 feet using 12-inch-thick hollow core planks.

Chair, drafting space. *Photo:* IKOY.

Rear entrance to swimming pool. *Photo:* IKOY.

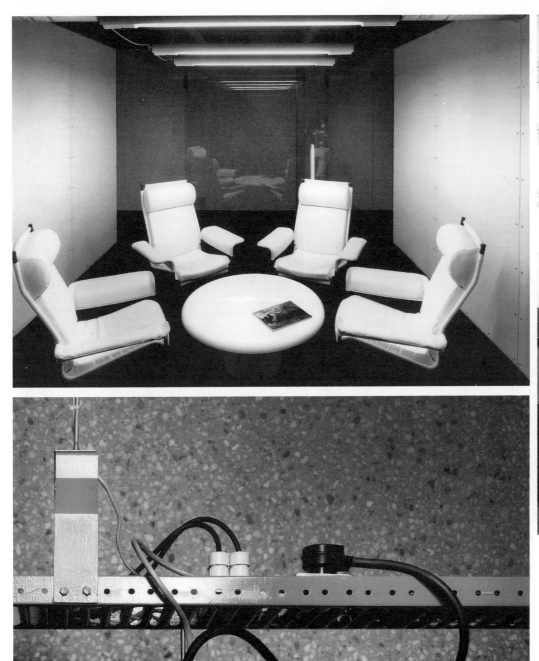

*Photo:* F. Wilson.

Exposed, crosstied steel tube wind braces give the end walls rigidity. Without them the building would topple over. The concrete panel side walls are too high to have any structural stiffening capability, and the glass curtain walls at either end have no membrane ability whatever. The best they can do is protect themselves from lateral wind pressures, which they do quite well. Steel plates connect the double Ts and hollow core panels to the walls.

The electrical system is a series of pans hung from the ceiling. There are no electrical plugs in walls, floor, or ceiling. All power is distributed by surface-mounted raceways. Light fixtures plug in and out individually. If a fixture within reach has a buzzing ballast it is plugged out and thrown away. If the buzz is from a ceiling fixture the youngest member of the staff is called, for it requires climbing an 18 foot ladder.

The mechanical system was designed by the architects and a tradesman. The heating and ventilating contractor told them to buy 4 rooftop heating and cooling units and plug them in and plug them out. They work perfectly at half the price of the system originally recommended.

It is true that the hot air is blown down over the curtain wall, which is frowned upon in the best heating and ventilation circles, but it works, and well.

There have been three major moves of furniture and electrical equipment in the past ten years. They were made by the staff on Saturday and Sunday with beer and sandwiches while kids, wives, and husbands splashed in the pool below.

## Factual Information

*Construction Time.* 90 days; started March 15, 1978; opened, furnished and operational, on June 10, 1978.
*Area.* 11,000 square feet.
*Cost.* $375,000; $34 dollars a square foot (1978 U.S.).

*Structure.* Walls: precast sandwich (insulation) panels, lower level 12 feet high, upper panels 8 feet wide, 24 feet high, 13 inches thick. Factory made with steel plates welded together on site. First floor is constructed of hollow core planks resting on cast-in-place grade beams supported on piles. Second floor is double Ts resting on sandwich panel bearing wall. Upper floor wall panels sit on the Ts, roof is 12-inch hollow core planks with built-up roofing.
Steel structure for wind bracing.

*Skin.* Metal and glass curtain wall at both ends.
*Mechanical.* Four roof plug-in units blowing air down from the roof.
*Electrical.* Standard electrical system, exposed. All wiring accessible from electrical troughs. The electrical trays are metal scaffolding planks turned upside down.
*Comments.* They put on three kinds of roofing. Two were inverted roofs (insulation on top of the roofing membrane), the third an old fashioned built-up roof. The two inverted roofs failed—one very quickly; had to be completely replaced for it could not be patched. There was so much water damage that they were lucky their insurance agent was an old friend. The second inverted roof lasted ten years before failing. The standard built-up roof remains in excellent condition.
All of the furniture in the building is made of industrial slotted shelving angles that come in two or three sizes. Masonite panels and metal scaffolding planks are attached to them.
The column and beam structure of the mezzanine is bolted wide flange sections connected with S sections. It can be unbolted and removed. The tempered glass panel walls and doors are clipped to the beams. The glass block panel is set in a metal frame that is bolted to a face plate on the floor below the topping. To remove the panel, the topping has to be chipped, the panel unbolted, and the trench filled with latex concrete.

# NORTHWEST LEISURE CENTRE
## The Award

The Northwest Leisure Centre was awarded a Canadian Governor General's Award by the Royal Architectural Institute of Canada in 1986. The following is quoted from the official catalog of the Royal Architectural Institute of Canada.

The client requirements were for a leisure/recreation centre capable of future expansion. Phase I consists of a swimming pool, a small multi-use gym, two multipurpose meeting rooms and the related administrative and service spaces. Phase II will include an ice arena, food services and racquet courts.

The complex is located on the corner of a small park within a major new subdivision. The pavilion context has allowed the building to clearly make its statement of identity and purpose.

The architectural planning is based upon a well articulated street concept which links the various activity pavilions, serves as the social focus, provides an effective administrative control and allows for a Phase II addition.

The choice of materials and the design approach for the assembly of components accomplished several objectives. The exterior and interior cladding is standard industrial steel panelling selected for reasons of cost and for Phase II match-up capability. The colorful and vigorous display of components serves not only its role of architectural expression, it also works extremely well with the overall leisure centre philosophy. There is an immediate user comprehension that this is a place for fun, fantasy and escape.

Phase I of the Northwest Leisure Center was developed by the City of Regina with the assistance of the Saskatchewan Housing Corporation; it is a major social and recreational element of a

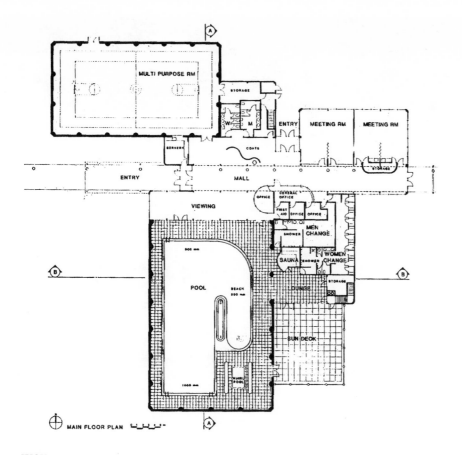

MULTI PURPOSE RM
STORAGE
W M ENTRY MEETING RM MEETING RM
SERVERY COATS STORAGE
ENTRY MALL
OFFICE GENERAL OFFICE
VIEWING FIRST AID OFFICE OFFICE
MEN CHANGE
SHOWER
SAUNA SHOWER WOMEN CHANGE
POOL BEACH STORAGE
LOUNGE
SUN DECK
WHIRL POOL

⊕ MAIN FLOOR PLAN

Plan. *Drawings:* IKOY.

twenty-one acre ongoing subdivision jointly undertaken by the provincial and municipal governments.

Owner's Assessment

Commodity: The building satisfies the functions that it was designed for and has proven flexible enough to accommodate additional uses that were not identified in the initial program.

Firmness: The Northwest Leisure Centre is energy efficient and sound. Some initial problems in the pool mechanical and rooftop heating units have been resolved. The atmosphere is comfortable in the various spaces.

Delight: The two aspects of the building that have prompted the greatest response are the "main-street" effect of the main concourse and the dramatic color scheme of the exterior and interior surfaces. The Centre is an exciting place to be and has received a large number of favorable comments.

Summary Comments: We could not be more de-

lighted with the response and use the building has received. Over 200,000 users a year have enjoyed the pool, gymnasium/auditorium and meeting rooms for a variety of recreational and social activities. All age groups use the facility. The multiplicity of uses at any time and the high level of use have made the Northwest Leisure Centre an unqualified success. We anticipate that use of the Centre for structured programs, social events and unstructured recreational activity will continue to grow. We will be initiating Phase II of the Complex in the coming year; this includes an ice arena, art studio, meeting and office spaces.

## As the Architects Saw It

The city of Regina wanted a community gymnasium, swimming pool, and arts and crafts center, with a hockey arena to be added in the future. Swimming is not competitive but a leisure activity. Regina is a prairie city in the middle of great grain fields. There are no lakes nearby. They wanted a year-round leisure center with water. In the summer it would be like the lakes and in the winter like Hawaii.

Civic swimming pools are always great money losers. People go, swim laps, and leave. The huge buildings have no more people in them than those that can swim simultaneously in the same body of water. Twenty citizens who paid a dollar each are subsidized by the rest of the community. This was the problem given with the same budget they would have spent for a "lapping" pool.

They received in return not only a pool but a community meeting place with meeting rooms for serious business like that conducted in a town hall. But the building is primarily associated with fun, relaxation, and social interaction. There are modest learning events and basketball can be played in a gym. Competitions are not held here. Swim laps, but do not get too serious about it.

Entrance, Northwest Leisure Center, Regina. *Photo:* IKOY.

Entrance, Chimney detail. *Photo:* IKOY.

When doing the laps in a rectangular pool the swimmer looks down and sees the green lines on the bottom and is directed. When they go to the lake in the summer or to Hawaii in the winter they swim out to the buoy or raft. They are effectively swimming laps there from one point to another as they do in the pool. Lake and beach became key words in the development of the pool. The lake and the beach, the board walk and promenade where there. Ice cream, hot dogs, and souvenirs were the design inspiration.

There is a street or a "promenade" through the building leading to the arena which would be the next stage of the complex. Part of the challenge was to deal with the problems not only of today but tomorrow.

There were mistakes made in this building. The rooms of beach and gym were too much alike. They selected and used interesting and colorful structure for a "fun" environment, but this was before they understood the importance of "attitudinal direction" which you will read about later in Chapter 7.

The beach area is a rectilinear volume similar to the gym. It should have been inspired by words like freedom, relief, difference, change, relaxation, easy, or "laid back". The choice of structure had more to do with making the building stand up than illustrating ideas and attitudes.

A new pool in London, Ontario, the London Aquatic Centre, recently designed by the architects (1989) deals with these words and ideas. The leisure pool room in London has a structure inspired by a merry-go-round and Roman Baths. It is fun and free.

Almost all buildings are composed of rectangular volumes. The beach and lakes are outside and trees do not make rectilinear volumes. The key was to remove the edges that define a room shape. That relief takes a person into a different environment radically different than any room they may have come from. This sets the tone and attitude reinforced by the other details.

There is no glass at the Northwest Recreational

Pool area. *Photo:* IKOY.

Windowless pool. *Photo:* IKOY.

Centre because the lifeguards said it would cause reflections in the pool and they could not see the poor drowning children. They argued more life guards would be required. So there are no windows in the recreational zones of the pool area at the Northwest Centre.

The building won a Governor General's award but the architects are disappointed. They won because it was a "pretty building" not because it has the attitude of a laid back, easy beach.

They learned they had all the correct techniques but the failure was in their ability to exploit all of the expressive possibilities of the structure. At London they did a round room using conventional techniques including light to create a lakelike attitude or ambience. The cost of an extra life guard is a small price to pay for a delightful space.

Architecture must market itself to the public. The challenge was posed to make a pool that will make money. The London pool will be rented to members of the community for use as a night club spa. In the daytime it has so much glass it is like being outside. At Northwest Centre you cannot tell if it is 10 in morning or 10 at night. A leisure center should use daylight and darkness as tones of change. Tan in the daytime, party at night.

The street works well. Its structure is an early experiment that was greatly refined in the corridor at Batoche (page 57). We did not succeed at Northwest, they say, for it did not solve the problem the way we wanted it solved. "We have great techniques to make things pretty but that is not what architecture is about. The problems did not generate the solution. Instead we found our answers in structure and paint."

They learned about the street at the Northwest Centre and Batoche came from that. This is the way that architects refine their art. A key to solving problems is to realize that many are generic, that is common to certain building types. Another example of generic formal development is the Computer Center galleria (page 83) that evolved from the Earth Sciences building (page 69).

Problems are almost never solved in the first attempt. Each problem must be met with a foundation of knowledge and a vocabulary of expression. Northwest is an early example of building vocabulary, learning new words and learning to use them poetically.

## Factual Information

*Construction Time.* 1981–1982, completed in 10 months.
*Area.* 25,000 square feet.
*Cost.* $2,000,000; $80 a square foot.
*Structure.* Poured-in-place concrete below grade to 5 feet above; standard steel frame; wide flange sections, steel joists and tube sections; steel deck-ing spanning between beams; no joists or purlins.
*Street.* Tubed steel structure, tube purlins supporting, and 1-1/2 inch decking.
*Mechanical.* Direct air; separate system for pool room vented to outside.
*Electrically.* Standard electrical system, lights, motors, appliances; combination fluorescent and incandescent bulbs. Special atmospheric fixtures.
*Skin.* First use of control grid; custom extrusions and painted steel corrugated panels, 12 feet by 3 feet in control grid; first use of radius corners; transformation of steel stud wall to thermodynamic barrier, expression of skin as skin instead of wall; control grid.
*Fitments.* Drywall on steel studs, plastic laminate screw-on, Plexiglas, glass block.

London Athletic Center round building. *Computer drawing:* IKOY.

Rendering of London Athletic Center. *Drawing:* IKOY.

## NORTHEAST PARK, WINNIPEG, MANITOBA
### Harborview

The city of Winnipeg, Manitoba dug an artificial lake, laid out a sports complex, and decided to build a parks building on a former city dump. They held a competition to select the architect. The competition program said the building should have something to do with the lake and must include change rooms for men and women, a pro shop, a dining room, a lounge, a banquet room, and administrative offices.

A lake in the city of Winnipeg is unusual. The architects went to look at towns in eastern Canada and were most impressed with Peggy's Cove a small, quaint, run down fishing village of 500 people in maritime Canada. Peggy's Cove became the model, run down and friendly—an ideal image.

How do villages grow on the edge of water? To begin, they do not grow large. All of the buildings are small. A series of tiny buildings multiplied, with fractured roof lines, creates the quaint lovely texture of a town. The idea of a village is important, and the square as meeting place is a key idea.

The city wanted one building. Village squares are not made from one building. A village is not like a city. An entire village can be seen from the highway but an entire city is never seen on the ground. Wholeness identifies the village place. The city is identified by individual districts and buildings. You never see the entire city and are always a stranger, but "village" means "friendly community."

To keep a park a lively place it must be operated 12 months of the year. In the summer there are golf, lawn bowling, tennis, boats on the lake; in the winter the lake is for skating, the hill for tobogganing, there is cross country skiing on the golf course—all outdoor activities, summer and winter. The village is to change clothes, pause for refreshment, cool off or warm up.

There must be a square. The one building was made into five buildings, three major and two minor structures connected with a covered trellis walk. Separating locker rooms and pro shop from each other and from the dining hall and connecting them with a covered walkway created a village square.

The square is entered from one side and crossing it brings the visitor to the docks and boats opposite the dining hall and lounge.

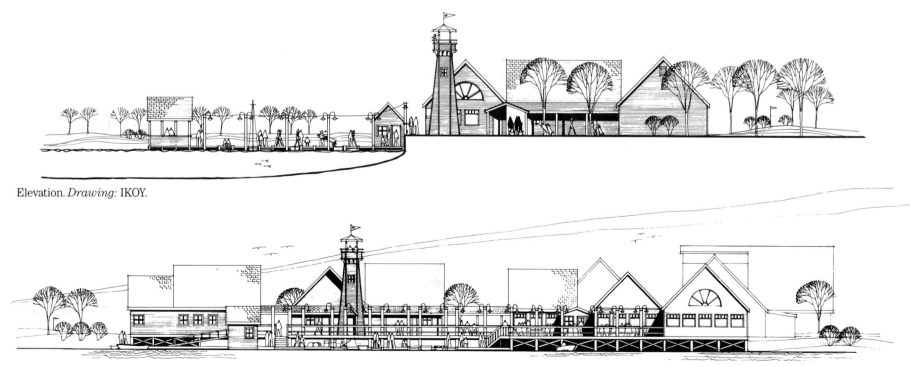

Elevation. *Drawing:* IKOY.

Elevation from dock. *Drawing:* IKOY.

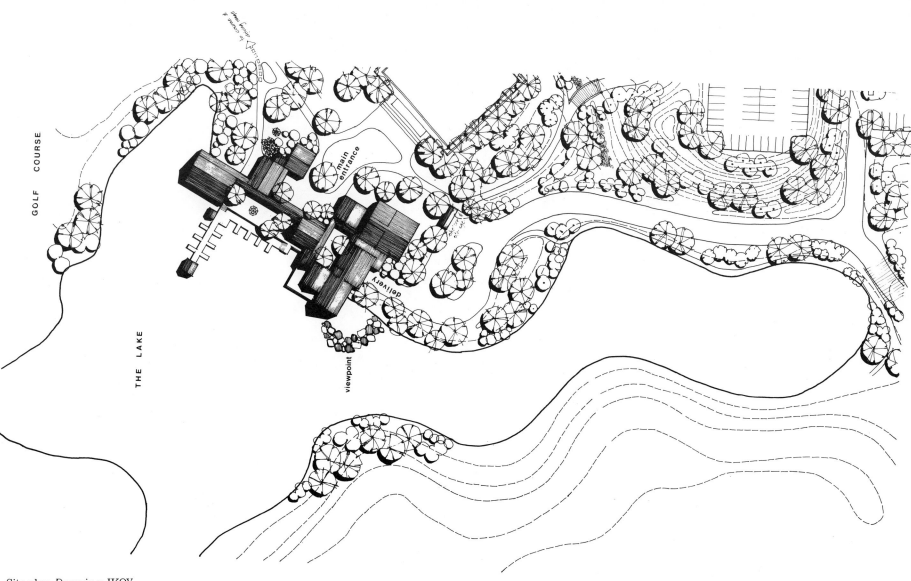

GOLF COURSE

THE LAKE

main entrance

delivery

viewpoint

Site plan. *Drawing:* IKOY.

*Photo:* IKOY.

*Photo:* IKOY.

*Photo:* IKOY.

Once anyone changed for skiing or golfing it mattered little if they went outside again. Village square and village were key. The formal references are fragmented coastal fishing villages, variations of pitched roofs which are not planned on a grid system. The lack of individual order merges into one form. The public called the village quaint and loved the texture.

The multi-building was built entirely of wood and there is a small tower for looking at the park and lake. It is a focal point reminiscent of lighthouse or church steeple and is seen from a distance rising from the square.

The entire "village" can be taken in a glance. The forms were inspired by the shapes of fishing villages but the buildings are not vernacular. Industrial trusses were used and the pitch varied. Wood joinery is exposed and sophisticated. It is memory, myth, and village nostalgia.

Photo: IKOY.

## Factual Information

*Construction Time.* Seven months, 1982.

*Area.* 12,000 square feet.

*Cost.* $640,000 (U.S.).

*Structure.* Driven timber and precast concrete piles and cast-in-place concrete grade beam; precast hollow core plank floor; wood stud bearing walls combined with engineered wood trusses; heavy timber, post and beam roof; frame with wood deck.

*Skin.* 1″ × 6″ rough sawn cedar boards installed with 4″ exposure (to the weather).

*Mechanical.* Roof-top combination heating–air conditioning units and gas-fired forced-air furnaces.

*Fitments.* Dual chimney, free-standing fireplaces; antique lounges, furnishings, and seating.

## RED RIVER COMMUNITY COLLEGE AUTO/DIESEL SHOPS
## The Award

The Red River Community College Auto/Diesel Shops building was awarded a Canada Governor General's Medal by the Royal Architectural Institute of Canada in 1986. The following is quoted from the official catalog of the Royal Architectural Institute of Canada.

### Owner's Assessment

Commodity: Red River Community College has occupied the building for approximately one year and reports the facility to be functionally satisfactory to the current needs. In addition, the design will readily accommodate future program and occupancy modifications.

Firmness: The final assessment of the building systems is not yet complete. The Department declines to offer an opinion until this definitive data is available.

Delight: The interior of the building is bright, airy and extremely pleasant to the eye. Natural lighting is well utilized and makes a significant contribution to the interior appearance of the building.

Summary Comments: The building is most pleasant and appealing, and makes an excellent use of natural lighting. The concept of having two vehicle vestibules in lieu of the traditional 10–15 garage doors has made a significant contribution to effective utilization of energy. This positive approach to energy conservation permitted greater use of glazing, which contributes to the successful interior atmosphere. Most significantly, however, the building was designed within time and budget constraints."

## As the Architect Saw It

Auto/diesel shop for training mechanics. Engines, machine, parts, tough kids, the greasers. They deserve a working environment at least equal to people working for IBM. Because they have grease in their hair does not mean they are not elevated human beings.

These machine shops historically reflect the Humphrey Bogart prison movies, but once one sees beyond the grayness of the prison there is a fascination in machines and engines. There was an opportunity to make a building to celebrate the machine and its parts.

Auto/diesel shops usually have a dingy shaft of light coming through haze and dust. They are always eerie, but spiritual. Ideally, a great deal of natural light is necessary. It is important to work on engines in a well lit room and comfortable surroundings.

The shop had to be designed to use only half the energy consumed by similar shops of this kind. When the program was analyzed, the only solution that would meet the energy consumption demands would have been a black, windowless box in the winter and a silvered, windowless box in the summer. But even a windowless box could not accommodate the 15–18 foot overhead entrance doors that would have been required to move equipment in and out and would be open most of the time, summer or winter.

Could architecture solve the energy problem that the engineering calculations could not? The program stated that the major room, the full length and one half the size of the building must be 25 feet high to the underside of the structure. The normal structural depth for long span trusses meant that the building would be a volume 29 feet to the underside of the roof deck, heated and cooled at levels impossible to achieve with the energy consumption specified.

The architects analyzed all equipment, including hydraulic lifts, and found that they could be accommodated by a 21-foot clearance. They then chose a spanning member 1 foot thick and smooth on the bottom. The cube was now 72.4 percent of the size programmed, a 27.6 percent reduction. This effectively reduced the energy demand by one quarter.

The cost of 8 feet of perimeter wall was saved. The length of the building was increased and a road run through it with a vehicular vestibule at each end. These were large enough to enclose the largest machines that would come into the shop.

The vestibules operated on the same principle as those for people entering or leaving a building.

Plans. *Architectural drawings:* IKOY.

North Vestibule.

Details. *Photo:* IKOY.

Drive in an airlocked space. The door closes behind and the one into the shop opens. The vestibules solved a crucial problem, that of the open door.

They had another advantage. A piece of equipment left outside in $-25°F$ temperatures is like a huge ice cube when brought indoors. The vestibule was equipped with hot water and steam lines to wash down the machinery. This warms the metal. The doors to the shop are then opened.

The building has more natural light than a comparative office building and consumes less energy than specified as a minimum in the building program. This proved that architectural thinking could solve problems that engineering calculations alone could not. Solutions were not derived with mathematics but common sense. A building with less cubic volume costs less to heat. An automatic door opening directly to the outside wastes more heat than a closed vestibule.

The architects described the building as follows in the award catalog:

The Auto/Diesel Shop strives to serve its users as being a functional machine—not only by proudly exposing its machine crafted components and organizing and ordering them in a manner expressive of the action of building, but by creating an efficient shop having qualities of firmness, delight, scale, grain, texture and light—which generate a special human quality.

The giant machine vestibules are the keys to the shop. Having the lowest energy consumption (850 mega-joules) of any building of its type in Canada. Even with the generous use of glazing, the selection of structural components, hollow core on box tube truss, reduced the cube, adding to the energy efficiency.

"But it is most aptly put by the students— "Moon Raker" they call it, they respect it, they love it."

## Factual Information

*Construction Time.* 9 months 1983–84.

*Area.* 60,000 square feet.

*Cost.* $4 million (U.S.); $66.65 a square foot.

*Structure.* Wide flange column, tube steel box trusses, 12 inch hollow core plank.

*Mechanical.* All air variable volume system, with large make up air to counteract air lost by vehicular exhaust; exhaust air directly to outside; pressurized airlines, gas lines for shop equipment.

*Electrical.* Variety of power supplies for shop equipment operation. Developed a rack; the minor mechanical that goes to the electrical runs on a rack accessible from all work and teaching areas. The mechanical and electrical price per square foot is higher than for an automated office building.

*Skin.* Curtain wall, steel stud, control grid, glazed and corrugated aluminum panels.

*Fitments.* Interesting—a material called "acustadeck" which is a regular structural flooring panel with holes for sound waves backed by sound deadening acoustic material. Used here as finished wall and ceiling elements. Attached to underside of hollow core planks with vibration isolation clips.

Melamine and sheetrock panels screwed directly to steel studs for partitions. Hardening agent put into concrete to withstand heavy impacts of dropped objects sometimes covered by battleship linoleum.

Detail. *Photo:* IKOY.

*Photo:* IKOY.

*Photo:* IKOY.

## BATOCHE NATIONAL HISTORIC SITE, RECEPTION AND INFORMATION CENTER, BATOCHE, SASKATCHEWAN
### Battle in the Bush

On May 11, 1885 three hundred Métis were defeated in a battle with Royal Canadian Mounted Police. The police, commanded by a British general, captured the Métis leader, Louis Riel, and took him to Winnipeg where he was hanged.

After the battle local wheat farmers, in a ritual killing of the site as the Romans had sown salt on the ruins of Carthage, cut down all the trees. This bare killing ground on the banks of the Saskatchewan River came to symbolize the last stand of mixed blood French and Indian rebels fighting for their land.

The architects were commissioned in 1984 to design a visitors' center to accommodate 25,000 tourists annually. Trees were planted by the Parks Department to return the land to its pre-battle condition. When grown they will shield the center from view and tourists can relive the stalking of police and rebel a century ago.

## As the Architect Saw It

Design a building to commemorate a bloody, century old, battle between mixed blood French and Indians and police. The site today is bare with a single small Catholic church whose only attraction is its isolation. It was not always like this.

The Métis were fleeing from the Royal Canadian Mounted Police, a paramilitary force. They crept through the woods and dug tunnel trenches. The attacking police would rather have fought properly on open ground in military order, but were forced to creep and stalk in the bush.

What can a building say about bush and battle? How can a commemorative center recall a conflict of frightened men, creeping through the woods to shoot each other?

What is the essential symbol of fear, stalking, and shooting? Is it gun bore, gun sight, rifling, metal, sneak, deadly hide and seek?

They chose the long hexagonal form of spyglass and rifle barrel. Nineteenth Century gunsmiths often fashioned hexagonal barrels. This is the link between bush and battle. A tube pointing at the church which is the only other man-made object on the site.

Put your eye to the V and site the parish church of St. Antoine de Padoue built in 1883, two years before the battle. It is an unholy contrast of horizontal gun barrel and vertical church steeple, a pairing of gun and church that contrasts the lawful killing in war and the "thou shalt not kill" of peace.

In the tube corridor the visitor spies on the church in the bore of a rifle and walks down it like a projectile aimed at the church. The visitor is then projected from the center to walk the battle site prepared by this experience.

Strong light and sun shadow patterns fall on the floor to remind the walker projectile of the spiraling in a rifle barrel that directs the bullet on its true course.

The trees will grow and hide the tube as furtive gun barrels were shadowed in 1885. The experience will be one of creeping through the bush. The three separate service buildings—administration, theater, and museum—are spaced as metaphor of the deadly game of flicked glance "peekaboo" between tree trunks played by the forest fighters.

There can be no mistake. This building is not a historic artifact. There is no material association between center and church. The center is brightly painted and clad in green tinted glass and corru-

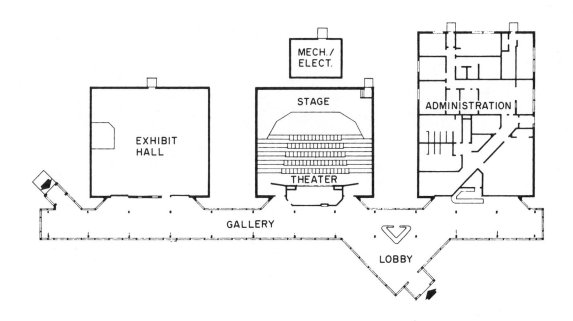

Capture of Batoche 1885. Courtesy of Provincial
Archives Manitoba. J. W. Curzan Sketch from *Illustrated
War News* .

*Photos:* IKOY.

*Photos:* IKOY.

gated silver aluminum panels associated with aerospace.

The deck fits within the two sloped surfaces. The impression is of whirling down a curvilinear spiral reinforced by sunlit diagonal shadows. Stripped patterns unify the tube interior. The corridor is used only in daylight. It is closed at night.

The steel corridor is entered through a steel arch. Inside, framing members are painted blue. The two column air returns are yellow. Walls and underside of the ceiling are natural finish corrugated aluminum. The glazing mullions of the barrel end form a crosshair sight aimed at St. Antoine de Padoue.

It is more than a corridor, more than a gun pointed at a church. It is a lethal tube aimed by the British Empire and pointed at the head of Louis Riel.

## Factual Information

*Constructed Time.* Commissioned in 1984, completed (1986).

*Area.* 18,500 square feet.

*Cost.* $1.5 million dollars; $81 a square foot.

*Structure.* The structure is hollow metal tube sections forming the columns and sloped roof sections. The purlins (horizontal members spanning between roof framing) are also steel tubes. The curtain wall has a dominant horizontal pattern. The boxlike buildings attached to the 236-foot-long hexagonal tube are one-story steel framed structures—a small office block, an 80-seat theater, and an exhibition hall.

*Skin.* Curtain wall with standard or natural anodized aluminum in control grids backed by steel stud partitions.

*Mechanical.* All air system heating and cooling.

*Electrical.* All standard.

*Comments.* The site is remote. Materials and labor had to be transported 200 miles from Saskatoon or Prince Albert. The curtain wall was sent 800 miles from Winnipeg.

# THE PROVINCIAL CENTER AT FLIN FLON, MANITOBA: A MULTI-PURPOSE ACROPOLIS
## The City

What makes a city a city? When does a town become a city? Few people have been as sure of the answer as Pausanias, the second century A.D. Greek traveler and geographer, and Earl K. Watson, the deputy mayor of Flin Flon, Manitoba.

When Pausanias came to a little place in Phocis called Panopeus he hesitated to dignify it by the name of "city" (*polis*) because it had no government offices, gymnasium, theater, or agora. It consisted of a few miserable houses and one or two ancient shrines. Panopeus in the Second Century A.D. was a Greek version of Flin Flon in the 1930s.

Flin Flon is a frontier town on the northern edge of civilization. It is seven hundred miles north of Winnipeg, reported to be the coldest major city in the world.

Flin Flon was born with the discovery of gold fifty years ago. "The town grew like Topsie," said Watson, "they built houses where they had tents, then when things got going they incorporated the houses in the town plan. A few people had to be moved but the city layout is very much like a mining camp ground."

The landscape surrounding Flin Flon is a corrugated lake-fissured land of scrub pine dotted with birch. It stretches south to civilization and north to the frozen pole. Flin Flon sits on a series of small hills or great boulders. Sparse soil gathered into rock pockets feeds lichen, grass, weeds and sometimes flowers around the miners rough built houses.

Houses were built by owners with help of friends and are painstakingly shaped from nostalgic memories of door casings, gable ends, railed stoops in Kiev, Glasgow, Seoul, Budapest, Delhi, Toronto, and Quebec.

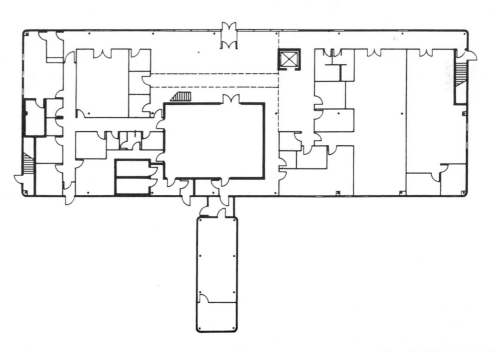

*Photo:* F. Wilson.

Some houses have storefront windows cut in their facades. Customers enter where families once rocked and gossiped on porch swings. There are also staunch residential holdouts that stand where they are and claim their right to a place on the main street, vender or no, asserting the rights of free citizens to stand among traders and wampum dealers or wherever they damned well please.

False fronted buildings are as much a mark of the universal brag of the frontier boomer the world over as were the pedimented wooden temples in Greek colonies. Both marked the difference between village and polis. In Flin Flon the false fronts say this is a city, not a town, "We have lots and subdivisions, choice sites, and land speculation. We have Shriners, Lions, and Odd fellows. We are 'humdingers,' a town going places."

## A Multi-Purpose Acropolis

The claim to city status is not brag. Flin Flon has a new Provincial Center standing at the end of Main Street three blocks from the mine smelter. And the Provincial Center nestles a court of law, a building within a building, in the center of the offices of government to prove its right to "city" status.

The Provincial Center is Flin Flon's Parthenon and the law court its statue of Athena. During the early years, when the tent village was turning to a wooden town, misbehavers were transported to surrounding cities for trial. When civic pride swelled sufficiently judges were flown in and miscreants faced their accusers in the high school gymnasium. Today justice is served properly in a courtroom entered through bronze doors.

Before Flin Flon attained city status its municipal offices were scattered in various rented spaces in the town. Today the offices of highway department, social services, and natural resources surround the court on a lower and upper level. This is where hunting, fishing, and driving licenses are issued and

Red and white mine buildings share town space. Two mine head frames are the town's high rises. The smelter sits at the town's north end in the middle of a wasted land of vomited earth from which the gold, copper, and zinc have been sucked. Next to it, rising as a huge exclamation point above its puddle of desolation, is the great smelter stack. It can be seen for fifty miles.

A few town blocks to the south of main street is a great open pit mine, cut vertically into the hard granite. House sewers in the town are above ground and boxed in sinuous wooden colons running between the houses. The igneous rock is much too hard to dig for anything less precious than gold.

Ordered rows of parking meters are Flin Flon's minor civic sculptures along the main street. The major civic decorations are graceful silvered traffic stanchions extending long arms to dangle traffic signal boxes over the center of street intersections. The boxes impartially allot time to tarry at the curb and command stop and go. The parking meters assert the right of the municipality to tax for use of curb and gutter.

Department store facades and movie house fronts along Flin Flon's main street are archaeological evidence of departed professional builders.

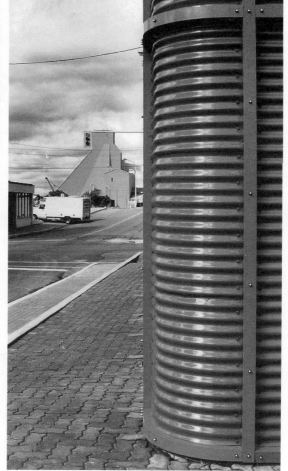

*Photos:* F. Wilson.

where social workers, foresters, and scientists protect the welfare of the people, the lakes, bear, moose, and wolf of the surrounding tundra and scrub forests.

The court, the jewel of justice, is symbolic of law, order, and civilization. It is a monument Pausanias would have examined with interest and noted in his journal. This is the architectural declaration that Flin Flon will no longer tolerate gunslinging minors beating each other over the head with crowbars on Friday nights. Mental cruelty can now be substituted. Differences will be decided by lawyers and the judge will dispense justice in a civilized fashion commensurate to each lawyer's eloquence.

# The Building

The Provincial Center commission was awarded to the architects by the Provincial Government. It was simply "their turn" to get a commission. Architectural firms donate money to various political parties, a practice not unlike offering temple sacrifices in ancient times. Donations, like sacrifices, are a "good buy." The cost of preparing a building proposal is at least $50,000, which is considerably more than the amounts permitted by law to be donated to political parties. We might say that normal temple donations were not required, so the architects made the city of Flin Flon a shrine in memory of "our turn."

The site was donated by the town and has a unique shape because the owners of an adjacent electrical shop refused to sell their property at a price the township could afford. The government told the architects the building would be a Provincial Center housing offices and a court and left the rest to them.

Sun angles are low at this latitude and darkness comes early in the afternoon four months of the year. The court is illuminated by the sun or electric lights through the glass walls. Visitors enter through a central atrium and face the metal-banded courtroom masonry walls and bronze doors. The court states the importance of the provincial building. Otherwise the offices are not unlike those of any modern administrative center.

Three metal bands, honoring the metals mined in the town, circle the court. The top and bottom are copper, the center zinc. The court doors are bronze, a refined metal reminiscent of the great Baptistry doors of Pisano and Ghilberti in Florence.

Flin Flon is the first link in the chain that begins with primitive copper and ends with civilized bronze. Copper leaves the pit as raw ore and returns to Flin Flon as smelted bronze. Justice behind bronze doors carries more "weight" than when dispensed behind wooden doors. Bronze is not the

*Photos:* F. Wilson and IKOY.

stuff of common structures, it is saved for the entrance to baptistries, banks, counting houses, and other buildings of substance. The return of bronze for copper dignifies the labor of the miners and rewards their efforts.

A suspension bridge links the two office clusters on the second floor. It is elevated above the bronze doors, saying plainly to those that cross over, "The law is our creation." The bridge has a slight sway reminiscent of lift cages in mine shafts. The solid masonry blocks of the courtroom walls contrast the steel's vitality.

The bridge is convivial, rebounding like the human body when stressed. Its ends bear lightly on the concrete plank floors at either end. Threaded cables suspend it at quarter points.

People in Flin Flon know machinery. They are comfortable with and curious about it. A townsman asked Watson if the Provincial Center was a heating plant?

## A Kinetic Context

The Provincial Center may or may not look like a heating plant but it looks like industry and industry is rooted in the mines. It is a bolted, red, corrugated box. Greek temples were colonnaded, rectangular, stone boxes. When the doors were open the statue of the god inside could be seen through the entrance doors, as the court at Flin Flon can be seen through the transparent glass wall of the Provincial Center.

The building is the same material and gender as the automobiles that pass it on the street, sit in orderly rows in the parking lot across the way, cluster behind it and stop at its entrance. The corner traffic stanchions are comfortable in its presence for they are as related to it as Greek sculpture was related to Greek architecture.

The facade is an industrial membrane designed to change as the functions within the building change. It celebrates the skill of building assemblers. Like automobiles it is an assembly of industrial parts, a triumph of industrial organization. The skill of to-day's buildings is found in fastenings as the skill of ancient buildings was displayed in masonry joints.

The automobile creates the primary context of human settlements in North America. The material and assembly of the Provincial Center is related to automobiles. Buildings are said to be harmoniously related to their environment when the architect searches out the outstanding features of surrounding buildings then aligns window heights, facade and cornice lines and matches the shape of building openings. But people in the street today see automobiles, not cornices.

The Provincial Center is a product of industrial technology. Each element was selected from a manufacturer's catalog and can be easily replaced by that manufacturer or two or three others. The parts are made in a factory and brought to the site in as large a piece as transportation will allow. Each fits in place as it should for it could not be fitted in any other way.

Labor has been reduced by simplifying connections. Parts are designed in large sections to minimize their number and set in place by machine power rather than human effort. The symbol of industrial buildings is not hammer, nail, saw, and chisel but the wrench.

The sophistication of environmental control is expressed in the exposed working parts of mechanical system as they run through the building and the boiler room plant is displayed behind a large window in a small building linked umbilically to the main center at midpoint.

The province of Manitoba has demanding energy standards. The Provincial Center was designed to meet them, using passive solar energy, a principle Pausanias would have recognized. The center's windows face west. During daytime working hours heat is gained from the sun through the glass. During the summertime the sun setting is northwest, almost north. The sun is far down. When the building closes at 5 PM, atrium space temperatures might be 78 or

*Photos:* F. Wilson and IKOY.

80 degrees. But work spaces are away from the windows and zoned for air conditioning. The sun angle that strikes the solid masonry courthouse in a golden glow not only highlights it like a statue of Athena but makes the Provincial Center one of the most energy efficient buildings in the province.

## Factual Information

*Construction Time.* 9 months, 1984–1985.

*Area.* 18,000 square feet (two stories).

*Cost.* $1.5 million; $84 dollars per square foot.

*Structure.* Steel pipe, tube trusses, standard joists, and hollow core plank.

*Mechanical.* Variable volume, all air heating and cooling system; return air through atrium; hung ceilings and walls enclose rooms as cubes in space. The corridors are return air plenums circulating the air around the room cubes.

*Lighting.* Standard, florescent lay-in fixtures in a lay-in tile ceiling.

*Skin.* 4-ply built-up roof; steel stud and commercial curtain wall in a control grid hung on wall clips. Glazed and infill panels of painted industrial corrugated aluminum.

*Fitments.* Public areas—plastic laminate (like formica) panels screwed to steel joists; private areas—drywall traditional application to steel joists; all flooring carpet.

*Comments.* Remote site. Most material and labor shipped 700 miles cost about 20 percent premium over a normal Winnipeg job.

*Photos:* F. Wilson and IKOY.

# DARTH VADER AND THE
# SOURDOUGHS*
## Earth Sciences

How did geology become the earth sciences? What are the earth sciences? Geologists are visualized by the community as kindly white-haired rockhounds who, like their sourdough cousins, engage in the constant pursuit of precious rocks in lonely places. Geologists and sourdoughs are indulged and secretly admired, for to the rest of us zinc looks like nothing, titanium like less than nothing, and most people chipping away for rock treasures are elated when they discover shiny mica called "fools gold," worth almost nothing.

Today geology is serious business and is no longer geology but the earth sciences. Earth scientists use sonar and aircraft, and cut rock samples with delicate, sophisticated saws in thin enough slices to examine under electron microscopes. Great scientific problems and complicated mathematical formulas are discussed and solved as geologists calculate how to drill to find ore and oil in the earth. They do not deal with rocks alone but with oil-producing rocks, and therefore use all the high tech equipment, mathematics, and research known to the oil industries of the world. Earthquakes are part of geology, and seismology is an earth science in its own right.

The university wanted a high-tech building to say that geology was a new, high-tech, computer, sonar, electron microscope, moon rock science doing important things in the world. It deserved respect and funding. This also had to be a building that could change to home economics should the university rearrange its building functions, as universities so frequently do.

High-tech is mixed with space weaponry in the

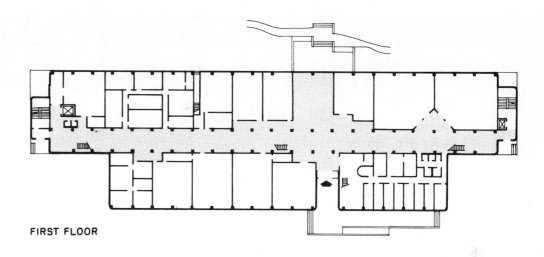

**FIRST FLOOR**

public mind. The military uses so much high-tech and the universities so little that universities cannot furnish a model of the symbol the university wanted. The high-tech laboratories at Oxford University are in Georgian buildings.

A laboratory can operate in any kind of building as long as it has proper fume hoods. Life in the laboratory is sustained by fume hoods. Exposure to the fumes of research kills researchers. Mistakes can be fatal and an array of 12 fume hoods can be a fearful sight even to the initiated.

Scientific equipment is a mystery because nonscientists do not understand the dangers in a scientific laboratory. Lack of understanding makes us conjure up the dark side, the mystery, the bizarre of Star Wars and Darth Vader.

What is the difference between an earth sciences building and a starship other than one travels space and the other is landlocked? The people in the building, like the actors in a television series, read seismic charts talk to computers, and belch scrubbed, hopefully thoroughly washed, no longer noxious chemical fumes.

The laboratories are benign to those that understand them and malignant to those that do not, which moves an understanding of them outside the realm of high-tech into that of superstition.

The building had to reflect all of these impressions, for the architects found that the earth sciences were as much a mystery to the university community as how a building is made.

The earth scientists wanted to expose their leading-edge science to the community. To do this the architects exposed slices of building using a technique of skin and transparency. They designed the building as a geode. It is like the dull surface of a nodule of stone broken to expose a cavity lined with fascinating, colorful crystals. The aluminum and steel of the building comes from iron ore and bauxite discovered by geologists. The columns are precast concrete sandblasted to expose the local stone aggregate.

What does geology look like? In most instances the results of this remarkable science, prospecting, analysis, testing under fume hoods ends as a report in a file drawer. It deserved better.

*Sourdough: a veteran inhabitant, esp. an old-time prospector of Alaska or northwest Canada.

*Photos:* IKOY.

## Site

The building site was a major issue. The architects examined four possible locations then proposed the one on which the building now stands. It is on the river side of a ring road that a previous campus plan specifically advised must be kept free of buildings. However, later university planners blocked the impressive ceremonial entrance leading to the heart of the campus with an athletic club. The original plan was turned inside out with an "anything goes" abandon.

The service road, with parking lots, agricultural barns, and equipment sheds, became the entrance to the university. The Earth Sciences Building, formerly located in a remote university "quad," is now a ceremonial gateway. The building stands above a sea of parked automobiles adjacent to the university's largest parking lot, symbolizing entry.

Across the street, barely concealed by a decorative wall of Tyndal stone, is a second parking lot. There was not enough room between the back of the building and the river to place a third.

During the cold, subzero winters the corridors of the Earth Sciences Building serves as transition from warm automobile to warm buildings for most of the campus buildings are connecting by underground tunnels.

Tunnels, the architects say, are a convenient way of moving people but a foul way to treat them. It is better to see sky instead of heating pipes when walking from place to place. University corridors are seldom more interesting than tunnels for the only way the walker knows where he or she might be is by the room numbers on identical doors.

The Earth Sciences Building has a warm, elevated stoa, three stories high, which they call a "galleria" to give it "class." This is the organizing principle around which the building is designed.

*Photos:* IKOY.

## The Galleria

The Earth Sciences Building is in reality a three story, multi-level, open movement corridor passing through, up, and down the building, with laboratories and class rooms attached like jewels on this central thread.

The galleria is a place of visual relief from laboratories and classrooms or a closed car interior in the winter time. It is a continuous lounge, the living room of the building. It is a place to hang out, lean on the rails and watch fellow combatants in the war against ignorance pass from one battle ground to the next.

The galleria is a display of visual and verbal interaction. Natural light from many angles enters at the beginning, the end, and at two central openings. It is furnished by the electrical and mechanical systems, switch gear, make up and return air boxes which are kinetic kiosks on the promenade. Instead of pasted messages they click, buzz, and flash lights behind glass fronts.

Classrooms and laboratories are no-nonsense, simple working spaces. Students can be seen working with microscopes and laboratory paraphernalia.

Galleria stairs are ingeniously fashioned of folded metal sheets, bent pipe, and threaded wire. These are convivial treads and risers for passing from one level to another. In addition there are strategically located, concrete-block-enclosed fire stairs required by law for leaving the building in haste and fear.

## Inside

The earth sciences building is elevated on a modest plinth of Tyndal stone to celebrate its sourdough origins, politely acknowledge its neighbors, and appease campus traditionalists. The building skin is dark gray anodized aluminum and tinted glass.

There are four lecture theaters available to botany, chemistry, physics, and mathematics, and when

*Photos:* IKOY.

not required by these disciplines they are scheduled by other university disciplines. As a result, students unconnected academically to the earth sciences or to any of the other sciences pass through and use the building.

If in 20 years, or tomorrow, the Earth Sciences Building becomes a Home Economics or Fine Arts Building the theaters would continue as they are, but should more scientific use be made of them provision has been provided for computer terminals.

Electrical systems are the nerves of modern buildings and are constantly being modified. Corridor walls are capped by a metal compartmented raceway carrying power and communication cables to laboratories, offices, and classrooms. Power is accessible from both sides and modifications made from the corridors so laboratory and classes are not disturbed.

Changes are inevitable. They must not interfere with work in other areas. They must be made quickly, dry and clean, without mess or sawdust.

Change is part of the building program. Mechanical, electrical, and plumbing systems are as much part of the building as columns, beams, doors, and corridors, and are as thoughtfully placed. Corridors distribute people and mechanical systems. Intake ducts, cable trays, junction boxes, plumbing and electric risers that distribute water and power and plumbing stacks that dispose of waste and gases are architectural features.

## Darth Vader

Students call the Earth Sciences Building "Darth Vader." Darth Vader is black and ominous. His community awards him great respect. He has very special capabilities and wars against the light and even his own son. The "dark side" is elevated and respected in *Star Wars*. The students appear to hold technology in veneration but are afraid of its dark side. Einstein is associated with Darth Vader. And although this kindly man did not make the atom bomb he is blamed for it.

Ironically the Earth Sciences Building is no more high-tech than Einstein was Darth Vader. Its plan, structural system, and finish is classical, bearing more architectural resemblance to a Greek stoa than to a space craft.

The galleria is a three-storied, colonnaded pathway. The structural system is the classic trabeated system with base, column, and frieze of hollow core plank. The ordered row of columns substitutes a haunch for the column capital. It is visually direct, consciously avoiding the mystery of technical complexity, as does a Greek temple.

This is not a simplification of a complex technol-

*Photos:* IKOY.

ogy but the clarification of a simple one. The ordered rows of columns spanned by stout beams creates a classical sense of order. The structure is clear and statically determinate. It is not optimized, continuous, or indeterminate and therefore not high-tech, but classical. Connections are exposed, for concealed they would violate classic principles.

If a building element looks as if it could be knocked down it is not properly visually connected in a classical building. Strong beams emphasize the sense of bearing and the beam to column connection is the key. There is no hint of the structural virtuosity of high technology.

The Earth Sciences Building answers some of the "why" of why buildings stand up. It is reassuring and can be trusted even though Darth Vader is suspect.

## Factual Information

Wallace Building
University of Manitoba
Winnipeg, Manitoba

*Costs*. Total cost for construction about $10.5 million—$1.6 million under budget; 130,000 square feet, two and three stories. (The building came in at $9,000,000, $1.5 million under budget, so a basement was added)

*Structure*. The building is set on piles, as are most major buildings in Manitoba, because the soil is predominantly clay. Precast concrete columns extend three and four stories high. Precast concrete beams span the columns, resting on column haunches. The column system allows the addition of another two stories.

Beams are spanned by 12″ hollow core concrete planks that are cantilevered into the central atrium corridor space on one side, creating the upper level walkways. The building skin is steel studs and an extruded aluminum control gird, which is capable of supporting corrugated anodized aluminum panels, or glazing. Hollow core planks, columns and beams are sandblasted concrete. Exposed ducts, switch gear, electrical raceways, and trays are factory-finished. Ductwork is run in the cores of the hollow planks.

The hollow core floor panels have excellent spanning ability and penetration characteristics. Cores are 9″ in diameter. Holes can be cut perpendicular to them, the full width of their diameter, 12″ on center, for distribution access. A maximum perforation of 9″ × 12″ is also possible without compromising their structural integrity. This allows almost unlimited access to distribution systems.

Plank loading capacity is 150 lbs/sq ft. Plank bridges can be moved or removed or additional bridges can be installed using a fork lift truck with an extended lift mechanism. A craneway has been incorporated into the structure to move heavy laboratory equipment. This also allows the shifting of building components.

Electrical and mechanical distribution systems are paired with the major beams of the structural system running the length of the building. Electrical distribution is located on the laboratory side of the beams and was installed prefinished and prewired.

The advantage is obvious. Factory labor is about $6 an hour and on-site labor costs about $24. The quality of the factory work is higher. Electricians simply connect to secondary distribution systems in the building. The more complex the wiring required, the greater the cost savings achieved using factory wiring.

Major air replacement is required, due to the loss from fume hoods and direct exhaust from laboratories. Heart pumps were selected because they adjust well to the floor core distribution system.

*Plumbing*. Toilets are located in individual units with sinks and lockable doors, which is unusual in large institutional buildings, and a first step toward a movable toilet system that will allow relocation of washroom units with a fork lift truck. Movable washrooms can then become part of the secondary, rather than primary plumbing distribution system.

*Fitments*. All partitions are steel stud and melamine covered panels. Security problems are severe, so all partitions must extend to the underside of the hollow core slabs. When walls must be relocated, panels can be detached, and the metal studs discarded. New metal studs can be erected, and the panels attached to them simply and quickly, as they contain no mechanical equipment or wiring. There are hung ceilings for soundproofing in less than 15 percent of the space. The mechanical elements in the remainder of the space are exposed as part of the architectural expression.

*Skin*. Steel stud, control grid, aluminum corrugated and curtain wall Kawneer-like curtain wall.

*Mechanical*. 4-pipe heat pump system which is a sophisticated fan coil system. Electrical energy costs are low in Winnipeg, so heat pumps can be used economically. Each heat pump unit has an electric motor. They collect the hot air and make it cold or the cold and make it hot. A series of water pipes exchanging heat pass back and forth through the building.

Will never use heat pumps again. The great number of machines and duct work required wrote an almost uncontrollable piping and power cable scenario, and required supply and make-up ductwork that goes to them. Heat pumps function extremely well but the architectural consequences of using them are extreme.

# RCMP FORENSIC LABORATORY, WINNIPEG, MANITOBA
## The Building

The Royal Canadian Mounted Police (RCMP) serve as Canada's Federal police force. They operate a network of regional crime-detection laboratories to analyze bullets, clothing, hair fibers, blood, and other potential evidence collected in criminal cases.

The building is a two-story rectangle placed partly below ground. Exterior walls are eight-inch-square glazed concrete block. "They wanted a nice building, a nice red brick building, but not a nice red brick invitational building," say the architects.

This is a research laboratory whose grim work is to scientifically investigate the physical evidences of crime. The laboratory technicians and scientists must, at all costs, preserve the exhibits from even the remotest suspicion of tampering, for they constitute life and death evidence.

The wonder of what is happening inside the building could not be satisfied by exposing part of the interior to public view. The architects were asked to place a pleasing building in the landscape but one that was completely private.

It is not the architect's task to "educate" clients but to understand their belief systems. The building says enjoy me, feel secure, and keep away. I am very good looking, but do not approach to bandy witticisms.

The building is like a Cold Stream Guard or a Canadian Royal Mounted Policeman in full uniform. Attractive but not inviting. There is little curiosity about what is going on inside of him. You do not expect surprise, delight, fun, or humor. It is expected that the right and proper things are happening. You expect impartial judgment and fairness, not curiosity. You expect investigation, rational analysis, and a totaling of the facts to arrive at an unbiased conclusion.

## The Challenge

The possibility of doing a "real" high-tech lab building was exciting to the architects. It was high-tech but for a paramilitary organization. Not only was the public excluded from the building but ordinary police were excluded as well. It was not a "high security" building in the sense of scientific or military secrets. Secrecy was guaranteed by law. Canadian courts take the sanctity of evidence very seriously, bordering on paranoia. Who would dare rob the building of the Royal Canadian Mounted Police? They did not know but would take no chances that someone might.

The first idea was a solid exterior wall. But scientists have to see out and light must come in so it was agreed there would be windows large enough to look out but not large enough for a man to come in.

The site was parklike. They wanted a fortress in the park, although a nice looking fortress in a residential district. It must say, stay away from me, please, backed by weapons.

This was quite a challenge for designers who had made a career of invitational buildings by exposing the inside of the building through the skin to the street. The designer was told by men in uniform to do a building you can not see into and not to use aluminum but something solid like "red brick."

The building must have the attitude of uniform and paramilitary organization. A starched and ordered building. A building that respected the police military point of view that looked like it was wearing a pressed uniform. The building skin is glazed concrete block with horizontal bands of anodized aluminum which decorate like the piping on pants seams or the stripes on uniform sleeves.

Windows are frameless and flush with the block. Their coverings are put on with special tamper proof screws. They are black and the walls grey, striping is silver bronze. The fume-hood vents on the roof line up in two ordered and regimented marching lines.

The building is set in the ground, which rises up and moves around it. The community calls it a "submarine." The architects think of it as a soldier peering over a trench. But submarine or soldier, protected by the ground around, dug in secure and ready.

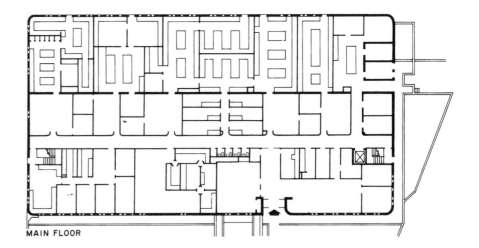

MAIN FLOOR

Front elevation and detail. *Photos:* IKOY.

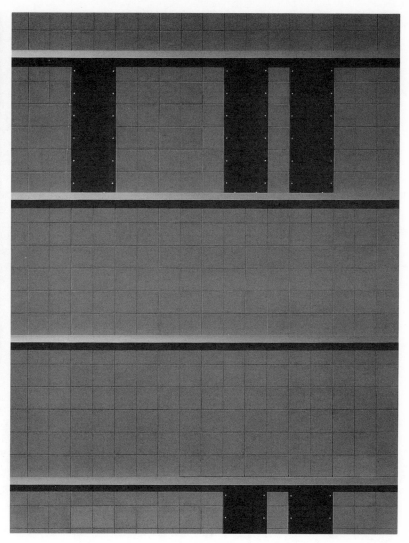

Entrance and corridor. *Photos:* IKOY.

## The Corridor

It is not a large building. The one common area is a single-story corridor. On one side are high-technology labs and on the other low-tech labs like photography and administration.

The corridor is 300 feet long, 7 feet wide, and if it had a hung ceiling would be about 8 feet high. Each door is the same as the other doors. No windows and no skylight for parachutists to sneak in.

Nothing bores and intimidates like a long corridor with repetitive doors. Only scientists, about 40 of them, use this corridor. These are not sheep or lepers but sensitive people.

The architect chose this building to challenge the entire idea of a one story corridor. The corridor was "peeled" to its basics. It did not need to be more than 7 feet wide. The structure chosen for the building had 11 feet to the smooth hollow core planks above. These were supported on wide flange beams with a single row of columns located on one side of the corridor 30 feet on centers.

Traditionally the columns are built into partition walls and hung ceilings will hide the beams. People walk down a sheetrocked, acoustic tile tube not knowing whether they are on the 1st or 12th floor of a building. If they did not take the elevator it is the first.

The column is the proudest part of any building and how column and beam are connected has endless fascination. The wide flange beam the engineer selected was exposed, the columns were rotated and web stiffeners put in the beams. Then the architect designed a "virtuoso" column. It looks like it is doing more than it is doing when it is doing what it does normally. The cost was 500 dollars each for ten columns, 600 dollars less than the cost of a hung ceiling.

The mechanical system uses fan coils. This equipment was brought to the edge of the corridor so that all maintenance could be done from there. All electrical switch gear is also exposed in the

Corridor of the U.S. National Bureau of Standards. *Photo:* F. Wilson.

corridor. Maintenance of electrical and mechanical equipment does not violate the security of the laboratory or disturb the scientists working in them.

Exposure of the building's working equipment and structural system are primarily responsible for transforming what might have been a sense-numbing tube into a fascinating one-story passageway that explains something about the science and technology on the other side of the doors.

## Factual Information

*General.* Completed in 1987, 30,000 square feet at a cost of $4.4 million, $146 a square foot.

*Structure.* Wide flange column and beams, 8″ hollow core precast plank.

*Mechanical.* All fan coil units; four-pipe fan coil heat and cooling any time of the year. No interchange of air from space to space; air heated, cooled, and circulated in space. A lot of air dumped outside, a separate make-up air system blows air into any lab and is blown out the fume hoods. Very little return air used in the system. Most air is either recirculated or blown out.

*Skin.* The skin is glazed concrete block, steel stud backup with 4–6 inches of insulation. The building is one story above ground and a half underground. Labs are serviced from a walk-in crawl space under them or from the public corridors. There is minimum requirement for the entrance of any tradespeople.

*Fitments.* Melamine panels or aluminum plate panels screwed onto metal studs or drywall on steel studs.

*Comment.* This building combines architectural high tech and scientific laboratory technology. 35–40 percent of the building cost is in scientific equipment. There are fume hoods, special lab counters, special rooms, such as a firing range equipped to measure the speed of a bullet. The rosewood veneers of an executive office are cheap compared to the dull gray or black of a scientists work top, which must be impervious to all forms of acid.

# COMPUTER CENTER, UNIVERSITY OF WATERLOO
## Tying It All Together

The University of Waterloo is recognized as a world leader in the production of data, routines, and programs for the use of digital computers. The work was generated by a blend of disciplines, primarily mathematics and engineering, dispersed in makeshift facilities haphazardly scattered in campus buildings. There was a computer science department located in the mathematics building, but the engineers work around the engineering complex and other interested scientists found space where they could.

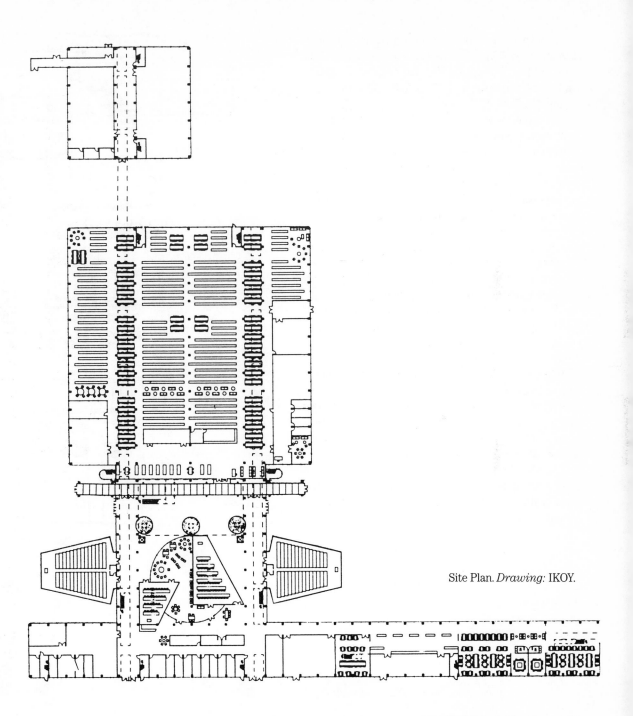

Site Plan. *Drawing:* IKOY.

The University held a limited national competition for the design of a building to tie it all together. The architects analyzed the competition program, walked over the site, and studied the university and its ambitions.

The problem was to design a building to enclose a new science barely 20 years old. It is a science that is reordering social, economic, and professional relationships—one that is widely accepted by the public but viewed with suspicion by traditional university disciplines. There are no traditions or visual associations such as ivy-covered tudor halls, gothic revival, or even modern boxes.

The Center must include 400 research offices and hundreds of laboratories. These will be used by professors, researchers and graduate students. There must be room for a major engineering–mathematics–science library and dining hall. There must be two multipurpose auditoriums, no classrooms, and very private offices, some designated as "high security."

There must be a physical link between engineering and mathematics. The size and the importance of the building establishes it as a new gateway to the eastern campus. It sits on what was formerly a secondary parking lot which has now been moved across the street.

The building must declare the prominence of computer science, even though not all agree that computing is a science, or agree on the appropriate visual references.

## How?
### The Key

The University stipulated that scientists must talk to each other. They seldom do. Researchers move in and out of their laboratories, day or night as the mood strikes them. They appear miraculously, do

*Design sketch:* IKOY.

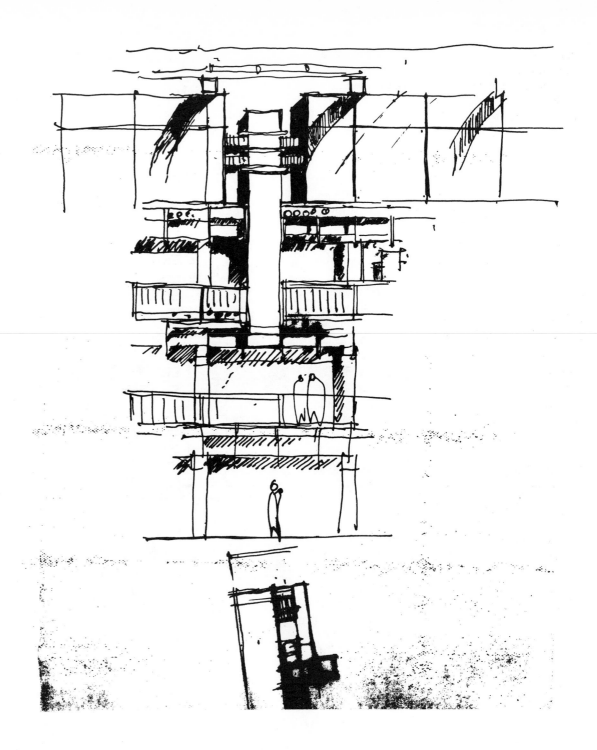

their work or whatever they do in laboratories, and vanish as mysteriously as they arrived. How can a building encourage community and individuality for eccentrics that treasure privacy above all else and lump community with faculty meetings, which they detest?

What does a computer building look like? An earth sciences building could express a triumphant transition from dull geology to moon rocks and space probes. In contrast to the wonders of rocket ships and distant planets, computers are definitely "blah." Small computers look like suitcases, and large, mainframe computers look like refrigerators.

The designers studied the computer screens in their office and discovered the fascination is not in the shape of the box but what's in it. The black box is not anonymous. Pictures are generated by a mysterious series of dots in a number of colors and a chaotic order is present in color, purpose, and line.

These patterns are not unlike minuscule wall edges, door frames, window mullions, ceiling channels, pipe elbows, duct hangers, and cable trays. Researchers find meanings in the dots and lines on their terminals as less adventurous people are instructed by letters, words and sentences in books. This could well be the stuff of an architectural language.

The computer's guts are a mystery to all but repairmen. Most of the people that use computers would rather not know they are there. Hackers are oblivious to what is inside the box as philosophers are disinterested in the techniques of neurosurgery. Most of those who use computers are content to leave the mind-boggling complexity of wires and chips encased in slick boxes, a mystery.

However computers, in contrast to other high-tech tools such as those used by dental surgeons, for example, are not sinister. They appear mysterious, but helpful. They do not threaten.

*Design sketch:* IKOY.

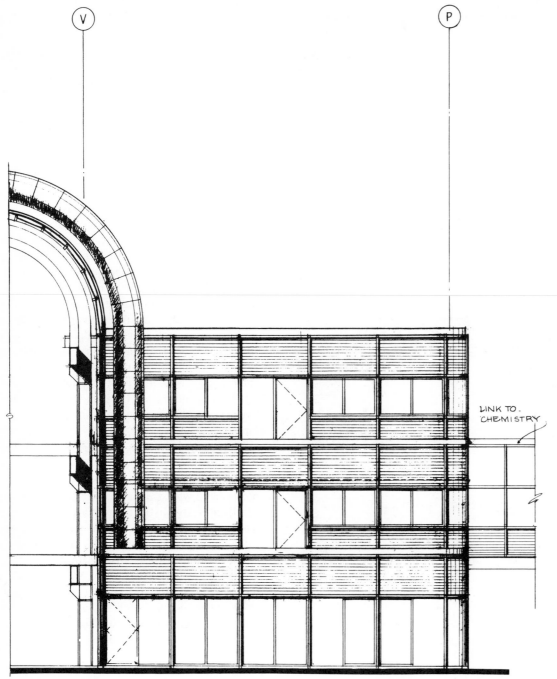

LINK TO.
CHEMISTRY

*Developed design sketch:* IKOY.

What would it be like to pass through the computer screen as an electric surge and move among those brightly colored lines and dots? If lines and dots were "real" and the people walked by, around and through them, would they be reassured by a sense of place as a Greek citizen was comforted passing by and through the familiar forms of temple and stao? This the architects said, is the key.

## Through the Looking Screen

There is always a background. It is not black but dark blue. When penetrated it is as if one passed through the "looking glass" into a chip zone. This is the wonderland of inner computer workings behind the brightly colored lines.

Microchips drive the computer; labs drive the Computer Research Building. Labs, like chips, have memory, route knowledge, turn energy on and off.

When the scientists, engineers, laboratory technicians, professors, and students come out of the chip zone they enter a galleria of brightly colored dots and lines.

People that work with computers talk to each other on computer screens. The great galleria is a talking zone in which the players in the building, the computer scientists, mathematicians, electrical engineers, systems engineers, mechanical engineers share information to energize in the dialog zone. Researchers do not socialize in their laboratories. Research is dross, only valuable when published with their name attached to it.

If researchers are coached from concentrated laboratory work they enter a zone of relief from demanding work. The lab is a chiplike cell full of energy sources where the occupant sits in front of terminals working intensely to squeeze out the last of the best idea.

When scientists leave the laboratory they should not step into a 400-foot-long corridor 8 feet wide and 8 feet high lined with green numbered doors.

Galleria from the outside. *Photos:* IKOY.

Vent from library below. *Photos:* IKOY.

People do not stop and talk to each other on mean thoroughfares.

They must enter a delightful place that speaks of their science and electronic communication. It should have sunlight, clouds, rain, or snow to remind them of the outside world forgotten in the laboratory.

The space must clear the brains cramped cells that have concentrated on a single problem for hours. It must welcome challenge and discussion. The building must do what universities are supposed to do, which is stimulate.

The building should stimulate like Oxford and Cambridge. There, dons, students, and scholars mingle in the colonnades around the quadrangles. The food is bad in their dining halls, but dining halls are places for conversation. Students do not line in them to grab a cheeseburger to take back and eat in their laboratories. The libraries and vaulted halls of traditional universities are the setting for great ideas, whether they are generated there or not.

Those who research and think in the computer center are there because this is where they want to be. They do not care about tenure. They are showered with job offers each promising more money than the one before. Money is not a motivator to great hackers. Better hacking and a better hacking environment is.

The building must be part of their desire to stay.

## The Building

The Computer Center is a gateway, a computer gate. The great glass-covered stoa leads to half the buildings on the campus.

The glass entrance facade transforms the people behind it into animated computer graphics. The brightly painted parts behind them are part of a gigantic dot-and-line CAD system.

In the hierarchy of building, structure is above the mechanical and electrical ducts, raceways, and junction boxes, but in the computer center the ducts are so large they obviously are not structure but environmental sculptures serving a life-support system.

In the corridor the electrical switch gear and computer communications cable makes it clear this is movement space for people and communication lines from lab to lab delivering and dispersing information.

The galleria, an architectural glass tube, is a metaphor for a cathode ray tube. The person is in the tube because the person is in it. There are lines, overlapping lines, columns, base details, handrails, raceways as elements of tracery like the stone ribs and lead fastenings of a gothic window, or the dots and lines of an incredibly enlarged terminal screen.

Yellow bars, 4 feet on center, placed overhead along the corridor mask and reveal the light and machinery of the building above. There is a choice of looking directly at the exposed parts or lowering the eyes so the light bars bar them from the line of sight.

Time has been told by water, sand, wax, the sun, and gears. It is now told by beeping microprocessors, buzzers, and voices instead of bells. The building is a place of beeps, buzzers, and voices, as gothic cathedrals were places of chants, chambers places of chamber music, and baroque churches places of fugues. The dots and lines of the computer screen have a physical presence that evokes the music of the microprocessor.

## Factual Information

*Construction Time.* Competition winner, awarded October 1984; construction started fall 1985, completed 1988.

*Area.* 320,000 square feet.

*Cost.* $24 million; $75 dollars a square foot.

*Structure.* Poured-in-place columns; precast concrete beams and 12 inch hollow core planks; bent columns that become roof beams are precast.

*Mechanical System.* Standard VAV, HVAC in terms of equipment supplemented by perimeter radiation. The four 9-inch-diameter holes in hollow core planks used for air distribution, supply, and return fed by continuous header duct. Header duct runs in public galleria. Acts as efficient active mass thermal storage diaphragm. The temperature of the concrete is raised or lowered by the air supply. The result is a 320,000 cubic foot heat sink.

*Electrical.* Electrically the building is extremely simple. The difficulty is in the communication cable between computer tables. User groups supply, install, and maintain computer cables. The computer people in the building are far more expert with the computer cables than any electrician, subcontractor, or electrical engineer. Electrical and communication cables are separated. Separate distribution system for electrical power. Almost all equipment works off 110 or 220V lines and 347V for fluorescent fixtures. The computer industry made most of the equipment to go into a standard office building. The robotics laboratory has special power requirements.

*Skin.* Curtain wall, anodized aluminum on steel studs combined with curtain walls and control grids; double exterior glazing.

*Fitments.* Lab partitions on steel stud system with removable drywall panel system.

*Comments.* Use of plank cores for HVAC resulted in tremendous cost saving because of elimination of metal distribution ducts; the smooth underside of planks used for bounce light to reduce glare on computer terminals. This allowed floor-to-floor height of 12 rather than 15 feet, which reduced the building cube by 20 percent.

The building at this stage (nearing completion) is like MTV. There are so many messages in the temporary structures of the builder. There are tools and tool boxes, stacked equipment. There are industrial boxes made by the same machines that make the building parts. Here and there the clear outlines of the building are revealed as the "plot" or story line amid the jumbled confusion, as the singer flashes in and out amid the various images of MTV. The TV images support the plot, elaborate it in under- and overstatement, by analogy and metaphor as do the worker's temporary structures and equipment.

The building parts in their boxes elaborate, overstate, and understate the building theme. Bins of connectors are multitudinous declarations of connections like a crowd at the beach. The connector in the building is a separate drama, like a man and woman, holding hands, walking alone along the sand at the water's edge. The bins, like the crowds of people on the beach, are connection possibilities. When there is connection it is apart from the chaos of the beach and gives a hint of potential within chaos. The bin is potential the connection is realization making the building and society a functional whole.

—Keenberg

*Photo:* F. Wilson.

# Chapter 4

# Architectural Language

## THE CLASSICAL IDIOM

The Classical idiom of the orders made up of stylobate, column, entablature and pediment has proven the most enduring of all architectural languages. Classicism has survived for at least 2500 years and continues to be spoken where people consider themselves well bred.

Practically every town in the Western world, large or small, has Doric, Ionic, and Corinthian buildings to shelter its banks, brokerage houses, law courts and libraries. Some of the greatest modern buildings—the Pantheon in Paris, the Capitol in Washington D.C., the Imperial Palace in Tokyo—have been designed in the classical language of architecture. Civic buildings in the cities of Southeast Asia, that have had nothing at all to do with classical civilization, proudly display monumental architectural essays in the classical language of Greece and Rome.

John Summerson, the English architectural historian, defined a "classical" building as one whose decorative language is derived from the architectural vocabulary of the "classical" world. The beginnings were the temple architecture of the Greeks and the religious, military and civil architecture of the Romans. Greek and Roman architectural structures and decoration were organized into orderly systems by the Renaissance. The systems were flamboyantly overdone during the Baroque era, copied and manipulated during Neoclassicism and the Beaux Arts, exploded in size by the Nazis to become the fun and games and furnish the material for the whity comments of Post Modernists.

### A Definition

The harmonious relation of parts which we could call the syntax of the classical language begins with the *orders*. These are divided into 5 standard varieties of columns and entablatures with standard ways of treating door and window openings, gable ends, and runs of mouldings. This orderly system allows the standards to be altered, but they must remain recognizable.

The goal is a "harmony" of elements achieved by a dimensional ratio of the sizes of the building and its parts. For example, the spacing of columns, "intercolumnation," is measured in column diameters. The entablature, pediment, and all other building elements must be variations of the basic column thickness or "module."

Vitruvius, in his third and fourth books of architecture, describes three of the orders, Ionic, Doric, and Corinthian, and adds some notes on the Tuscan. Vitruvius considered the orders an acceptable way of talking architecture if one wanted to show one knew what one was talking about. The formalization of the orders and combining them with the arches, vaults, and domes of the Romans was the contribution of Renaissance humanists.

Alberti added a fifth order, the Composite. Serlio a century later published the first fully illustrated

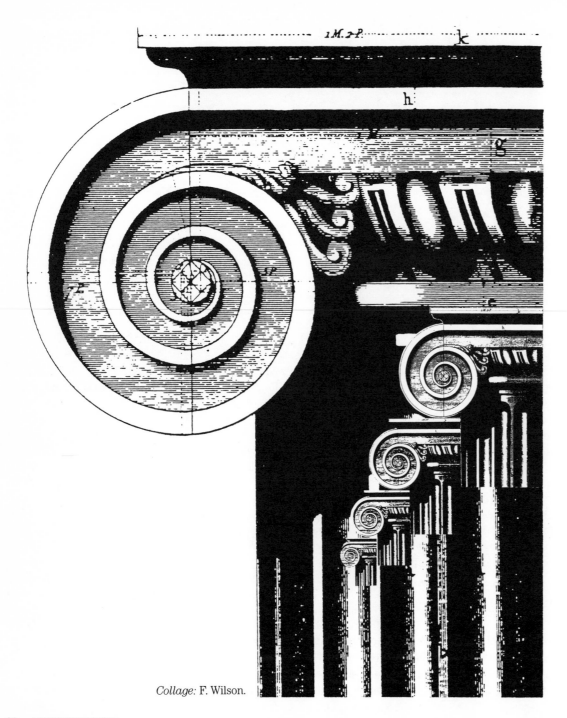

*Collage:* F. Wilson.

architectural grammar of the Renaissance. Serlio arranged the orders according to their relative slimness in the ratio of diameter to height, in the sequence Tuscan, Doric, Ionic, Corinthian, and Composite. Almost every 17th and 18th Century primer of architecture began in the same way.

A building may have the same proportionate harmony, but not the trappings of classical architecture. It is not therefore "classical" says Summerson. For example the porches of Chartres Cathedral are classically proportioned but the building is unmistakably Gothic. To be classical the building must make some reference to the orders.

In summary the classical language of architecture uses forms whose combination are known, recognized, and understood by a considerable community. The classical syntax is found in the harmonious arrangement of parts or elements and the way they are combined to form architectural phrases, clauses, and sentences.

The language of architectural elements may appeal to the eye as poetry to the ear, but buildings have utilitarian functions as language has meaning. Classical buildings must be stable and lasting, and must satisfy and accommodate the purposes for which they were built.

There has been a slow development and refinement of the fundamental elements of classical architecture through the ages. What began as structure was decorated, and as the utilitarian functions of buildings changed the structure itself became decoration. The wooden columns that supported early Greek temples were decorated, replaced in stone, and became the Doric, Ionic, and Corinthian orders. By the time of the building of the Colosseum in Rome (70–82 AD), the mighty concrete brick and stone structure used the classical orders of architecture purely as decoration. There are three-quarter round, Doric, Ionic, and Corinthian columns for the first three stories and a Corinthian pilaster at the top supporting nothing at all.

Corinthian columns in the Pension building, Washington,
D.C. *Photo:* F. Wilson.

The North facade of the New York Stock Exchange,
Manhattan. *Photo:* F. Wilson.

# WHAT WERE THE GREEKS TALKING ABOUT?

The classical language of architecture is recognized the world over but the meaning of its forms and decorations is almost forgotten. Classical ornament, according to George Hersey, is derived from sacrificial ceremonies. Its decorations are the instruments of sacrifice which the ancients felt it necessary to remember and record [1].

Greek art is full of sacred trees. Sacrifices were made before them. Temples were built in sacred groves, gods and goddesses appear in their branches. Trees and groups of trees were decorated with sacrificial instruments and the results of their use. The victim's remains, bones, horns, and sacrificial paraphernalia, urns, lamps, fruit, flowers, and weapons are the decorations of Greek art, as Hersey demonstrated. Masks, spears and skulls are suspended from alters and trees trimmed in the shape of primitive columns.

Why wrap a courthouse in garlands and streamers used to decorate sacrificial oxen? Why call a gable by the name of a bone and leather drum, *tympanum,* that was used in Bacchic rituals? Why, as Pugin, the anti-classicist, asked, "Do we worship the blood of bulls and goats?"

This was the question "modern architects" asked and answered in the words of Henry van de Velde, who said in 1902 that the ideal was to "recognize the meaning, the form, the purpose of all the things of the material modern world with the same truth as the Greeks, but do so in a 'modern language.'"

The new language Van de Velde wrote five years later should express the form and construction of all objects in strict elementary logic and justification for their existence. Form will be subordinated to the essential use of the material. Ornament used only to the extent that it respects and retains and essential appearance of the basic forms and construction.

Adolf Loos wrote his famous article "Ornament and Crime" in 1908. And in 1914 Futurist architects

The real thing at Paestrum (Italy), c. 450 B.C., East front from South. *Photo:* W. Loerke.

Antonio Sant'Elia and Filippo Tommaso Marinetti declared in a manifesto, "The calculation of the strength of materials, the use of reinforced concrete, rule out 'architecture' in the classical and traditional sense. Modern building materials and scientific ideas do not lend themselves to the disciplines of historical styles."

Modern materials, they said, should not be forced into the limiting structural forms, the heavy curve of arches and massive appearance of marble. The apparent fragility of reinforced concrete and steel should be respected and appreciated.

An architecture of reinforced concrete, iron, glass, textile fiber, substitutes for wood, stone, and brick should result in an elastic, light architectural idiom, they claimed.

By 1910 modern architects were ready to dispose of the garlands of sacrifice, and the sacred trees of the Greeks. Buildings with the new materials and knowledge of the 20th Century were to find beauty in the expression of their materials, techniques, and utilitarian functions. Ornament, if it became necessary, should derive from contemporary life rather than sacrificial paraphernalia.

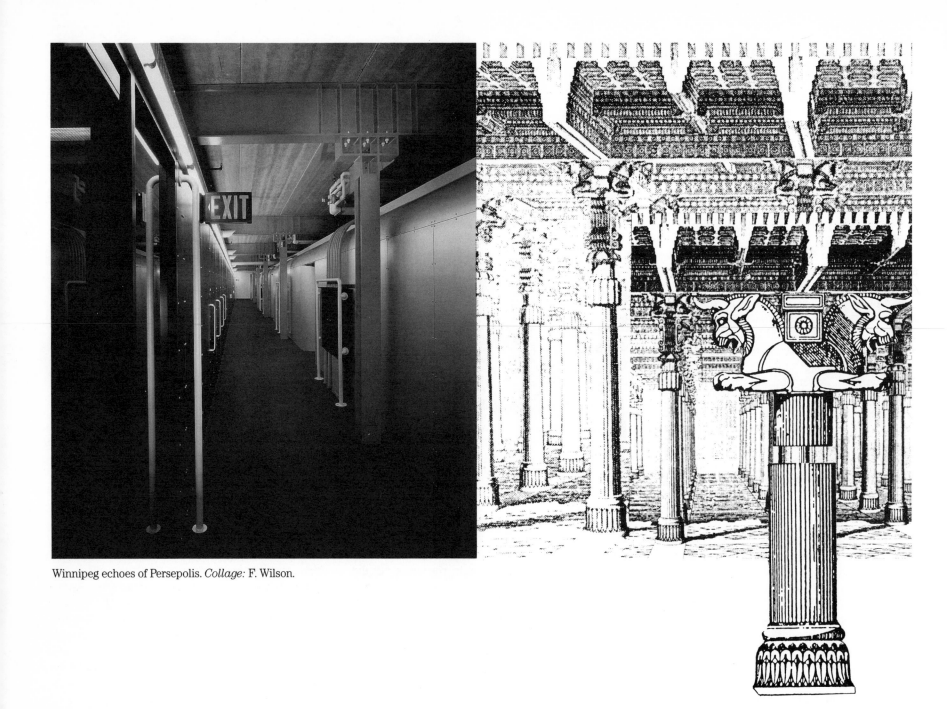

Winnipeg echoes of Persepolis. *Collage:* F. Wilson.

The language of modern architecture became an international language with the publication of Johnson and Hitchcock's book *The International Style* in 1932, and lasted almost fifty years. In the late 1960s the dominance of modern architecture was challenged by a succession of enthusiasms, including a return to historic references by postmodernists.

The buildings shown here are not classical, modern, or postmodern. They do follow the search begun by the modernists in the early years of this century to express the functions of the time with its materials and techniques. But these are now entirely different than they were when the first strident manifestos of modern architecture were written.

There is a difference between 1910 and now. Today's "modern architecture" must respond to a group of inventions centered around the computer and rapid advances in electronic technology as well as the new materials steel and reinforced concrete that fascinated van de Velde, Loos, Le Corbusier, and the others.

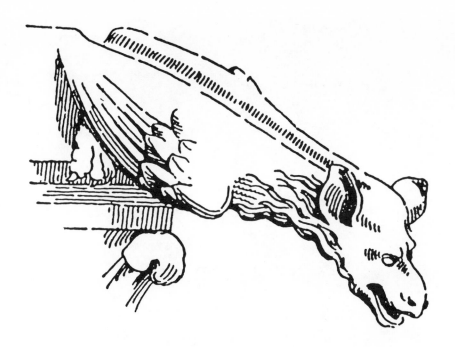

The gargoyle of La Sainte Chapelle, Paris, for rainwater runoffs. The gargoyle of the auto diesel shop at Red River Community College for diesel fumes. *Photo:* IKOY.

A Chac at Kaba Yucatan c. 1200 A.D. and a tension rod
socket c. 1979 watching you. *Photos:* F. Wilson, IKOY.

Chacs or rain gods were worshipped as masters of life-giving rain and masters of the storm. They were often portrayed brandishing a symbolic flash of lightning and are found on almost every Mayan temple frieze in Yucatan. Uxmal, Yucatan. *Photo:* F. Wilson.

Twin chacs of power and communication with fluorescent lightning tube, and draped cable noses. IKOY offices, Winnipeg. *Photo:* IKOY.

# THE SOUND OF INTERACTIVE OBJECTS

Advanced electric appliances, photocopiers, automatic bank tellers, FAX machines, word processors, answering machines, talking key rings, all interact with their users in a different way than ordinary objects.

Designers now deal with artifacts that sense, and say what they feel. As objects become "articulate," our response to them influences their design. The object is no longer a single entity but instead linked to other objects in a network of communication.

There is an invisible interface between human language, gestures, and the computer, wrote Ezio Manzini [1]. Computer science influences human thought, language, and conduct. The demand for a "user friendly" interface determines the quality of machine–person relationships, he continued.

There is no formal point of reference to judge interactive objects, for the components that make the objects "intelligent" are invisible. We do not see them or what they are doing. Function is flexible. Different actions are performed. It is impossible to categorize objects in traditional ways, wrote Manzini. For example, an ordinary appearing personal computer can run a nonsensical computer game, precipitate a "run" on the stock market, or launch a missile. The division between work, which has been traditionally functional, and play, which has been traditionally frivolous, has no physical distinction.

The range of communication between person and object changes from calculator keyboard to electronic dials to advice spoken by a camera. Form has little to do with function. The shape of a key finder, electronic game, heartbeat recorder is not an indication of the seriousness of their functions. The technology of sensors, actuators, displays, and digital and analog controls is invisible to their users.

The computer chip writ large at the Computer Center, University of Waterloo. *Collage:* F. Wilson.

The attitude of an olympic pool. *Rendering:* IKOY.

The questions designers must now answer are degree of automation, whether to talk to a washing machine or arouse its interest with tactile sensors. Should the user press a button or a sensitized membrane, use a hand print or whistle? Manzini asked.

The interactions between human and inanimate objects is programmed by their form. Chair and buttock are programmed for each other by physical shape of both. But the interactivity of "smart" objects is no longer a program inscribed in the physical shape of arse and chair seat.

Inanimate objects interact with users passively. Pacificity is a given characteristic. The new generation of "smart" things modifies behavior according to external variables. Light sensors turn lights on and off when they detect movement in the room. Sprinkler heads flood the room with water when the temperature raises a given amount. Contact with "smart" objects is time related. They are no longer passive but interact with their environment. A thing of beauty is no longer a passive joy forever. Today it might jump and bite.

## How to Talk to Architecture That Talks Back

Microchips do not influence the shape of the "thing." So far objects with the "smarts" tend to assume traditional forms much as the classical orders descended from Greek temple architecture serve to express bank and car wash.

The "smart" credit card and wrist watch are examples of this process. The card is used to make purchases—but it also remembers what you spend, calculates, plays radio music, and opens hotel room doors and runs on a solar cell. The watch tells time, calculates, measures distances walked, projects TV, remembers telephone numbers, and monitors heart beats. An interactive glove is used as a means of translating spontaneous hand gestures into machine language, and a "mouse" draws pictures on a computer screen.

Inanimate buildings are taken in at a glance, acknowledged or ignored. Interactive things can demand attention. A malfunctioning burglar alarm will keep a neighborhood awake all night. A malfunctioning mechanical system in a sealed building causes its evacuation, an eccentric elevator might trap its passengers for a weekend. Interactive objects are both convenient and scary.

As we move today from an industrial to what some call a service society, the language of classicism, modernism, postmodernism or any of the gradations between could be and are used as a design language for interactive buildings. We do not know if the language used is archaic, appropriate, or postmodern.

What is the "correct" form for buildings that talk back? Past forms can be used, it is true, as we use watch and credit card as types, but this is as temporary a solution as marble ionic columns on a steel skyscraper. The smart credit card and watch do not look exactly like their old, dumb forebears. There are subtle differences hinting at new forms. The credit card has a solar cell, the watch has added buttons and bulk.

The smart watch and credit card are like the uppermost row of Corinthian pilasters on the Coliseum. They are no longer watch, credit card, or Corinthian column. We need new words.

## EXCERPTS FROM A MODERN ARCHITECTURAL DICTIONARY
## Some Words

### Attitude

We can begin our search for a modern language with a further definition of *building attitude*.

The way a building presents itself to an observer may be described, in a summary way, as its attitude. In this definition, the term *function* must be taken in its broadest, most comprehensive meaning, that is, not only its physical function as gymnasium, post office, law court, apartment building, office building, bridge, or the like, but also its psychological function—human exercise, speedy communication, government (impersonal, majestic), private enclave, cheerful work space, flying road, etc.

The viewer's comprehension of the building is directly proportioned to his or her apprehension of it. Therefore, each building connection must explain itself by visually demonstrating its relationship to other building elements.

There must be no mystery in why the building stands (its structure), where its edges are (its skin), why the interior climate is different from the outside (its mechanical systems), where its energy comes from (its electrical systems), where one is going to go or has been (its plan), and how its spaces are subdivided (its fitments).

### Talking Structure

The term *structure* includes the total structure in all its aspects, physical elements, and manner of assembly. When the designer brings the total structure into close harmony with the broadest definition of its function, he or she has created a building. Every part then contributes to the telling of its story. That building strikes an attitude which any one can read.

The building structure is the building skeleton. It explains the building form and demonstrates why the building stands. It gives comfort. Structural elements take the loads. Their size, geometry, and connections make forces visible and understandable. This is the most important message the building can convey. There may be primary, secondary, and tertiary structures, structures within structures, each adding levels of assurance.

The structural material determines the type of connection. "Dry" materials such as steel frames and precast concrete columns and planks are erected at high speed. "Wet" materials—masonry,

At the beach in a merry-go-round. *Rendering:* IKOY.

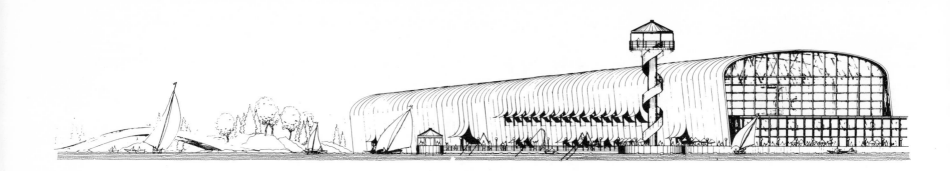

The no-nonsense olympic shed and the laid-back
rounder. *Renderings:* IKOY.

stone, cast-in-place concrete—are put in place
slowly. The connections between materials explain
the difference between wet and dry. Bolted steel
connections say fast erection.

Column bases and capitals are exposed in "dry"
construction, are not hidden in the slab as with
poured-in-place concrete. They are seen as firmly
planted in place and column-to-beam connections

plainly state how loads are received and moved on.

Welded column-to-beam connections are visually
ambiguous, in contrast to bolted connections. The
composition of the steel the architect selects is not
revealed in the rolled steel sections, but the joinery
of a pipe column and a wide flange beam becomes
part of an architectural language.

Exposed structure says the building is designed

to be changed. Emphasized building connections
such as column capital and base with floor slabs
resting on beams with junctions clearly expressed
point out the possibility of disconnection. The proportion of connections at all levels (beam to column,
slab, panel, and stud) add to this impression.

Connections exposed to express a hierarchy of
size and shape explain the difference between

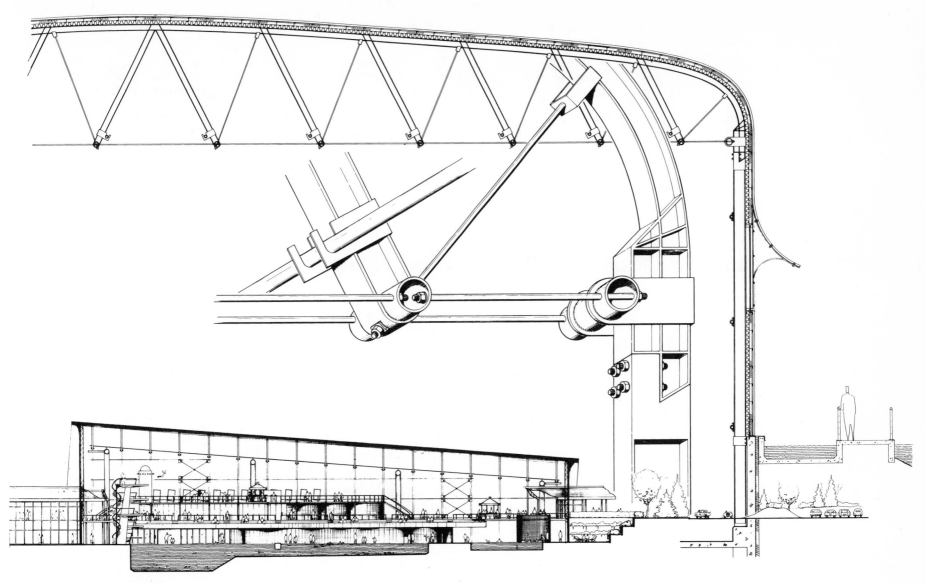

Straining truss. *Drawing:* IKOY.

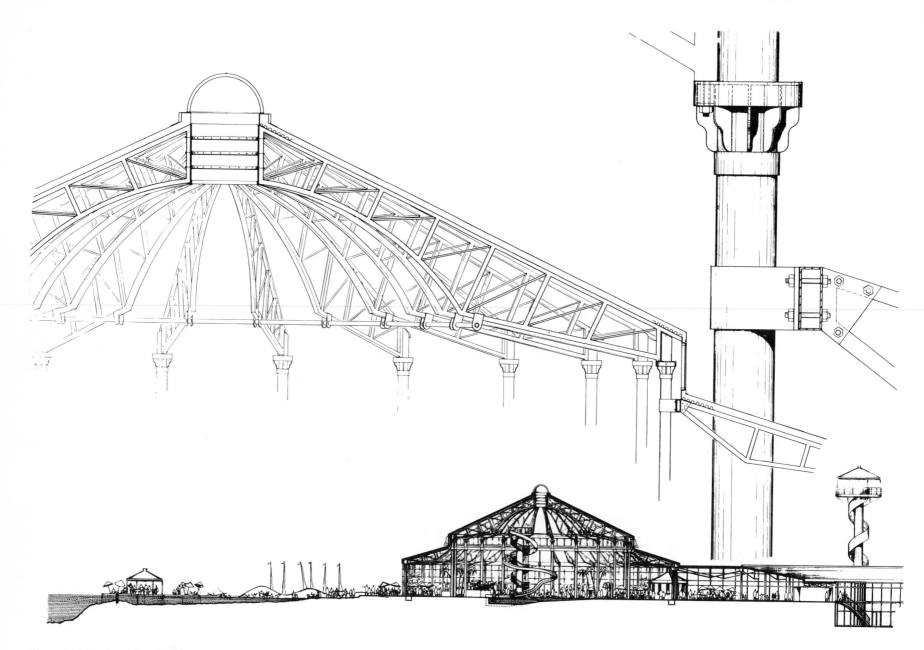

Trussed circle. *Drawing:* IKOY.

structural and temporary fastenings. Structural connections are physical links, while a laminated panel screwed to a metal stud partition is a temporary functional fastening.

The structural components are the key to the building's attitude for it literally structures the building's shape. All other elements are minor themes.

## Some Phrases

### Two Attitudes—Country Club and Leisure Center

Country clubs and leisure centers differ, and the selection of their elements must express this as clearly as the selection of Doric, Ionic, or Corinthian orders expressed, man, maiden, or matron in classical buildings.

Any large shed can cover a swimming pool, a multipurpose gymnasium, or a hockey rink, and if large enough can cover them all. A recreational building is a place of relaxation, enjoyment, and fun. That attitude must be apparent and influences all component choices.

Country clubs provide a very special leisure. Their members play formal golf and wear appropriate clothing at all times, particularly at dinner. They are restrained, aloof, and, simply, not much fun.

In contrast, people "shoot a game of golf" on public courses. This is a different leisure attitude.

One expects beer drinking and arguments over football or baseball, loud laughter, jokes, expressive consternation in the sand traps.

People do business on the country club greens and give each other "the business" on the public courses. Common people fart, cultured people break wind. The differences must be incorporated into the building posture at country club and public golf course ticket shed.

### Olympic Pool

Buildings with swimming pools can be like "going to the beach" or competitive looking structures where compression and tension structural members are in competition. They can be "lean and mean" expressions of athletics that demand you begin practice at 5 o'clock in the morning with minimal comfort, no wooden bleachers but cold steel or concrete. Exposed electrical switching gear express the tension between two incompatible elements, electrical fire and water. If mixed, water and electricity spell injury and death. Safety is essential but the potential for conflict, as it exists in sports, is evident. Sport is a peaceful exercise of warlike activities. Pulsing lights added to switching gear, with "stop" and "go," on and off, can be reminiscent of pin ball machine competition.

The starter is installed on a podium as the supreme arbiter. Although actual decisions are electronic when swimmers touch the wall, the expression of the importance of the starter is essential. The starter is a significant symbol. Pucks move much too fast to be seen at a hockey game and the audience cheers when the red light goes on.

The use of standard open web joists in this building would not be "lean and mean" but cheap. The building attitude is aristocratic, like that of a Watusi warrior. An olympic pool with a 10 meter diving board is an exotic gladiatorial arena. Training rooms have the aura of sacred space, for athletes revere training as worshipers revere ritual. (See the Northwest Leisure Center for a public pool, Chapter 3, p. 36.)

## REFERENCE

1. Hersey, George: *The Lost Meaning of Classical Architecture;* MIT Press, Cambridge, Mass. 1988.

2. Manzini, Ezio: "Interactivity," in Ottagano, *Design in the Information Environment,* p. 74, Whitney, Kent, and Knopf, New York, 1985.

# Chapter 5

# Materials and Machines

## MYTH AND MATERIALS

The "rightness" of a building material for a specific use is decided by more than its strength or ability to support loads, to withstand moisture and survive under adverse conditions. It must seem "right" to the architect. (See Attitude Chapter 4, p.- 91, and Fragments, Chapter 7, p. 139.)

Through long study and association with the materials of building the architect gains an understanding of them. But their selection is only half determined by physical characteristics, for almost any building material can be substituted for another with adequate physical properties and the building will not fall down.

Each material has a "quality" that makes it "right" for its particular use. Rightness is determined by a belief system that distinguishes the architecture of one age from another and one architect from another. For example Augustus is said to have found Rome a city of brick and left it a city of stone. Stone in Roman times was far superior to brick. Yet thin stone facings on a modern building is much less durable than brick or even aluminum, the material of beer cans.

## Vitruvius

Vitruvius thought that trees were pregnant in the springtime and used all their natural vigor to grow leaves and fruits, making them empty, swollen, weak, feeble, and unfit as a building material during this season of the year. They began recovery in autumn, their leaves withered as they drew nourishing sap from the ground, and they were compressed by the strong air of winter. Trees should be cut at this time.

The nature of materials were defined in terms of fire, air, earth, and water, and their usefulness for various building functions depended on the amount of each primordial element possessed. In siting a town, Vitruvius advised, marshes should be avoided for they bring with them mists and mingled with the mist, the poisonous breath of swamp creatures.

In many instances advice Vitruvius gave two thousand years ago, when separated from its myth, is good advice today. Some of the myths of modern architects may seem equally queer to future building scientists.

A fundamental challenge of modern architecture was to find a creative use of the new materials which science and industry provided. A philosophy of industrial architecture demanded new thinking about form and material.

The spans which stone can bridge, either as beam or arch, are limited. The longest Roman arches were 60 to 80 feet. A draped, high strength steel cable can stretch over a mile. The physical proportions dictated by these limitations established the sense of rhythm of Classical, Gothic, and Renaissance architecture. Reinforced concrete or steel have entirely different span ratios to depth of section and therefore structural geometry. Longer spans are achieved

Materials and machines; robotic auto manufacture. *Photo:* General Motors Corp. Stairway, Earth Sciences Building, University of Manitoba; Earth Sciences building from the parking lot. *Photos:* IKOY.

with thinner members. The greatest difference is in the use of gravity.

Stone buildings were held together by the pull of gravity. Gravity is the glue. Stone was stronger than mortar. Buildings were complex and beautiful balancing acts. The great daring and exquisite precision of thrust and counter thrust of the gothic arch against flying buttress balanced by pinnacle, all channelling forces to the middle third of the buttress at its base, is as thrilling as an acrobatic balancing on a high wire.

Modern materials have joints as strong as or stronger than the materials they hold together. Continuous, indeterminate structures are created. Reinforced concrete and steel framed buildings depend on strength of section.

When the floor slab is cantilevered beyond the columns the wall becomes a membrane. Sheets of glass change the wall to a transparent air barrier. The building is peered into as well as out of. Privacy disappears in a passing glance. New materials generate new perceptual experiences.

# Modern Myth
## Brick

Brick fitted to the size of the hand has been part of the human memory since before recorded history. The brick was designed to form a bonded, monolithic mass. Mortar is weak. Bricks are strong. Continuous mortar joints are planes of weakness. The secret of the brick is "broken," noncontinuous joints. That is why they were bonded in english, flemish and common bonds. Mortar keep the bricks apart, bonding keeps the wall together.

Before modern times the brick came from the earth and rested on it. The Pyramid was an ideal form, for it became wider at the bottom, expressing the accumulation of weight as it reached the ground.

When brick is suspended in the air it becomes a "machine" product. It is glued onto panels, lifted, like concrete or metal panels, by cranes. Brick is like paint. The historic bonded structural system becomes decoration as the columns applied to the Colosseum in Rome. But the ghost of the hand that determined the size of the brick remains.

## Glass

Glass is a poor thermal but a fine air barrier. As a transparent skin it allows light in and people to look in and out. It welcomes heat in the winter but must shut it out in the summer. It is an alchemist's material. Scientists have applied coatings to it which changes these fundamental properties. Glass continues to fascinate modern architects and manufacturers. It was the material that changed the most after the "energy crisis" of the mid-1970s.

## Precast Concrete

Although this material is concrete, the architect should think of it as steel. Its site connections are similar to steel, as are its erection characteristics— not at all like poured-in-place concrete. Precast concrete must be supported by beams, where poured-in-place forms slab, beam, column, and column capital in one piece. Precast concrete planks run in one direction. A poured-in-place floor may be two-directional.

Both steel and precast concrete are dry. Both can be made in large elemental pieces at the factory and lend themselves to high-speed site erection with cranes and few connections.

## Prestressed and Post-Tensioned Concrete

This is concrete that is precompressed in the zone where tensile stresses occur under load. Consequently cracking of the concrete due to tension is avoided. The usual technique is to tension tendons of high-tensile steel in the concrete. Prestressing is classified as pre-tensioned or post-tensioned depending on whether the tendons were tensioned before or after the concrete has hardened.

## Steel

This material offers shape and the assembly of shapes—beams, trusses, columns, and connections. It is important to develop a steel shape vocabulary. There are at least 15 varieties of wide flanges. There are H, I, and S shapes, and all can be combined with square, round and rectangular pipes and tubes.

There is a family of light metal sections that can be used for light industrial buildings and interior structures, walls, and partitions. Hollow steel sections can be combined with rods, cables, joists, and tube trusses that will support varying depths of deck. Deck is a horizontal membrane.

Jigged hollow steel trusses are precisely and economically fabricated at the factory. They are visually more comprehensible than wide flange beams, for they show load direction through their struts. They accommodate the passage of pipes, conduits, and ducts, and offer little obstruction to their passage. Because of this the height of the building is reduced, walls and columns do not have to work as hard.

Steel is made in factories and its qualities controlled. It is plastic material that can sculpture the physical forces imposed on the building. Today steel is formed, analyzed, sized, and manufactured without the intercession of the human craftsman. Computer software is connected directly to computer manufacturing programs. The designer's concept moves from computer screen to finished factory product in a single design operation.

## Bolts

Bolt heads fastening metal panels are the size of the jaws of a wrench, a tool that simulates the action of turning thumb and forefinger. It is a memory of this action, even though the massive building sections held together are far heavier than a person can lift.

## Wide Flange Beam

A wide flange beam is a quietly beautiful object. It is an early nostalgic reminder of the uniqueness of machine craft. It expresses its purpose and the society that produced it. It is an industrial "found object" to be used "off the shelf" that becomes part of the visual delight that makes a building architecture.

## The Rationalization of Labor

" . . . For while the painter may fill a plane within his composition with continuously changing details, the architect is usually forced to create a regular method of subdivision in his composition on which so many building artisans will have to work together. The simplest method, for both the architect and the artisans, is the absolutely regular repetition of the same elements, for example solid, void, solid, void, just as you count one, two, one, two. It is a rhythm every one can grasp. Many

people find it entirely too simple to mean anything at all. It says nothing to them and yet it is a classic example of man's special contribution to orderliness. It represents a regularity and precision found nowhere in Nature but only in the order man seeks to create." [1]

The order Rasmussen describes was achieved by organizing and training great numbers of workmen working by hand and with simple machines, expending great physical effort. The world surrounding them was predominantly natural for most people lived on the land. The natural world is without straight lines, square corners, perfect circles, and no two of anything exactly alike. Repetition and "one two, one two..." order did represent a precision found "nowhere in Nature."

But when mechanization achieves exact, precise duplication, the square corner, perfect circle, endless repetition becomes the norm for urban populations. Simple repetitions speak ad nauseum to "man's (and woman's) special contribution to orderliness" in such overwhelming abundance that human senses are dulled and perhaps eventually altered.

Plaster and gold leaf ceiling, Metropolitan Life Insurance Co.

Precast concrete window boxes, lower Manhattan. *Photo:* F. Wilson.

*(Left)* Repetitive patterns of steel highway bridge.

*(Right)* Construction site disorder from which the work is organized appears international. New York City building site. *Photo:* F. Wilson.

## Organization and Design

Buildings can be built well or badly, with skill or lack of it, be ugly or beautiful. They can not be built without work. Buildings are complex undertakings. Work must be organized. Evidence of organized work is as old as the history of villages and cities. Kiln fired bricks were in use by 3,000 B.C. Brick manufacture was common before recorded history. The Hebrews in bondage in Egypt made bricks for the pharaohs according to the Bible. The great "households" of the Egyptian nobles were manufacturing centers. By the Pyramid Age there were smiths, carpenters, masons and other artisans organized as building teams [2].

Construction site Montreal, Canada during the building of Habitat, 1967. *Photo:* F. Wilson.

*(Right)* Magneto assembly line, Ford Motor Co. 1913.

Imhotep is said to have been the first architect and to have designed the step pyramid of Zoser at Sakkara, at the beginning of the third dynasty, 2778 B.C. [3]. He may have been a scribe acting as Zoser's "project manager."

Builders worked at repetitive tasks organized into complex structural compositions before recorded history. The introduction of the assembly line by Henry Ford in 1915 simply mechanized this activity.

Archaeologists have identified markings of at least a hundred different makers of Attic pottery in the Sixth and Fifth Centuries B.C. Vases were mass produced. Several workers might be collected in a single workshop and different operations divided among them. Classical Greece exhibits the germs of a factory system with specialization of labor [4]. The English poet Percy Bysshe Shelley's "Ode To a Grecian Urn" was written to a "no deposit no return" container for the export of wine and olive oil.

At the end of the Fifth Century, the father of Demosthenes, the most famous Attic orator, owned a bedstead workshop employing twenty slaves and an arms factory with thirty-two. Free citizens as well as resident aliens and slaves worked on piecework contracts for the Athenian State, at fluting temple columns [5].

Mass production is universal in all early cultures. It must be accepted as a universal building principle.

Packaging Andersen Window Frames, 1905. *Photo:* Courtesy of Andersen Windows.

The Temple and progeny. *Collage:* F. Wilson.

"Palace of the Governor," Uxmal, Yucatan. *Photo:*
F. Wilson.

The great stone "temples" of northern Yucatan were mass production products. One of the most impressive, the "Palace of the Governor" at Uxmal, is 300 feet long surmounted by a mosaic frieze 10 feet high on all four elevations, with a surface area of 7,500 square feet.

The frieze is built of stone mosaic pieces between 8 and 24 inches in length and weighing between 55 and 175 pounds. There are 150 Chac masks roughly 3 feet wide and about two feet three inches high.

The 150 masks have 300 eyes, 300 horns, 300 hooked fangs, and 300 ears, each formed of two blocks, and each ear, had an ear plug, making 600 ear pieces and 300 plugs. The entire composition was composed of over 20,000 carved stone mosaic pieces. Mortar joints are about one-third of an inch, less than half the size of a contemporary brick mortar joint.

The stones were worked in teams. One worker rough cut, another dressed them on four sides, and a third did the more skillful cutting. All three worked with stone tools. The "palace" is but one of 40 or 50 buildings on the site, and the site is but one of hundreds partially restored.

Seven hundred years later a European architect issued a manifesto threatening dire consequences if the world did not immediately mass-produce buildings.

"A great mass-production revolution has begun," Le Corbusier wrote in 1923 in *Vers une Architec-*

Part of prefabricated "mask" at Kabah, Yucatan. *Photo:* F. Wilson.

*ture.* "Industry furnishes new tools to adapt to a new epoch, animated by a new spirit, that of industrialized building. The problem of the house is a problem of the epoch. We must create the mass-production house, the mass-production spirit." Le Corbusier concluded with the battle cry "architecture or revolution."

Why mass production should send Le Corbusier into such a tizzy is hard to understand. Mass production of building components has been part of every epoch. The columns of the Parthenon were mass produced and Socrates, as a young stone cutter, may have been one of the production workers. The great pyramid and the "Palace of the Governor" at Uxmal in Yucatan was put together of mass produced parts by a stone age culture in the 11th or 12th Century.

Sometime during the 1830s the 2 x 4 and the cut nail revolutionized the concept of industrialized housing in the U.S. By the 1870s there were freight rates for portable buildings. An entire prefabricated town could be purchased in St. Louis and shipped west, houses for $200 and civic structures for $1,000.

Following World War II major industries no longer involved in war production turned their attention to building. Attempts were made to revive the ambitions of the early modern architects to manufacture houses like automobiles. The Lustrum house, one of the first attempts, was backed by the U.S. government. The Reconstruction Finance Corporation granted Carl Strandlund, an engineer and inventor who headed Lustrom, fifteen and half million dollars, and later granted additional loans.

Strandlund was given a surplus war plant to convert to housing manufacture. The plant when in operation could produce four houses an hour, almost 100 houses a day. The heart of the factory was a conveyor belt moving at 20 feet per minute. The Lustrom house had a floor plan covering 1,025 square feet. It was built of mass produced steel parts. Automotive assembly line techniques were

Entrance to inner chamber Kabah. *Photo:* F. Wilson.

5,000 buildings were built with SCSD components, including schools, hospitals, warehouses, and office buildings. David MacFadyen, president of the National Association of Home Builders (NAHB) Research Center, is using the same technique today (1989) to encourage major manufacturers to develop sophisticated electronic, plumbing, and mechanical components for the "Smart House."

## From Mechanization to Automation

The computer in manufacturing has inspired design engineers to investigate new techniques of computational analysis. Supercomputers, those that have exceptional capacity and speed, take engineering beyond the restraints of physical testing and observation. For example, aerospace engineers have used computers for over 20 years. Aerodynamic research is among the largest of any scientific field. Aerodynamics has revolutionized the aerodynamic design process [6]. The supercomputer is as important as or more important than the wind tunnel.

The computer goes beyond the wind tunnel. The tunnel shows what is happening in model form; the computer shows this but adds what might happen if what is happening continues to happen.

The supercomputer examines details the wind tunnel can not. Straining of great quantities of data reveals patterns undetachable in the output of smaller computers. For the first time computational analysis can provide insights missed in physical experiments.

Aerodynamicists using wind tunnels tried repeatedly to solve a problem concerning the positioning of a jet engine nacelle and wing. Wind tunnel tests repeatedly showed failure; computer analysis agreed but in addition revealed the actual flow mechanism that created drag.

Model testing requires several months, computer analysis a few days. Auto manufacturers use supercomputers to design new cars for fuel savings and

used, including the conveyor, automatic assembly equipment, sheet steel stamping, wall, roof, and ceiling panels. The porcelain enameling process was used for exterior steel panels attached to steel framing.

There was glass fiber insulation and rubber gasketing to cut down thermal conductivity. But the project failed.

The exact cause of failure is not known. Following efforts to mass produce houses also failed. The Alside house was tried in 1964 and failed, and only one reinforced plastic house designed for Monsanto

as "the house of the future" was ever built. It was exhibited at Disneyland and later broken up with sledge hammers.

A major step in the direction of the rationalization of the building industry was made by Ezra Ehrenkrantz's School Construction Systems Development (SCSD) Program in California in the late 1950s and early 1960s. Ehrenkrantz's goal was to develop new products, encourage manufacturers to work together to create "systems." SCSD guaranteed a product market.

Although only a few schools were built, at least

save millions in design costs. They are used extensively in crash simulations.

In construction, supercomputers model stress and earthquake resilience of major projects such as bridges, nuclear-reactor containment vessels, skyscrapers, arenas such as that at Calgary and the Saddle-dome in Alberta.

The beginnings of building automation can be seen in the connection of computer-aided design programs and manufacture in the space frame industry, and the software programs of metal plate fasteners in the home construction industry. In these industries designers compose on computer screens. Building fragments are calculated and sized, and the information is fed to automated cutting, sawing, milling, assembly, and packaging machines. Human workmen unwrap the building parts on the site and put them together.

Automated engine assembly line, General Motors.

## Transition

Despite these advances in other industries and in housing manufacture automated manufacture has little effect on building design today. General contracting and bidding procedures discourage the effective use of automation. But as buildings are visualized more as industrial products and construction sites as assembly plants, contracting, bidding, and assembly procedures will adjust.

On-site building assembly for industrial buildings is planned for the use of simple tools and simple connections so assemblers can readily comprehend the logic of the work. The division of labor has created extreme differences in skill levels. At one end is the designer, whose time is very valuable, and at the other is the anonymous, semiskilled worker marking time until their place can be taken by a smart machine.

## SCIENCE AND BUILDING TRADITION

Not a single recent primary invention that made industrial cities workable—the telephone, elevator, vented plumbing trap, steel frame, fresh water delivery, subway, internal combustion engine—was invented by an architect. Architects did not consider these architectural problems.

In the past architects considered mechanical inventions part of the architectural profession. They invented the catapult, the tortoise, and the siege tower to break cities apart. They invented the round tower to withstand battering rams and the star shaped city as a defense against iron cannon balls. In all of architectural history except for the past century or so, building and mechanical problems were integral parts of the same solution. Vitruvius devotes almost all of his tenth book of architecture to engines and machines.

Facade of World Bank Building, Washington D.C. *Photo:*
F. Wilson.

## The Romans

The Romans moved hundreds of tons mechanically but did not consider the accomplishment worthy of recording. The stone drums of the column of Trajan, even though hollowed to make a system of stairs, weighed over 40 tons and the topmost was lifted a 100 feet.

In 1546 Domenico Fontana moved the 327 ton obelisk in front of St. Peters and was so proud of himself he wrote a book describing this accomplishment. But we do not know how the Romans erected this obelisk in the first place, or for that matter how they hoisted any of the 22 others they pilfered after the conquest of Egypt.

Augustus ordered the first obelisk erected in the circus Maximus and the others arrived shortly thereafter. The obelisks were standing in Egypt when the Romans arrived. They took them down, dragged them to the Nile put them on a raft, floated them to the mouth of the Nile. There they loaded them onto a specially constructed ship, sailed it to the mouth of the Tiber, transferred the obelisks to a raft, pulled the raft up the Tiber took the obelisk off the raft, hauled it through the streets of Rome and erected it, and never wrote a word about the entire operation. This was a run-of-the-mill, all-in-a-day's-work task for the architects of the Roman army.

What did impress Romans was a boat big enough to stow an obelisk. It was described in detail and we knew it lay off what later was to become the port of Ostia for quite some time. It was a very large boat. Ostia was not yet an official port when the obelisks arrived, so they were hoisted from boat to raft off-shore. When Ostia was made the port of Rome the obelisk ferry was filled with stones and sunk to act as a jetty. They then built a 40 story lighthouse on top of it. Boat and lighthouse are part of recorded history but not moving 22 obelisks from Egypt to Rome.

The Romans had a "sightseeing" attitude about technology like the German *Kunst und Wunder.*

Technology had to be something to wonder at, like a huge boat. What to us are surprising technical achievements pass unnoticed unless they are markedly unusual. But their wonder was short lived, for after they had moved a few obelisks they no longer mentioned the boat, and when the port builders of Ostia needed a breakwater they unceremoniously sank her full of stones as a lighthouse foundation.

The Romans accepted technology as a natural outgrowth of building. It was simply a thing architects were expected to do well and usually did. If the results were strange and spectacular they were worthy of *Kunst und Wunder.*

## Gothic Builders

Gothic builders earned considerable incomes as masters of all phases of the work. They were as much engineers as architects, they used and invented machines as well as designed buildings. The sketchbooks of Villard de Honnecourt, born at the turn of the 13th Century and professionally active between 1225 and 1250 (Gimpel, p.-120) are full of drawings of machines, including one for perpetual motion.

During the building of the great dome of the Cathedral of Florence, Brunelleschi (1377–1446), who was trained as a goldsmith, designed various machines for hoisting and facilitating the work. The mechanical arts and architecture have been inseparable through most of building history.

## The Industrial Revolution

The technology of the industrial revolution was not invented in a single burst of genius. Much of it was known to the Romans and the builders of the Middle Ages. What we term the Industrial Revolution was the introduction of the steam engine as a power source. The machines that steam first powered were medieval inventions powered by wind and water. The windmill was as common a sight in the middle ages as industrial smokestacks are today.

The sketchbooks of 15th and 16th Century engineers and architects are full of variations of crane, hoist, and traction-engine. The architects who built the great churches, halls, and palaces of medieval and Renaissance Europe did not have the resources of manpower enjoyed by the Romans. Single towns with very small populations built great cathedrals and town halls, which they could not have done without the help of medieval machines.

Illuminated medieval manuscripts show winches turned by cranks, and flywheels steadying the revolutions of their axles. Small cranes raise building stones and gibbets hold pulleys free of the work so the material can be lifted more easily. Windlass, pulley, lever, and screw were inherited from the ancient Romans. Power was transmitted in the late middle ages by complex trains of gears, pulleys, and drums driving one another through cable-belts or chains. The water powered industries of the Middle Ages were familiar to every carpenter and mason, and the master mason was master of them all.

The Industrial Revolution was a power revolution beginning with the steam engine, then moving to internal combustion and then electricity as energy sources. The new engines drove building machines used since ancient times. The Middle Ages replaced the power of human and animal muscles by the power of wind and water. Renaissance builders refined the motors and the Industrial Revolution invented the steam engine and electric motor to drive them. Until very recently architects practiced the art of mechanics and engineering as well as the art of architecture.

## New Inventions

New inventions—elevator, flush toilet, glass wall, steel frame, telephone—changed the way buildings were used, but not until after the Second World War did machinery change appreciably the way buildings were built.

The early "Modern" architects designed buildings

Space frame glass pyramid tops I.M. Pei's Le Grand Louvre three-story underground addition, Paris, France. *Photo: Courtesy of I.M. Pei.*

to look like efficient machines, but they were constructed by hand craftsmen. Le Corbusier's "machine for living" was not a machine at all but a machine metaphor.

As proof of this, energy from a single source such as a steam engine could not be used on construction sites. The systems of gears and pulleys necessary to distribute power would have obstructed all other building activities.

Building work except for excavations was hand work until the introduction of small electric motors. These did not make their appearance in large quantities and were not used effectively in construction until the 1950s.

Building hardware, cast iron building facades and columns were common for well over a century. But industrially manufactured building components on a major scale did not appear until after World War II.

Aluminum was not used for window frames, door hardware, or electrical conduit until the 1950s. The industrialization of building that Walter Gropius dreamed of in 1913 did not take place until the 1950s and 1960s. Plasterboard, fiberboard, metal studs, and plastic bathtubs are recent additions to the architect's design vocabulary.

The Empire State Building, completed in 1932, was not air-conditioned and had double hung windows. Air conditioning was not in general use in the U.S. until small, plug-in window units were introduced in the mid-1950s. The first mainframe computers were installed in the 1950s, but computers had little effect on buildings or their design until the introduction of the personal computer in the mid-70s.

The great surge of change in mechanical and electrical equipment dates from the energy crisis in 1973. It was the personal computer, like the plug-in air conditioning unit, coupled with the energy crisis, that revolutionized work, communication, and building design.

## The New Machine Basics

Machines do what people cannot. Or they do in minutes what people do in days. Handcraft is disappearing from the construction site. Machine products have become more complex and design is more and more involved with the selection of industrial products.

Machines are operated by machine operators or driven by computers. Others are programmed by systems engineers and some are so complex that computers operate robots programmed to make the product. The skill and cunning of the hand, as we have known it in the past, is no longer a significant contributor to the building art of industrial nations. Machines do some things better then people, but others less well. The division of labor between hand and machine has become more complex than it was in ancient times.

Designers unaware of how machines operate tend to specify tasks difficult for machines to accomplish. Architects who thoroughly understand the forms peculiar to hand work created by hammer, chisel, saw, plane, and rasp and those peculiar to machine extrusion, stamping, and casting can use both successfully. If machine or hand is forced to perform tasks unsuited to it the forms are costly and ugly.

Assembly is the key to industrial buildings. The major cost of building is in fitting and attaching building elements. The architect balances the additional cost of manufacture against the on-site cost of assembly. Building today is neither hand nor machine craft but combines handcraft and machine craft in a unique transitional period.

The additional cost of engineering in the manufacturing of products that simplifies their connection is cost effective. Modern buildings are characterized by the simple erection of sophisticated building products attached with primitive connections such as bolts and washers, clamps and turnbuckles.

The ideal of machine craft is found in the program for the erection of structures in outer space: "one hand, no tools, no sharp edges." The aim of engineering genius is to create a structure an idiot can erect.

The clearer the method of assembly is indicated in the design the stronger is the crucial link in the chain from factory product to finished building. Clarity of design and ease of erection speed construction, improve quality, reduce costs, and increase profits.

The materials of handcraft have been wood and stone cut and fitted on site; the "wet materials," plaster and concrete, poured and smoothed in place; or masonry units held together with mortar. The objective is a monolithic building. The opposite is characteristic of building assembly. Materials are dry, manufactured in large sections, and lifted into place by cranes. The building is sectional, bolted,

Connecting hub of a space platform in McDonnell Douglas underwater aerospace tank, California, 1987. Below, hub detail. *Photo:* Starnet.

Bees and honeycomb, auto paint baking tunnel. *Photo:*
Courtesy of General Motors Corporation.

screwed, and fastened in units. Hand work is limited to connections. The wrench is the symbol of the assembly of industrial products, as hammer, saw, nail and trowel, brick and mortar, iron and rivet were the symbols of pre-industrial handcraft building.

Today's connections are different from those of the past. Column-to-entablature, entablature-to-pediment connections were fashioned to last. The rapid change of building use demands connections capable of fastening and unfastening without changing other parts of the building or the human activity in the affected areas.

### The Problem Is . . .

The modern building machine has enough *Kunst und Wunder* to spark the interest of even a jaded Roman military architect. It also incorporates enough mechanical devices to "blow the mind" of a Gothic builder and is actually becoming a "machine for living," flushing its own toilets and running its own elevators. This has changed architectural ideas, the relative price and value relationships of the building fragments in relation to time, the ordering systems of design and the language of architecture.

## REFERENCES

1. Steel Eiler Rasmussen, *Experiencing Architecture,* MIT Press, Cambridge, Mass., 1959, pp. 128–129.
2. Childe, Gordon: *What Happened in History,* Penguin, Baltimore, MD, 1942, p. 120.
3. Fletcher, Sir Banister: *A History of Architecture,* 18th Edition, Scribner's, New York, 1975, p. 17.
4. Childe, Gordon: *What Happened in History,* Penguin, Baltimore, MD, 1942, p. 208.
5. Ibid, p. 209.
6. *Scientific American,* New York, Vol. 256 Number 4, October 1987.
7. Gimpel, Jean: *The Medieval Machine, The Industrial Revolution of the Middle Ages,* Penguin, New York, 1976, p. 120.

# Chapter 6

# Cost and Value

The surest test of the civilization of a people—at least, as sure as any—afforded by mechanical art is to be found in their architecture, which presents so noble a field for the display of the grand and the beautiful, and which, at the same time, is so intimately connected with the essential comforts of life.

—William Hickling Prescott (1847)

## PRICE AND VALUE

What makes a building so valuable that a society demands its builders use their utmost skill to create architecture? The answers are not the same for all societies. They differ today from those of the Golden Age of Athens when the Parthenon was designed and built, and differ from the 12th and 13th Century values when Chartres was reconstructed into the cathedral we admire so much today.

Great architecture is always expensive, at least more costly than common building. Is it possible to have great architecture without great cost? If a society is willing to invest large amounts of materials, labor, and money is great architecture assured? What is the relationship between cost and architectural value?

Does anyone know the value of the Parthenon or Chartres Cathedral today? What do we know about their value when we know the square foot cost to build them?

Value and cost expressed in mediums of exchange are seldom the same. Cattle were used as a standard of value in the ancient world but precious metals such as iron, silver and gold were used as means of payment to symbolize cattle. Cattle and precious metals are only related in that the exchangers agreed both were valuable.

Since a building is an accumulation of building materials and materials have a price, does their accumulated cost constitute the value of the building as buildings are priced today?

Value and cost are crucial architectural questions. Architecture will not be created unless it is considered valuable. Today the deciding measure of building value is building cost. What is the relationship of cost to value?

Buildings of the past that we consider great architecture today have long outlived the values that inspired their building. Neither the worship of Athena nor medieval Christianity has survived, yet the Parthenon and Chartres Cathedral are universally recognized architectural treasures of great value.

## The Parthenon

Pericles developed the Parthenon as part of the Acropolis "package" during Greece's Golden Age in the 5th Century B.C. The sculptor Phidias is said to have been the "artistic director" and three architects, Ictinus, Callicrates, and Mnesicles were employed on the project. The cost of the Parthenon was one of the largest budget overruns in history, never surpassing until the building of the Sydney Opera House, completed in 1973. The Athenian treasury was first bankrupted then the treasury of

Athens' allies of the Delian league was looted to finance Pericle's development schemes. The price of the Parthenon was estimated at $150 million in 1985 dollars, or $500 a square foot. Philip Johnson's A.T.&T. Building, reportedly the most expensive office building ever built at the time of its construction.

As building progressed criticism of Pericles grew. He was attacked through his mistress, Aspasia, who was accused of running a sporting house for intellectuals. Aspasia, a brilliant woman, is reported to have written the general's (Pericles) speeches. His impassioned plea in her defense, probably written by her, moved him to tears and won her acquittal on the morals charge.

But Phidias carved a very small portrait of Pericles and himself in a battle scene on the shield of the statue of Athena. This was a much more serious offense than pandering to lecherous intellectuals. What today would appear a modest act of self expression was considered an impiety by the Athenians. Phidias went to jail and is said to have died there. Pericles was banished but later allowed to return to Athens and lived to see the Parthenon completed.

The Parthenon took 15 years to build. It stood as a sacred temple to the virgin goddess, Athena Parthenos. In 334 B.C. Alexander the Great nailed 300 suits of Persian armor to its exterior columns to celebrate a victory. Emperor Demetrius I housed his courtesans there and the Byzantine Emperor Theodosius made it into a Christian church dedicated to the Virgin Mary. The Turks converted the Parthenon to a domed mosque in the late 1400s and added a minaret.

Two centuries later the value of the Parthenon was little more than that of a shed. Turkish officers used the building as a powder magazine, and on the

Corner of the Parthenon. *Photo:* Gift from a student.

evening of September 26, 1687, German mercenaries manning Venetian mortars lobbed a shell directly in. The building exploded and burned for two days. When the fire died the center of the building was gone, the walls and 28 columns had collapsed.

The Parthenon remained picturesque rubble until the latter part of the 18th Century, when Greece became a tourist attraction for the "beautiful people" on the "grand tour." Lord Elgin, ambassador to the Turkish Sultan, salvaged surviving pediment statuary, but later, when his personal fortunes declined, he was forced to sell them to the British Museum.

The Parthenon was restored sporadically toward the end of the 19th Century, and by the centennial of Greek Independence in 1933 appeared almost as we see it today.

In spite of staggering initial cost, hard times, rough use, theft, and restoration the Parthenon is considered by the Greeks and much of the Western world as one of our most valuable building.

## The Cathedral Builders

In the Middle Ages, the "fabric" of the church was taken to mean everything pertaining to the construction or maintenance of the cathedral, including the acquisition and administration of funds. The fabric was controlled by the "chapter," and the bishop was rarely consulted or took major responsibility for cathedral building or maintenance.

The chapter consisted of churchmen with special privileges. Gimpel writes that during the first half of the 10th Century several cathedral chapters had their revenues separated from those of the bishops and their independence grew from then on. The canons were not obliged to live in the cathedral city, and were to a large extent free of episcopal control.

Flying buttress.

They could dispose their movable property by bequest and many became quite wealthy.

The chapter was, Gimpel says, roughly equivalent to a modern commercial developer and city planning commission. They solved the same order of problems, expropriation, financing, and contracts and met difficulties similar to those encountered by today's developers, and they were no less ingenious at raising funds.

The chapter at the cathedral of Saint-Lazare at Autun asked the confessors to remind their faithful that dishonestly gained goods must be turned over to the fabric. They incited the young religious fraternities to energetic effort in organizing collections. Clerics who arrived late for religious services were fined and the money went to the building fund. Orators from the pulpit described the spiritual gifts accorded benefactors of the cathedral. An orator at Amiens in 1260 promised that aid to the cathedral would bring the donners 27 days closer to Paradise than they were the day before the contribution if subsequent sin, envy, and lust did not cost them the indulgence, which could be repurchased at slightly higher rates. [1]

In addition even in death the building benefited. The chapter decided that anyone desiring to be buried within the walls of the church would have to pay for the privilege.

Relics were displayed and viewed at a price. Three months after a fire had ravaged the cathedral at Leon in 1117, canons and several laymen left the city with relics saved from the fire which consisted of a piece of the Virgin's veil, a fragment of the Holy Sponge, and a part of the True Cross. They returned in the fall with funds to repair the damage.

Cathedral building costs, like present-day space exploration, can not be measured in usual values. Builders pushed their skills to the utmost as astronauts do today. They took incredible chances. Cathedrals collapsed. The great cathedral at Beauvais fell three times, and following each disaster its builders rebuilt it higher.

The cathedral was both the town's physical and information center. It conveyed messages in stone, wood, glass, inlaid marbles, and gold. God's house was the earthly image of the Heavenly Jerusalem. It was the house of adoration but also the house of the people.

The people did not have access to the sanctuary of the Parthenon. They viewed the building from a distance. The Christian church, by contrast, demanded the faithful contribute to the construction and that it be large enough for the populace to meet inside.

The cathedral portals invited the passer by to enjoy sculptured figures. During the 12th Century, the book of images, the data points of the Christian faith, opened itself, as the pages of an eternal periodical, on frescoed walls and vaults. Then little by little, as gothic architecture progressed, the medium changed, windows became larger and wall space smaller, light was brought into the church, and the spaces for painting large frescos were gone. The book of images was transferred to stained glass windows. These projected illuminated, and now animated messages, with every change of exterior light. The rose window became the equivalent of our big screen TV.

At Chartes Cathedral the guilds took the best possible location for their windows. They installed them close to the side aisles or in the ambulatory nearest the worshipers, while glass donated by bishops and lords was relegated to the clerestory windows, high above. The cloth merchant, the stonecutter, the wheelwright, and the carpenter, each had himself depicted in a medallion in the lower part of the window donated by his guild, as close as possible to future clients.

## Uffizi Gallery

The Uffizi palace in Florence, Italy was built in the 16th Century by Giorgio Vasari for Cosimo I de Medici as public offices. It now houses the state archives of Tuscany and the Uffizi Gallery, one of the richest art collections in the world. No one can say for sure the present value of either, although it is certain both former office building and art collection have appreciated tremendously in value.

## Sydney Opera House

The Sydney Opera House was built because a London symphony conductor of Belgian descent needed a concert hall in Australia. Australians excel in outdoor sports and are largely indifferent to opera. The conductor interested a politician, who became obsessed with the idea. A worldwide competition was held and won by a Danish architect Jorn Utzon. The building was started before any one knew if it could be built, how much it would cost, or when it would be completed.

The architect resigned midway in the project. Three local architects took over the job and reversed the building's functions. It was completed after 16 years of planning and 14 of building. The politician died during the first stage of construction and the conductor during the second. The project was designed as it was built and ended as a design by committee. It finally cost 1800 percent over budget.

The Sydney Opera House celebrated its 15th anniversary last year. It is universally acclaimed a historic monument and one of the world's great buildings, comparable to the Parthenon, Chartres Cathedral, and the Taj Mahal.

Dramatic tales of triumph over adversity such as this are the stuff of "penny dreadfuls" rather than architectural history. Why after a series of disasters any one of which would have scuttled a speculative office building, a corporate headquarters, or a municipal recreation center did the Sydney Opera House survive to become a world famous monument?

Media coverage of architecture gleefully reports mistakes, arguments, and failures as exceptional events. They are not, except in the building of unin-

Early model of Sydney Opera House. *Photo:* W. Brindle, courtesy of Australian Information Service.

spired buildings. Speculative office buildings are built by the thousands without any media comment at all. In contrast, risk taking is the stuff great architecture is made of and comes with the territory.

It is of course ridiculous that architecture should be so unstable, changing radically every fifteen or twenty years, but serious architecture does that. Commercial styling is much more reliable. "Architecture changes as it involuntarily follows the mood of society," wrote the Australian architectural critic Robin Boyd.

In all discussions of the failings of the Sydney Opera House cost overrun is uppermost. Why?

Like all great architecture it eventually proved to be a bargain and in keeping with the fast pace of modern change it changed from an outrageously expensive building to a bargain in a little over 15 years. Thirty years of media attention has increased its value to an extent that like the Parthenon it cannot be thrown away. The government tourist offices of both governments would rip out the tongue of anyone that dared whisper such sacrilege.

Great architecture has always been good for busi-

ness. The pilgrimage churches in Chaucer's time were essential features of the pilgrimage and thrived accordingly. All today's package tourists need to see in Australia is the "Opera House" to say they have been there. All else is window dressing.

The Opera House pays off in terms of bottom line. The estimated price was $7 million and final cost quoted at $120 million. Its replacement was priced at $500 million in 1988, roughly a 420 percent increase over a 15 year period. This is an impressive return on investment even for junk bonds. Which would you rather have?

Sydney Opera House, 1989. *Photos:* Courtesy of Australian Information Service.

Casting yard for rib vaults. *Photo:* Courtesy of Australian
Information Service.

# VALUE, PRICE, AND PROFIT

The Parthenon lost and gained its value over 2500 years and Chartes over 800, the finished Sydney Opera House tripled in value in 15 years. The cost of a building today changes in a year or two and can be estimated to the penny before it is torn down. These are unusual cases, interesting mostly because of their dramatic change in value. The usual decisions of architects involved in designing less spectacular buildings are devoted to more mundane decisions, but the principle is the same. The architect sets a strategy or plan of action, makes choices to enhance the building's attitude in terms of time and appearance.

Money influences every building decision, including the choice of materials, construction methods, quality, and appearance. It can be a simple act such as choosing between painted steel, painted aluminum, or anodized aluminum panels. These panels may be similar in weight, color, and configuration. But in terms of quality, steel is the least valuable and anodized aluminum the most, for painted steel will peel and rust, painted aluminum will peel but will not rust, while anodized aluminum will neither rust nor peel and it is not known how long it will last, for it has successfully withstood rain, wind, sun, and building stresses for over 35 years and remains in good condition.

Painted steel may cost $2 per square foot, painted aluminum $2.5; and anodized $4.45 (in 1985 dollars). Brick veneer is $5 dollars per square foot, and its mortar must be repointed at least every 25 years.

If long-term efficiency is desired, then the material's functional life span is the determining factor. Choices are, in reality, qualified and quantified by money. The architect is called upon to consider, test, and know all the characteristics of all the materials that can be used within a given budget, then select the most efficient and longest lasting.

If a building can adjust itself to accommodate changing uses it maintains and can increase in value. As an example, a building of 100,000 square feet that cost $1.5 million in 1950 may cost $8.5 million to replace in 1980. If the building has adjusted to new uses over time it has increased considerably in value. If not, it is only worth the land on which it sits.

Money buys value and value is tied to building purpose. As long as the building remains useful it has money value which often exceeds an equivalent interest growth if the money is left in a bank.

The ability to adjust is often paid for in first costs such as the selection of anodized aluminum panels, but such costs are minimum premiums paid for long-range gain. Therefore building transformation that assures continuous usefulness has an equivalent money value, quantifiable in dollars. Budget is the balancing factor. Building costs are set by the market and building value by the architects decisions.

# CHANGE AND VALUE

Change today is rapid and inevitable. Unless it can be made easily it will not be done. When minor adjustments in the building are not made they quickly become major obstructions to economic operation. The building is no longer viable as an economic tool and is discarded.

Traditional building materials such as stone and masonry are difficult and expensive to change. The majestic carved columns of New York City's Pennsylvania Railroad Station, built between 1906 and 1910, designed in the tradition of the Ecole des Beaux Artos by McKim, Mead and White based on Roman "thermae," with a 108-foot-high central hall, was torn down and replaced in 1965 by a new station with a 9-foot-high hung ceiling over much of its floor area.

To avoid a similar fate each system, component, element of a modern building is designed to plug in and out, bolt on and off. The timeless value of a building is no longer determined by the strength of building materials and how long a building stands but by how long it remains useful. The design problems are radically different as is the building's appearance. Yet the result must be as pleasing as the Parthenon and Chartres.

# DIFFERENT VALUE SYSTEMS— PRIVATE SECTOR AND GOVERNMENT BUILDINGS

Different values direct the design of private sector and government buildings. The value of a private sector building is determined solely on its "cash flow" and occasionally on land value when this is greater than the building's cash flow. The building is valuable as long as it is useful. Use is determined by the number of people willing to pay to use it.

"Cash flow" is the amount of money the owner makes from the operation of the building. Once a private sector building can not compete on an equal footing with a newer building because it is not as "fashionable," flexible, or technologically advanced it must reduce rent to compete. Rent rates diminish and vacancy rates increase, and the building is scrapped.

The government pays once for the building and is the owner, occupant, and operator. Flexibility and technology may be important but "fashion" is of minor importance. The government has a monopoly on government departments. There are not two departments of transportation competing against each other. There is only one and the community must go to it for service.

If the department operates inefficiently or gives poor service there is no competitor to mark or monitor efficiency. The flexibility of the building is not as important as it is in the private sector, for it is very difficult to appraise the efficiency of government departments. There is nothing comparable to them.

When governments talk about budget and deficit these are annual operational deficits. In the private sector the equivalent of government deficits would create insolvency. Government assets are not listed in annual statements. One of the assets of the American people, for example, is the White House. How valuable is the White House or the Senate Office Building or the Capitol? If these buildings were to be sold and rented back the government would realize hundreds of millions of dollars. The Capitol might sell for three billion U.S. dollars or thirty billion yen.

Government buildings represent a staggering value. The Pentagon is worth at least as much money as the Empire State Building. The government has buildings all over the land and in foreign countries as well. They may not be the best or the most efficient buildings but they are the real estate holdings of the tax payers of each country, and rich countries have more buildings proportionately than poor countries. Buildings are a good guide to the wealth of a people.

Design does not have great significance for government bureaucrats. If the building satisfies the demands of the originating program and is executed within budget and on time design is secondary. In contrast, the private sector has few long-term goals. The private sector wants the building to be on budget because they have predicted cash flows.

In contrast to government buildings, sophisticated developers market fashionable buildings using "style" to rent them at high prices. They do not ask that the building last 300 years or have any social significance. They tell the architect to design a highly marketable building that will appeal to the community at that moment in time.

The developer spends 10 to 20 percent more on the building to make it more fashionable and hopes to increase revenues from 30 to 50 percent. Generally fashionable design is more marketable.

There is a great difference between fashion and design, although they are often confused in marketing. Fashion increases immediate appeal while design increases the building's value by increasing its ability to perform.

Fashion is decoration that creates an image and illusion of function. For example, thin marble veneer creates the illusion of expensive, long-lasting material. In reality many of these veneers have proven unable to withstand normal weathering and are replaced at enormous expense. An 80 story building in Chicago had the stone veneers removed and replaced at a price of $1 million dollars per floor in 1989.

The profit incentive gives special meaning and value to the building. It substitutes, in modern times, for the worship of Athena that created the Parthenon and the veneration of the Virgin Mary that gave us Chartres.

# REFERENCE

1. Gimpel, Jean: The Medieval Machine, The Industrial Revolution of the Middle Ages, Penguin, New York 1976, p.66

# Chapter 7

# Design Decisions

Architectural design is a plan of action. It directs the choices of material, techniques, and technology to create buildings with commodity, firmness, and delight. The designer initiates a strategy for making choices and initiates the actions that will transform the idea to reality.

Vitruvius organized the rules of architecture into ten books. Even though historians say he was an uninspired designer his fame as an architect continues for 2,000 years, which shows how important architectural rules can be.

All buildings are built by rules. Sometimes they are set by custom, experience, and building lore, and sometimes they are made up on the spot. Buildings are complex undertakings involving huge social resources and the energy of hundreds, sometimes thousands of people. An ordering system is essential even though, as we said at the beginning, the system may be followed and great architecture not result.

Buildings are complex products. A simple product is something like a golf tee, pencil or a toaster.

Automobiles and buildings are complex products. Simple products have simple functions. Complex products have multiple functions.

It is wrong to define a building by its function such as a bank. Banking is the human activity that takes place in the building and to be used as a bank it will have hundreds or thousands of different functions. The same building could be used as a discotheque, a car wash or bowling alley. Its functions would change but it would remain a building.

Imaginary or unmade buildings in all of their parts and functions are, unfortunately, too complex to understand in their entirety by the designer. Designers therefore divide the building into fragments of simpler understandable elements. These can be:

- Structural, (see Structure, Chapter 3)
- Mechanical,
- Electrical,
- Skin, and
- Fitments.

To comprehend and create elements the designer

must have a set of strategies or a plan of action. This is essential. The designer first strives to understand the attitude of the building (see Chapter 4). The attitude is what the building is: What does the building feel like? What is essential to it, what not? This is a sense or understanding of the building that can not be explained directly in words but is described in metaphor or analogy, or feeling like words used in poetry.

The designer's plan of action measures the relative weight of time and value and balances these against the building's attitude to establish priorities. First these are set within the plan of action, secondly the fragments are arranged in orders of importance. The fragments may have different priorities from project to project. Structure is not always first.

When architects design fragments they choose materials and methods of working that will strengthen the attitude of the building. The choice of every part, in every detail, is directed by the plan of action to create a comprehensive attitude that

*Collage:* F. Wilson.

will survive for a decent interval with an appropriate value.

The attitude of a building can survive extreme transformation. As an example the temple of Jupiter, Optimus Maximus, at the Capine hill in Rome, was built about 500 B.C. by the Etruscans. It was famous for its ceramic decorations and bore the named the Etruscan sculpture that did them. They had a life-size quadriga (a four horse chariot) on the roof as a victory symbol.

The entire temple was built of wood with wide column spacing. The wooden fragments were gradually changed to stone. When this took place its looks must have changed dramatically. In one restoration, 80 B.C., the dictator Sulla, who ravaged Greece "like a plague of locusts," took columns from a large temple of Zeus in Athens which itself had gone through two or three restorations and was then unfinished. Sulla helped himself to the marble columns and shipped them to Rome. They were huge columns, about 60 feet high. He also sent the entablatures. Sulla considered columns and entablatures like fragments of an erector set. He cared little about "style." To the Romans it was a temple to Jupiter and must have the best possible attitude. They very probably gave these parts to the architect and builders and ordered them to put them in the building.

The original temple of Jupiter had probably burned for the second time. They delivered the columns, said here are the parts, do what you can. The Greek marble columns could have been put in the same location as the wooden columns, but not the entablature. The wooden spans would have been too great for stone so they may have designed another entablature.

The temple burned once again and was again lavishly restored. The temple symbolized Rome as the city's foremost historic monument. The attitude was there, all that had to be done was assemble the fragments.

It may have been symbolic that the columns came from the temple of Zeus. It was the major temple of Zeus in Greece and had been built at about the same time the Etruscans built the original temple to Jupiter. The temple to Zeus in Athens had been planned on a huge scale in an open field and never completed.

There were various sanctuaries in Ancient Greece. Some were international and not associated with sanctuary cities like Delphi and Olympia. The temple to Zeus beyond the city limits of Athens may have been meant to appeal to all Greeks as neutral ground. Whatever its intent, the fragments of the temple of Zeus were appropriate in Roman eyes to express the attitude of a temple and sanctuary of Jupiter.

Ordering systems embrace three basic decisions which govern all others. The first is, "What is it"? What is the building's attitude? The second is time. All buildings must eventually fall down, as all people must eventually die. The architect's task is to assure a decent interval between the two events. How long is this to be? The third is the "reality" it expresses, how will it look. Attitude and time influence this decision. We discussed building attitude earlier. How is the building to survive for a "decent interval?"

Time and the grim street sweeper at 127 John St., New York City. *Photo:* Dirck Halstead, courtesy of William Kaufman Organization.

# TIME

For a building to survive over time it must transform itself. Survival is tied to usefulness. The industrial development of the society in which the architect designs determines the ability to incorporate transforming elements.

Changes in the community affect the building which incorporates the products of industrial change and encloses changing social patterns. If the building parts are available in the "store" and purchased "off the shelf," as is common in the industrial nations, the building can be built rapidly and changed quickly. If built by hand it will have to be changed by hand. Most buildings are a combination of the two.

Change is fashionable and a reality as nations change from manufacture to information and service industries. Change is a building "style." The cranes that lifted building parts during construction are now incorporated as part of the building's permanent structure. They now perch on the top edges of Lloyds of London and the Hong Kong Bank. The building appears as if it could be taken apart piece by piece and reassembled by the clerks operating the word processors inside but may be a bit more difficult than it appears.

The industrial building philosophy proposed by Le Corbusier early in this century could not be realized, for the industrial capability of achieving it had not been developed. It is possible today but buildings look nothing like Le Corbusier imagined they would.

Buildings are more complex, include more components, and have incorporated many more disciplines than they did in the 1920s. Many of the parts added, such as elevator, mechanical, electrical, and communication systems, are the responsibility of professions unrelated to architecture in the traditional sense. The building must be designed to allow the constant updating of new forms devised by new production methods designed by professionals previously unassociated with building. Among the most recent of these are communication experts and wire managers.

The difference in the time of obsolescence of mechanical and architectural features demands that the mechanical elements be distinct from the building elements. The life expectancy of a building structure may be 50 years, while a heating and cooling system will be out of date in 15. It must be easily removed and newer equipment easily put in its place. New, state-of-the-art, machinery must be plugged in. The time required to substitute new for old is much greater in cost than the equipment and the workmen's salaries. If the facility is a bank, the cost of a single day's lost operation could be more than the cost of the entire building.

The test of a successful building assembly is in how easily and quickly it can be taken apart. A contemporary building can be compared to a sailing ship. It is a complex, expensive, product floating in a fluid market. It must constantly shift its cargo to remain afloat economically in the shifting tides of technical change. This ability keeps it afloat.

*(Facing page)* Changing New York City. Site of the World Trade Center. Cofferdams in place for landfill, 1968. *Photo:* Courtesy of Port of New York Authority.

*(Right)* Models of the World Trade Center, 1966. *Photo:* Courtesy of Port of New York Authority.

Renewal of New York City. *Photos:* F. Wilson.

The key to designing shiftable building assemblies is: minimum number of pieces, dry materials, light large sheets and sections, cranes, robotics, men guiding machines.

To build is to use solid materials to create space protected from natural extremes of hot and cold, wind and rain suitable for particular functions. Historically the ideal has been a lasting stable structure that satisfies the needs for which it was built and ideally achieving maximum results with minimum means.

These conditions: stability, durability, function, and maximum results with minimum means are to be found in Vitruvius's ten books of architecture. They were rules that could be applied equally to mud hut and marble palace and were summed up in Nervi's phrase "building correctly." Today an additional rule has been added—the ability to change.

All building changes must take place quickly with minimal disruption if the building is to remain economically valuable and therefore standing. Change is normal in the 20th Century. Social patterns, technical developments, economic growth or decline that in the past required three or four hundred years to complete their cycles today are born, reach maturity, and die in twenty. Patterns of change must be accommodated or the building discarded.

"Modern" 1950's buildings are now obsolete. The cost of adjusting them to contemporary work and social patterns exceeds the cost of new construction. Designers today are exploring the possibilities of systems, components, elements, designed to plug in and out, bolt on and off.

Building programs are only descriptions of a building at a single moment in time. Research in 1988 indicated an average building 40 years old had alterations amounting to three times its original cost. Based on the present rate of accelerated change projected 40 years in the future these figures may well exceed ten.

Buildings seldom "wear out," they become obsolete. A concrete building frame may last 500 years; the building's use may change in 5. Paradoxically the solidity of a structure may make it inflexible and signal its destruction.

## Recycling

The architect's clients treat his or her buildings as traders deal on the stock market: they buy them today believing they will be worth more tomorrow.

Rehabilitation and restoration of Brooklyn's Borough Hall. *Photo:* F. Wilson.

Taurus molding, Brooklyn Borough Hall. *Photo:* F. Wilson.

Clients expect buildings to increase in value. The idea of the disposable building is a remnant of the affluence of the 1960s. It was discarded in the early 1970s with the energy crisis.

Buildings today must be designed to be modified, transformed, and recycled quickly and economically. They must hold their position at the leading edge of technology and service even when the function of the building is as drastically changed as

the conversion of an auto/diesel shop into a classroom space for a mathematics department.

Recycling takes existing warehouses of no particular historic value and changes them into apartment blocks and office spaces. They are interesting as apartments because they can get more square feet of livable space with higher ceiling. But mechanically and electrically they often prove to be disasters.

Human adaptability allows cities to maintain their historics memorabilia yet provide reasonable functional space for new uses. But it must be understood that these buildings were never designed to be recycled. Nobody anticipated different functional uses for them. Their designers could not have foreseen sophisticated communication equipment, energy conservation and HVAC systems. Some recycled buildings were built when radio was the chief form of entertainment, air conditioning consisted of opening a window, and the world's high speed auto racing record was held by a daredevil who had traveled 60 miles an hour.

## MOVEMENT

Buildings are built to accommodate human movement. If the building is not and the humans in it do not move it is a prison or a tomb. Cities are gigantic movement systems of trade, commerce, power systems, disposal networks, and the passage of people. Buildings are small, intimate extensions of movement. Successful cities and buildings have given top priority to time and cost when they were designed. No one knew this better than the ancient Greeks.

The Greeks unified their cities with a simple covered walkways that ingeniously directed movement, unified all of the varied activities of the city into a cohesive unity. It allowed renewal by changing activities without destroying buildings. The idea was so successful that it lasted well into the Renaissance, when one could cross Rome without getting wet. It survives today in the arcade of Balogna, the great GUM department store in Moscow and present day shopping malls, which are modern versions of the stoa.

## The Stoa

The Greek stoa was like an electrical "cable tray" in a modern building. It was the multipurpose movement container of Greek cities. Like a cable tray that

Auto stoa for assembling coupes, Detroit 1987; Tourist stoa for assembling views, Batoche. *Photos:* Courtesy of G.M. and IKOY.

carries power to all parts of a modern building and branching off supplies energy to move machines and activate electronic equipment, the Greek stoa channeled human energy inside its colonnaded front for merchants, schools, temple, or administrative office. The stoa was a conduit for Greek life found in all Greek cities and their colonies.

This was a very simple and adaptable building, consisting merely of an open colonnade, normally with a back wall, to which the columns were joined by a roof. It had many architectural uses; it could form an entrance porch or a facade; it could be placed on one or more sides of a court, could form an internal or external peristyle or independent architectural unit.

The stoa played a vital part in Greek architecture and Greek life. The Athenian orators constantly include the stoas among the glories of the city; Demosthenes couples them with the masterpieces of the Acropolis, the Propylaea and the Parthenon, and with the ship-sheds of Peiraeus.

Colonnades have been used to channel human movement in many ages and lands. Before the Greeks the Egyptians used them in temple courts, as did the Minoans and Myceneans in their palaces.

Sometimes a light colonnade was placed against an existing wall to create a stoa. Large stoas associated with shrines had an outer row of Doric columns and an inner row of Ionic columns to give greater spaciousness and dignity.

The Greek city was unified by the stoa. City water fountains were placed at critical points in the city plan, usually an intersection or near one. In hot climates the fountain is extremely valuable. Stoas flanked the fountain and made the city distinct. In Antioch the main street was a mile and a half long with a stao on both sides. The stoa at Palmyra still stands.

The colonnaded stoa was an independent, freestanding unit channeling the activities of Hellenic cities, and was as characteristic of them as the power lines are of a modern metropolis.

## Christian Church

The early church adopted the Roman basilica form of building because of its movement system. The Romans had designed basilicas to hold, control, and regulate the flow of large crowds. Old St. Peter's and St. Paul's in Rome and all their innumerable progeny eventually substituting piers for columns, altered the basilica scale, narrowed the breadth, raised the height, adding towers and crossing lanterns, and the result was the Christian church. All had low shed roofs over side aisles and steep pitched trussed or vaulted roofs over the high central aisle, which can be read in the Romanesque and Gothic West Fronts.

This was a processional church, a movement system going from this world to the door of the next. The journey began at the atrium outside its entrance, entered through the doors into the great nave and ended at the altar. The side aisles were parallel conduits.

## Processions of Power

The crucial movement in a modern building in a manufacturing or service/information society is power. If power is blocked the deprived institution can not function. Manufacturing and electronic technologies demand power and access to it. The computer is at the heart of cabling systems focusing mail and message delivery, data and information transmission between people and computers and computers and computers in both manufacturing and service.

As the need for power grew from the early years of the century, equipment was powered through direct access from the building distribution system. Desks and equipment radiated out from columns and walls that housed fixed power outlets. The power system adapted itself to the structural and architectural systems. Today the reverse is true. The core design of the building determines primary power distribution. The core sets limits on the amount of power transmitted through the electrical system from the utility's main feeder line to the floors. Structural components can limit power access by blocking conduits that distribute wires and cables through floors and ceilings. If they do they must be redesigned. Structural and architectural design accommodates the power system.

The power, lighting, electronic, and communication (PLEC) system can deliver only the kind and amount of power permitted by core and distribution system design from the building core through either ceiling or floor systems to where the power is used.

Ceiling distribution systems use conduit, metal raceways, or flexible conduit cable to run wires and cables through the plenum (the space between the ceiling and the floor above it). Wires and cables are routed from the plenum to work stations through vertical, hollow "power poles" or through flexible "infeed" cables. Ceiling distribution can also incor-

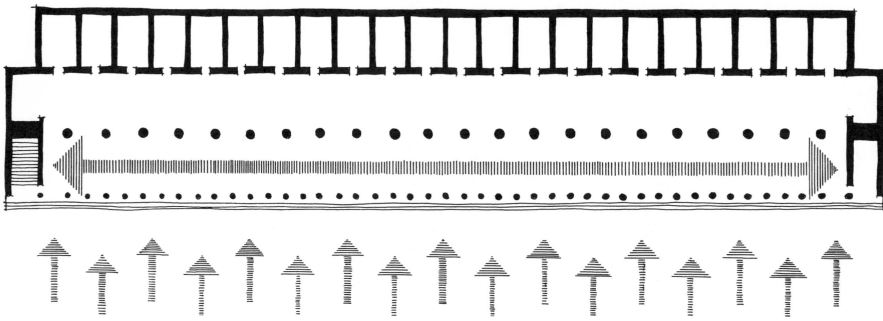

Movement system stoa plan. *Drawing:* F. Wilson.

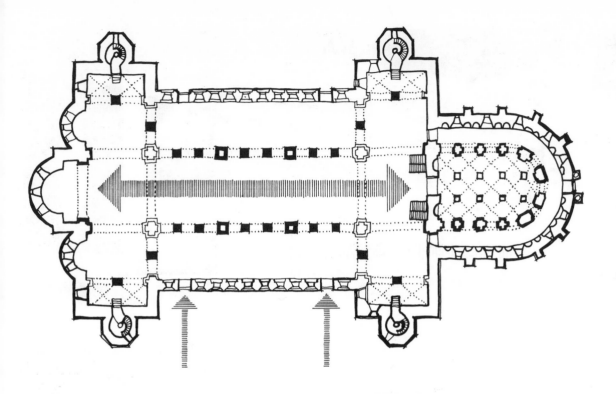

Movement system early Christian church plan.
*Drawing:* F. Wilson.

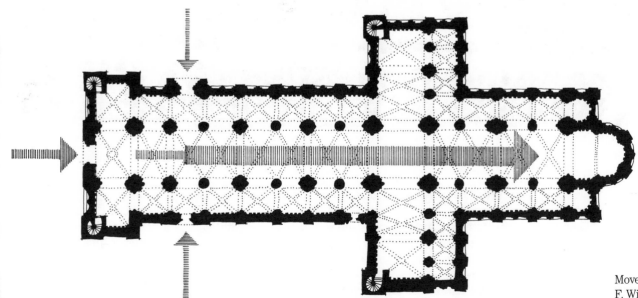

Movement system gothic church plan. *Drawing:*
F. Wilson.

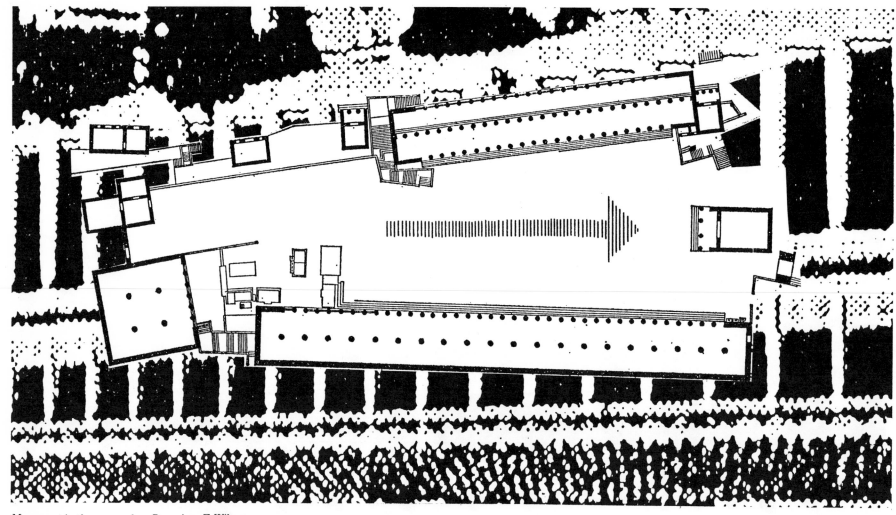

Movement in the agora plan. *Drawing:* F. Wilson.

porate a standard "poke-through" system of delivery in which access to the floor above is gained from the plenum below. As much as possible of the building is accommodated by these systems.

Wires and cables may pass through furniture, space dividers, and panels to reach the equipment they service. Hollow channels in panels, work sur-

faces, and furniture allow vertical and horizontal distribution throughout an area at various heights. Some furniture surfaces and panels come already electrically wired at the factory. Others store wiring and cabling out of sight under work surfaces.

The majority of today's offices are open with only fixed exterior walls. Partitions of various heights

provide spatial separation and privacy and support work surfaces, storage bins, shelves, files, office furnishings, and most of it is wired.

Business organizations relocate 40 to 50 percent of their microcomputers per year on the average, some even more frequently. Work areas are in a state of constant change.

Plan and interior of early Christian church. *Drawing:*
F. Wilson.

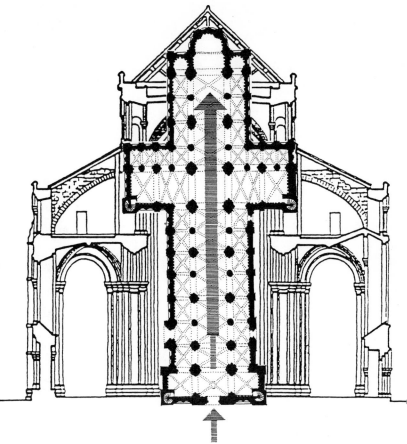

Plan and section of gothic cathedral. *Drawing:* F. Wilson.

## Mechanical Systems

The building's mechanical systems constantly respond to climatic changes, number of people in the building, and the heat and fumes generated by machines. Systems have become increasingly complex. They must be constantly maintained, adjusted and repaired.

The cost of mechanical equipment far exceeds architectural features. In the interior alteration of a bank the electrical contractors bill will be six to ten times higher than the supplier of partitions, hung ceilings and floor coverings.

The economics of energy consumption force the frequent change of mechanical equipment. New equipment pays for itself in saved energy costs in three or four years. If not installed the building becomes too expensive to operate. But the entire mechanical system is not changed. The most crucial is the machinery. Pipes and ducts can be left in place through several replacement of primary units. Minor distribution systems to rooms as their uses and sizes are altered is in a constant state of flux. The parts of the system that require maintenance, tuning and change are located in public movement space so that tradesmen can work on them without entering the building functioning areas.

## Mechanical Movement

the mechanical systems of a building is its only moving part. It responds to climatic changes, occupancy variations and energy consumed by office machines and light.

Boilers, fans, cooling towers create climate and in a sealed building are a life support system. But this is not the heart of the building as sometimes claimed, it is its bowels. When not functioning or sluggish the entire building, no matter how tastefully designed or how expensive its materials can not be used by human beings.

Light guided movement system. *Photo:* IKOY.

Red River Community College. *Photo:* IKOY.

## Plumbing

Bathrooms are the major focus of plumbing movement systems in most buildings. Historically plumbing is cut through the structure and becomes a permanent element of the building and is difficult and expensive to modify.

As the rooms of the function zones of the building continually change they change around the bathrooms or can not change because of the location of the bathrooms. There are also problems in buildings that require numerous sinks, such as brothels and laboratories. In essence the heart of the building, which is its living spaces, must be designed around the building's anus. Every time a room is relocated the sinks must be moved.

Pipe work must be controlled and hung ceilings installed where plumbing flexibility is required. In laboratory buildings hung ceilings are used to conceal the profusion of spaghettilike pipes. The plumbing system has not yet been solved satisfactorily as part of the building movement system. It exists in limbo between the permanent architectural system and the growing flexibility of electrical and communication systems.

## Electrical

The building's electrical systems have two major purposes. One is to provide power, the other is to give light. Modern buildings use electrical power at various intensities: 110, 220, 347 volts etc. Some of these are permanent, others are specific to a single building function; for example 347V is used only for fluorescent lighting.

Electrical power distribution must be designed to supply new power for changes in the needs of the building's machinery, and its computer and communication systems.

The city or utility usually supplies power to the building through transformers. The city or utility owns the transformer. It is best located outside the building, for the city or utility must have access to it. The primary transformer sends power to step-down transformers which change high voltage to lower voltages. These are boisterous, noisy devices that are best isolated in remote building locations. When they must be repaired major wiring is involved, which will disrupt all activities around them.

Electrical switch gear equipment, telephone pull boxes, and communication terminals, on the other hand are convivial. They can be placed in the building's public spaces, which are the human passageways to the building's function zones. If the electrical distribution system does not pass through floors or walls then partitions can be moved by building maintenance staff without involving outside electrical contractors.

Primary electrical distribution, which is the major nerve center of the building, is carried through raceways or channels which feed into cable trays. These distribute the wires to the working spaces of the building to power machines and instruments. These are best left open so that cable and conduit can be fed into them easily. The power passes from cable trays to wall-mounted wire molds or power poles for access where equipment is plugged in and out.

## Watt Festival

Evidence of the building's movement can be displayed. Electrical switch boxes with lights blinking on and off are small power festivals that can become part of the interactive language of architecture. These tell of the poles and sub-hubs of power. There is a seeming magic in a step-down transformer and the sight of electrical "stuff" coming through is a significant building event.

## Tempus Fugit

Buildings push air and power, and the architectural language will often express a sense of air and power movement through the building. Movement tells time, and there is a contrast in building movements—for example, electricity flashes by in milliseconds while a brick mortar joint takes 25 years to deteriorate and a foundation below grade without reinforcing rods may take 500 years to fall apart.

## Light and Color

Light and color are perhaps the most spectacular of all movement systems. The sun was the principal source of light in the ancient world. At night light came from fires, lamps, and torches. There were clamps on columns to hold torches and lamps. Greek lamps are found by the thousands, more numerous than coins, in archaeological excavations of Greek cities.

Color depends on light, and buildings were sited to catch the sun's variations as it moved, morning and night, north, south, east and west during the year. Vitruvius counseled winter dining rooms and bathrooms with southwestern exposures. "They need the evening light and the setting sun faces them in all its splendor but gives less heat and adds a gentle warmth to that part of the evening", he said.

Modern architects select and plan the building's attitude from a variety of light sources. Illumination serves more than the function of seeing, for light reinforces the comprehension of the building.

Theater light generates mood and character. Medical research proves we do not need a great deal of light to see. But the right kind of light is essential. Light must be safe for the human eye. It is not the quantity of light but the quality that helps us see well. The governing factor is not lumens or footcandles but the purpose of the light and its attitude. Light must describe and define structure and floor, wall, and ceiling. It must clarify building surfaces.

Electrical engineers skillfully design complex building power distribution systems. This is not the same as designing light. Usually they distribute

light as they distribute power, as a mathematical challenge. If it lights it functions. This is not enough and is the reason that architects use lighting designers as consultants, for they work with ocular qualities, the definition and theatrics of light rather than its quantity.

There are regulations and codes governing the use of power in buildings. There are step-down transformers, switch gears, insulated cables, and grounding wires and rules for installing them. Yet there is no building code, regulation, or rule that promises light will be safe and satisfying to the human eye.

Lighting and power differ. Power is measured for degree of performance. Lighting changes with the purpose of the spaces, the cost of operation.

Designers may study three hundred shades of green and select one. Once applied to building surfaces light will strike the color on different planes. The color will vary on each. Choice of lamp causes the color variation and there is no color without light. Most light is cast by fluorescent lamps. But daylight enters and modifies the color. Special purpose lamps modify color. The building is comprehended because of color modifications.

Color clarifies a building and defines. Art is not in the color but in definition and perceptual stimulation as the light strikes surfaces.

Modernists in architecture, early in this century, painted interiors shades of white, bone, ivory, or beige. But the dynamics of light transform a space with four matched white walls, white floor, and white ceiling into innumerable shades of white. Color in building is constantly transformed by lamps, shadows, clouds, and intensities of daylight. The architect does not pick a single hue as does the painter but a color, transformed by light variations to constant movement.

Luminous columns, Pension Building (Building Museum) Washington D.C. *Photo:* F. Wilson

Light transforms the uniform color exterior panels at various times during the day at Batoche. *Photos:* IKOY.

Light transforming interior color at Computer Center
and Earth Sciences buildings. *Photos:* IKOY.

# THE APPEARANCE OF REALITY

In the late Third Century B.C., Philon of Byzantium stated flatly that the oldest Greek buildings do not exhibit correct form. "Some parts of buildings, though they are of equal thickness and are straight, do not seem to be equal or straight, because our sight is misled by different distances." It is by trial and error, taperings and inclinations that the parts of the structure will appear well shaped, that is, agree with our vision of them, and "this is the goal of that art [architecture]."

Stylobates were curved, architraves slightly pitched forward, columns tilted. These adjustments make the building appear "right."

The aesthetic problem architects face today as in the past is to make things look as they are whether they actually appear as the artist sees them or not. Our eyes do not tell the truth. The brain is constantly translating optical illusions into real shapes and forms. We see an ellipse and know it is a circle and that strange polygons in perspective are really squares and rectangles. Our brain changes the figures we actually see into true shapes. How it does so is a scientific mystery even today.

But architects have known for at least 25 hundred years and perhaps longer how to curve the parallel lines to make them appear straight and how to tilt figures to make them appear plumb and true. Our brain converts the eyes' impressions to conclusions. The form of an object most be consistent with the building's attitude. The task of the architect is to make it so.

## Fundamental Principles

Vitruvius had an idea about how to make a building decision. He established organizing principles as have all architects from the building of the Parthenon to Cristopher Alexander at the University of California with his notes on the Synthesis of Form in 1964.

Vitruvius wrote that the building's attitude, which he called harmony, depends upon things in their proper place, with members of a height suited to their breadth and a breadth suited to their length. They must be a proper agreement between the members of the work itself and relation between the different parts and the general scheme in accordance with a certain part selected as standard. The work will then be harmonious because it has been constructed on approved principles. There was a proper way of proportioning a building front and Vitruvius was reciting the proper formulas for doing so.

Vitruvius divided temples into five classes and distinguished them by column spacing. These ranged from the pycnostyle, where the spacing was one and a half column diameters to the araeostyle with a spacing of four diameters, which is "further apart than they ought to be," he wrote. If the columns are spaced too closely together, matrons cannot pass between them with their arms around each other. They also obstruct the view of the door and the view into the temple. If too far apart they put too great a strain on the stone lintel above.

Column height was determined by column spacing. The pycnostyle was 10 diameters high and the araeostyle 8. The proportions of the temple facade were decided by the column diameter and all other dimensions and proportions followed the selection of this measurement. If these instructions were followed then the front and other three sides of the building would have harmonious proportions which any man or woman of good taste would recognize.

The architects of the Renaissance recognized the principles of Vitruvius but refined them and added a number of their own. Vitruvius based his observations on column and beam constructions. The Renaissance incorporated Roman arches, vaults, and domes and had to accommodate Vitruvian principles to a form of architecture Vitruvius had not considered, but the building front or face must be harmoniously proportioned none the less. To move or alter any part of it would be to destroy these relationships and the beauty of the building.

## Renaissance Face Lift

The front or facade of the building posed a major attitudinal problem in church architecture for the Renaissance humanists. The problem arose over the clash between Renaissance theory of the church and its appearance and the early Christian-Medieval development of the church building and what it became. The Renaissance believed a church should be a temple and called it that. In their view churches should be like ancient temples, which were elevated, isolated from other buildings, and very grand.

They were shocked that early Christian churches were modelled on ancient basilicas, which were commercial or legal structures. The Renaissance also considered the central plan superior to the longitudinal rectangle of the basilica.

The early Church avoided temples. It was not until the 7th Century that some ancient temples such as the Pantheon and Parthenon were converted to churches. As described earlier in this chapter, the Christians had adopted the basilica form because it was ideal for holding and regulating large crowds, which ancient temples were not designed to do. Eventually piers were substituted for columns, the structure was narrowed and heightened, and towers and crossing lanterns were added, with low shed roofs over side aisles and steep pitched trussed or vaulted roofs over the high central aisle, fully expressed in Romanesque and Gothic West Fronts.

The Renaissance wanted to make this standard church look like an ancient temple. The early church was a processional church, going from this world to the door of the next at the altar, and the side aisles were useful for these long processions.

In contrast the temple housed an image which was viewed by devotees through the open portal. They remained outside. The temple facade framed the door and the door framed the image. The church needs three portals, the temple one. The church needs windows, the temple does not.

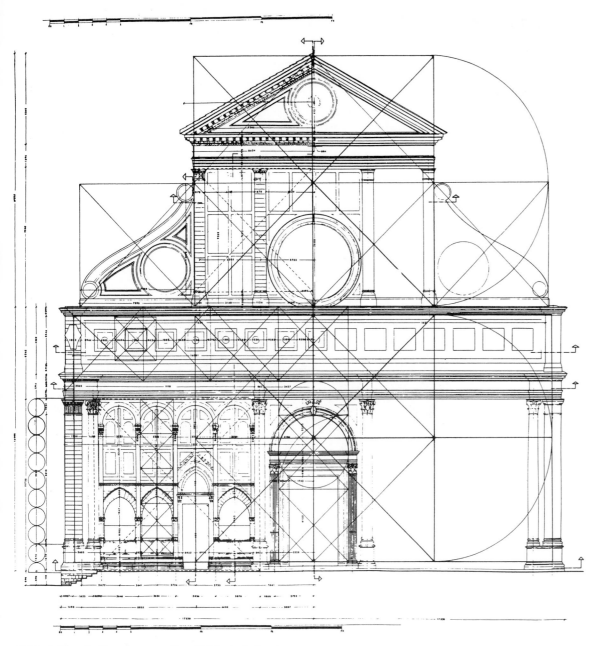

S. Maria Novella, Facade proportion (P. Electra) Courtesy of Architectural Design and Acroshaw Ltd. Vol. 49, No. 5-6, 1979

A church, the Renaissance thought, should be made to look like a temple yet retain its three portals, the windows, and the transept. The statement of temple could be made only on the facade. The facade was detached from interior design and the solution found in the superimposition of two temples. One temple roof covered the low side aisles and one the high central nave.

Although the stacked temples did not look very much like the temples Vitruvius described in his ten books of architecture, the same principles of proportion, symmetry, order were followed for 500 years.

## SKIN DEEP FACADES

Charles-Edouard Janneret, the future Le Corbusier, proposed a system of mass produced prefabricated housing in 1914 designed to restore devastated towns in Flanders. The system cut the link between construction and architecture. The "column and slab" Le Corbusier proposed formed a structural system independent of architectural elements. Interior partitions were no longer load-bearing and could be placed as the occupant desired. They did not have to attach to the exterior, so windows could be placed freely.

This was not a new idea: it had been discovered and used a quarter of a century earlier with the introduction of iron and steel framed buildings designed in the United States. But Le Corbusier's advocacy of the idea in manifesto and proclamation and inventive uses of the concept changed building facades to building skins.

The frame, Le Corbusier said, is completely independent of the functions of the plan. It simply supports the flooring and the staircase and is made of standard elements that can be fitted together.

Le Corbusier was inspired by machine manufacture. His model was the automobile and airplane. When humans wanted to fly, they first tried to fly like a bird, he said, and for hundreds of years they failed. But when they thought of a "flying machine" they solved the problem in ten years. "Let us face the problem of housing as a "living machine," he concluded. Le Corbusier did not mean living in a machine, but was thinking of the problem as the Wright brothers had though of the problem of flying as a mechanical, scientific solvable problem.

Le Corbusier was searching among new materials to find new solutions. Space in cities was scarce and valuable. The cost of buildings had quadrupled within a decade. Industrial mass production like that introduced by Henry Ford a few years earlier and used for the manufacture of airplanes and railway carriages might be an answer. Space is calculated to the square inch by these manufacturers, and there were new materials such as steel and reinforced concrete capable of creating new building forms.

The building Corbusier proposed was supported on columns or pillars, walls and partitions were non-load-bearing. The columns left the corners and stood in the room. The slab cantilevered to the outside walls. The fireplace was no longer part of an exterior wall and stairs could be placed where they were most useful. Exterior walls could be opened or closed. There could be a "free facade" with ribbon windows and glass walls.

Glass walls are more difficult to use than ribbon windows. Glass forms large, empty, uniform spaces. Under certain lighting conditions the spaces become blank holes punching through the unity and equilibrium of the design. Interior life is exposed to exterior view and glass is extremely sensitive to heat. It passes the sun's heat in when it is not wanted and passes the building's warmth out when it is wanted inside. Le Corbusier countered this difficulty by inventing movable screens (the *brise-soleil*) which were only partially effective. The problem of glass was not effectively analyzed and satisfactory solutions proposed until the energy crisis half a century later.

## The Curtain Wall

After World War II Le Corbusier's creative talents wandered to great architectural sculptures. The strip window disappeared into the magnificent south wall in the church of Ronchamp built in 1950–53. Le Corbusier had however helped launch the "curtain wall" and the endless multiplication of column and slab construction in the skeleton frame.

The great strength of steel and concrete made it possible to build higher and the patterns of modern cities are now determined by skeleton structures as decisively as the patterns of medieval cities were determined by the timber frame.

Skeleton structures are built of steel and concrete columns and beams rigidly connected. Load-carrying members are reduced to minimum sizes and there is a clear distinction between structural

Ronchamp by Corbusier. *Photo:* Courtesy of French Tourist Office.

Corbusier's facade from inside the Carpenter Center at Harvard University. *Photo:* Courtesy of Harvard University.

and nonstructural building elements. Rectangular elevations enclose box-shaped buildings divided into cellular spaces by regular column spacing. The building is the sum of individual cells whose internal organization is subordinated to the structural function of the skeleton.

The facade pattern is glass, metal, precast concrete or stone panels as space-enclosing skins strong enough to withstand wind loads and support

themselves. A grid system of intersecting lines is the dominant feature of the facade. The facade column or mullion spacing accommodates the connection of interior partitions to the exterior wall. The spacing of the window divisions indicates the sizes of interior working spaces. These are dimensioned to accommodate office furniture. The curtain wall is sized by the dimensions of a filing cabinet.

The spandrel or horizontal floor slab is either

thickened or the slab turned up or down to form a beam. As a rule floor bands are broader than columns. The structural pattern of the grid is based on the relationship between slender columns and the heavier horizontal floor bands. Each grid begins and ends at the corners, and the usual solution is to make the corner columns the same as all others.

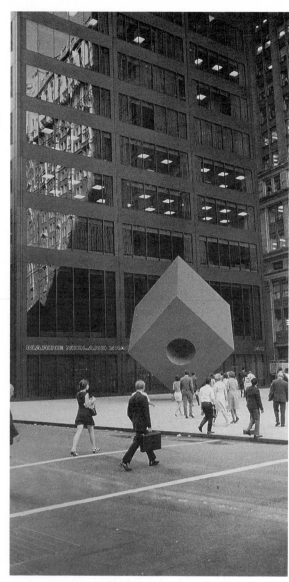

The curtain wall at Marine Midland Bank through its
Noguchi sculpture. *Photos:* F. Wilson.

# Thermodynamic Barrier

In the 1960s the curtain wall became the "building skin" and is thought of as a thermodynamic barrier. After the Arab oil embargo of the early 1970s architects began to examine facades, curtain walls, and building skins very carefully. Identical elevations in all directions were prodigious energy consumers. Harmony, form, and function became secondary to the heat transfer characteristics of thermodynamic barriers. And, because daylight is free and electric light expensive, the transparency of the barrier is important. There must be a relation to the uses of the room behind the facade and an ability to change the facade's opacity or transparency as the uses of the interior space changes which is a far cry from the harmonically proportioned symmetrical Renaissance facade.

The design of a building enclosure that can alternate as an opaque or transparent membrane poses different problems than designing a permanent building facade. One solution to a changing building front is to consider the spacing grid of the curtain wall as a control mechanism.

The "control grid" permits the skin to be perforated, that is, opened and closed at will to insert opaque or translucent panels. In contrast to the symmetrical classical facade that cannot be altered without either marring its perfection or redesigning the entire front the thermodynamic barrier can support random penetration, dictated by the need to let light into or close light out of the building's interior.

The control grid must establish a dominating design pattern that can be altered without changing the "attitude" of the building elevation. The building's occupants are no longer bound by the demand to plan interior activities on the characteristics of the external wall. As the demands of the things people do within the building change windows are inserted or removed without compromising the building's exterior pattern.

Facade and thermo dynamic barrier. *Collage:* F. Wilson.

Himawari system in use at Ark Mori building in
Ark Hills, Tokyo; 19 lens, Himawari. *Photo:* Courtesy
of Himawari.

## Activated Elevations

The next step after establishing the advantage of an adjustable thermal barrier is to mechanically or electrically activate the building skin and bring light in by other means. Present building research is moving in this direction.

"Light pipes" now carry sunlight into dark building interiors, and diffraction lenses bends light from the facade deep to the back of dark rooms. Light may soon also be bounced from building facades by diffraction gratings into dark city canyon streets.

Intelligent building skins can predict the weather, according to research done at the Dept. of Building Science, Sheffield, England. New materials and technique permit dynamic rather than static response to variations in external climate. Local weather is predicted over a period of several hours, and sensors activate building response.

Electrochromic panels activated by passing an electric current through an electrochemically active polymer film sandwiched between two panes of glass changes the color from clear to blue gray to obstruct optical clarity. Color changes with current intensity and remains at the tint opacity when the current is turned off. The power used is negligible. The amount needed to activate a square meter of glass is equivalent to that consumed by a 100 watt incandescent bulb in one or two seconds of use. However, eye glasses and motor cycle helmets will probably be successfully manufactured before large areas in buildings are economically feasible. Current research (1988) is working on an astronaut visor to cut down the glare of sunlight.

Laboratory investigations of technology for core daylighting extend the window using hollow rectangular "light ducts" with reflective interior surfaces to conduct sunlight from the building's surface to its core continues. A few buildings have been designed using this technology.

Holographic diffractive structures like those used in a credit card hologram change the way light

Himawaris exhibited at Tsukuba Exposition, Japan. *Photo:* Courtesy of Himawari. Daiwa House in Nagoya with Himawari. *Photo:* Courtesy of Himawari.

passes through a window. They are clear, lightweight, stationary devices that track the sun through the course of the day and through the seasons of the year. They can be programmed to redirect a range of solar angles. Systems dynamically respond to non-optimal solar positions exterior to the building envelope and redirect sunlight to areas deep within the core of the structure and control glare on the perimeter.

The basic idea is to use these diffractive structures (gratings) as lenses. Most daylighting excludes sunlight because it is too intense. The gratings break the sunlight into component parts and the individual colors can be projected or all combined as white.

The Himawari (Japanese for "sunflower") light collection and transmission device tracks the sun and use Fresnel lenses to focus sunlight into optical fibers which "pipe" the light to the desired location. The device was developed by Kei Mori, of Keio University in Tokyo. There were 79 himawari systems in use, mostly in Japan in 1987. They illuminated private homes, museums, office buildings, hospitals, schools, resorts, and nursing homes.

Light enters the himawari through a protective acrylic resin capsule. Hexagon-shaped, honeycomb-patterned Fresnel lenses capture incoming parallel light rays. The rays are focused onto the polished input ends of fiber optic cables. The capsule filters out some ultraviolet light while the Fresnel lenses filter out almost all remaining ultraviolet and about 60 percent of the infrared rays. A tracking system keeps the lenses trained on the sun and returns the sunflower to face the sunrise when the sun sets. The sensor sends information to a small internal computer which directs the tracking of the pulse motors.

Possible uses for the Himawari in future cities. Proposed "marine ranch," utilizing Himawaris. *Photo:* Courtesy of Himawari.

Light is sent through "light-pipes." The spectrum is almost identical to that of natural sunlight. The light brings less heat, ultraviolet, and infrared radiation and is therefore useful in clothing stores and art galleries to avoid fading and discoloration. Plants flourish and the himawari may be useful in treating medical rheumatism.

Curtain walls of buildings have been used for actively heating and cooling buildings since 1968. Vertical mullions, horizontal transoms, and glass units form a weathertight, hermetically sealed, insulated assembly. Water, adjusted to the desired temperature, is circulated through the interior profiles of the units. Although the total surface of the gridwork oriented to an interior space normally is larger than the surface of a conventional radiator, the space can be heated and cooled without additional radiators if a heat exchange system is incorporated in the gridwork profiles.

In a scheme proposed in Germany curtain wall mullions are connected to a normal heating system with water or air circulating through them.

When the building skin is activated incorporating dynamically variable properties such as low-voltage electrical distribution systems, simple sensing, logic, and control devices connected to computers that monitor building services the entire building is then animated.

As exterior walls selectively darken, lighten, change color, carry imagery, and display information and as the building facade becomes an information screen will this 21st Century version of the "rose window" advertise the "New Coke" or have a better attitude?

Reflection of the World Trade Center in neighboring curtain wall building. *Photo:* F. Wilson.

# Chapter 8

# How It Works—A Scientific Barn

## THE PROBLEM
### The Site

The client had a program and a budget. The building was to be built on a century-old experimental farm sited on an ancient river bank. The river is now a mile away. The proposed site location was on the flat land between river and hill. Spring runoffs created a lake half a mile wide and 18 inches deep where the building might have been.

The site was moved to higher ground. For most architects the rise in ground would have been of little consequence, but to flat prairie builders the new location was a "hill." There was a view over the farmland to the river, and beyond that the city skyline of Brandon, Manitoba a farming community of 35 thousand.

There were two outstanding forms on the landscape. One was a red dairy barn 75 yards to the west, the other an arboretum to the southeast. The

barn was old. Farmers no longer build barns in Manitoba. They erect metal machine sheds instead. The arboretum was unique. The scientists had planted every known species of tree they thought would survive in the killing cold of northwest Canada. Most of them did. The grove was now a mature forest of trees exotic to the prairie and different from any other arboretum on earth.

This was to be a laboratory building, but quite different from the Earth Sciences Building, Forensic Laboratories or Computer Research Center. The scientific and technical problems might be similar but these buildings had been built in cities or on a university campus.

This was to be a laboratory in the middle of a farm. A great modern laboratory building, on a slight rise of ground in the middle of a rural "nowhere." It would be "laboratory building" ten times the size of a barn, which is by far the largest building in a cluster of farm buildings.

The farms of western Canada are miles apart. Nowhere would a person see six in a single sweep of the head. Usually one sees a barn, a house, a silo and more and more and more wheat fields. The big red barn on the site was unusual, the arboretum was unusual, and an urban laboratory the size of ten barns would be the most unusual of all.

## A Word Image

Words in the mouth trigger images in the minds eye. The first was "laboratory" and then "farm." The visual images of laboratory and farm were completely opposed in visual images and scale. They discarded them. What is a farm. What is akin to a farm? What is a laboratory about?

There are three symbols of the country, the grain elevator, the barn, and the church steeple, currently being replaced by the microwave tower.

*Laboratory* was easy. There is the idea of science

and the idea of scientific farm. There was an arboretum and the sense of wheat and barley. But there is little architectural inspiration in wheat and barley. *Farm* was discarded. Farm buildings and the way they are built on the farm was pondered. This yielded two exciting situations: barn and storage bins. Both are dominant elements of Manitoba farms. Storage bins are short and storage bins are tall. Call them silos. The idea—*scientific barn.*

Then there were a series of insights. The laboratory building on the farm became the scientific barn. Barns have a major presence. They are constructed seriously of no-nonsense materials. They have a presence and a natural affinity with silos.

Once the idea of the scientific barn was chosen there was a flood of inspiration about how to design a big building where traditionally small buildings stood. The concept of scientific barn influenced the shape, volume, profile, connection structure, materials, and all other decisions.

## What Is a Barn?

The huge "ten times larger" building, no longer ashamed of its size, was treated as a barn. Barns are better to live in than farmhouses. Barns are utilitarian buildings with great human space. They are built almost as if cattle are preferred to the people that live in the small rooms of the farmhouse.

Barns are places of industry and experiment. Historically many experiments were done in barns—Alexander Graham Bell, Einstein, the Wright brothers used them as fitting places for experiment.

The barn is a model for industrial buildings. But the barn was not to be mimicked. It was not a barn for pigs and cows but a barn for science. A place for research and experiment. A place to elevate the human spirit in the search for knowledge not a reproduction but a metaphor.

It must be a place where scientists who do not go home for lunch because they are located so far outside the city would stay and talk to each other. It must be a place for talking and working together. The problem of encouraging scientists, engineers, and technicians to mingle was like those faced in the computer center. But in the scientific barn it was more natural. The scientists are appointed by the government and expected to share information. Information cannot be secret. The building must be designed to heighten inspirational interaction among the scientists.

A building galleria was designed as a meeting place. It is a street of visual sharing. The view is stimulating, traveling over and through the arboretum, down the hill to the valley and then to the city on the other side of the river.

## How to Make a Scientific Barn

The building structure could not be made of wood. It must be made of steel or concrete. The first idea was to use hollow steel sections to mimic wooden timbers connected by metal plates. It was too literal.

Round pipe columns were chosen because they were visually, without doubt, steel. Wide flange steel beams were connected to them. They were obviously steel, common and cheap like barn framing. It is extremely difficult to connect a wide flange beam to a pipe column, and more difficult when the roof slopes. The connection is reminiscent of the metal plates used to connect barn timbers near the truss ends, where wood cannot handle the crushing stresses.

The architects returned to a "metal vocabulary" they had used 10 years earlier in the IKOY office building wind bracers. They wrapped a plate around the round pipe and created a simple seat. The wide flanges were simply dropped into these factory-made connectors. Erection was simple, direct, and inexpensive in the grand tradition of plate and timber barn structures.

The structural inspiration is from the barn, but reflects the spirit of science and technology, not pigs and straw. It is not a building for square dancing. It is not a place to roll in the hay but one to satisfy scientific curiosity.

It is inspired by the simple, direct, and visually powerful means of heavy timber barn construction.

## OF BARNS THEN AND NOW

Farmers no longer build barns. They build garages for their equipment. Hay is rolled into big round mounds and stored under black plastic sheets. They pick it up with a forklift truck and drive it to the cattle.

The symbol of the barn as we know it is of barns built 40, 50, 140, or 150 years ago. Barns turned into garages when farm animals were traded in for combustion engines. Today's barn equivalent is the all-metal "Butler Building." This is a metal mechanical shed that serves as protection and repair shop for farm machinery. No working farmer has built a heavy timber barn for the past half century.

The barn is as historic a symbol for farming as the

classic Greek temple is to banking. The drive-in automated teller is today's banking equivalent of the farmer's metal machinery shed.

Farmers today store their own grain to play the commodities market. When commercial grain elevators are full or they cannot sell their grain they must keep it. The silo is not for silage but for speculation. An emerging farm form is the squat round building to store grain when they can not sell or do not like the price. The old silos, for silage, are used on animal farms. The grain farm has shorter storage bins.

Laboratory experiments increase farmers' profits. If the scientists find a barley that ripens three weeks earlier with four inches less rainfall the farmers will prosper. Laboratory research is in both plants and animals. The building has value for all of Canada, for the entire country will benefit from its successful research.

## SCIENCE IN THE BARN

Farmers are pragmatic scientists and inventors. During the winter when the crops are in they tinker with the machines in the barn, fix old ones, and make new. They are exceptionally innovative. And the scientists working in the scientific barn may well have grown up on a farm. They may have gone to agricultural school and instead of becoming chemical engineers they turned to agricultural chemistry. Who is more likely to be fascinated by biology and plant science than a grain farmer's son or daughter?

Early factories started in barns and barn structures, yet we associate barn buildings with animals. When we describe agriculture and wish to simplify our definition of it we say "farming." But in reality agriculture is a very exact science. This science is pursued in the laboratory. A laboratory cannot be regional or "vernacular," it is scientific. The memory of the barn in the scientific barn is to reconnect the scientist to the land.

Plant scientists use growing chambers; these are not greenhouses. They may be green or white boxes 6 x 9 feet high, some are 15 x 15 x 9 feet high. There is an array of computer controls at the front door of the box and the complex, compact equipment on the box roof rivals a submarine life support system.

The controls regulate temperature, light, and humidity and simulate changing sunlight. Environmental conditions are under absolute control. When plants are grown in greenhouses conditions change from year to year and differences in plants may not be due to genetic change but environmental conditions. Agricultural scientists demand exact information. They replicate and measure all factors exactly.

Temperature variation within a quarter of a de-

gree and light variation must be known and recorded exactly. Humidity is measured and temperature varied. Days and nights are created in the boxes with all of the attendant changes and each change measured. Exact records are kept. One laboratory can grow the same wheat that is grown in Winnipeg, Manitoba, Florida, California, Australia, and Buenos Aires by duplicating the exact growing conditions of each of these locations on the earth's surface.

This is not a farm were you sow seed in the dirt, squat, and watch. There is science and technology involved that equals the Earth Sciences (see p. xxx), RCMP Forensics (see p. xxx) and Computer Research (see p. xxx). The farm at this scientific level is comparable to Orwell's 1984. The scientific barn is plotting the future of farming.

Doctors talk of genetic splicing of DNA. Agricultural scientists have been working with the plant and human equivalent long before medical scientists. Farm animals and farm plants have been genetically modified for centuries. This is a place that can create modern Frankensteins. It is not a backwater research facility.

They have experimented with cows, wheat, and barley. No one was alarmed when they bred bigger and stronger cows and steers with more meat per pound. They have grown wheat with bigger heads and no one was alarmed when they spliced genes.

The scientific barn is the place where they do these things, interact, and share ideas. A place to generate reverence and dignify the idea of work, ideas, and the people that work with plants, animals, and ideas and promote their interaction.

## Designing Interaction

There are levels of transparency. The labs are glazed to the galleria—the walkway—they look outside through the galleria and borrow its natural light. In the forensic lab no one other than the scientists could look into or enter them. In the scientific barn visual participation is encouraged. There can be jokes with Alex. The research library is located next to the galleria and the cafeteria is in it. The conference centers where scientists and farmers meet open off the galleria.

Everyone passes each other. When farmers go to eat they walk by the glazed labs and see how the research is conducted that will give them better yields and safer crops. It is important that scientist talk to scientist and farmer talk to scientist.

Farmers on their farms are isolated. This allows the farmer to share his pragmatic knowledge with the scientist and scientist inform the farmer. The stoa-like galleria is an architectural device to diffuse information.

## The Computer

What do hackers and agricultural scientists have in common? To begin there are a lot of PCs on farms. But it is interesting that there is not a lot of computer technology in the scientific barn.

The labs are not loaded with computer terminals. There is a central computer area connected to satellite computer clusters that talk to each other and speak to others across Canada. The computer is used as an information vehicle. The environmental chambers are plants in computers. They are computerized test tubes.

Computers at the computer research building are used for researching and inventing new ways for computers to disseminate information (see p. xxx), but in the scientific barn the scientists use the computer and programs developed elsewhere to do more than they did formerly with test tubes. It is similar to the virologist who, when given an electronic microscope, can see what he could not see with a regular microscope. Agricultural scientists using the computer can search for answers where they could not search for them before.

# PRELIMINARY DRAWINGS

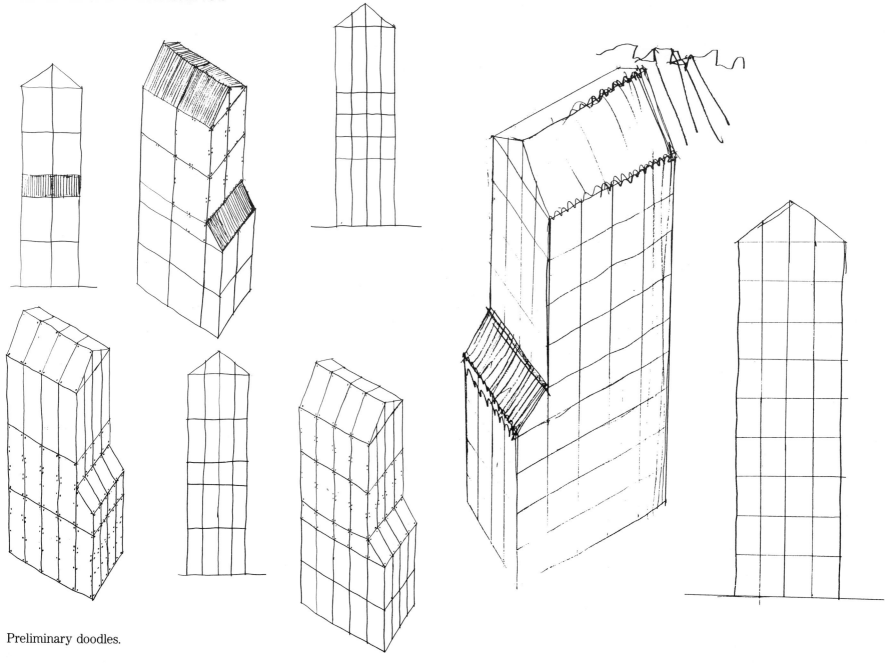

Preliminary doodles.

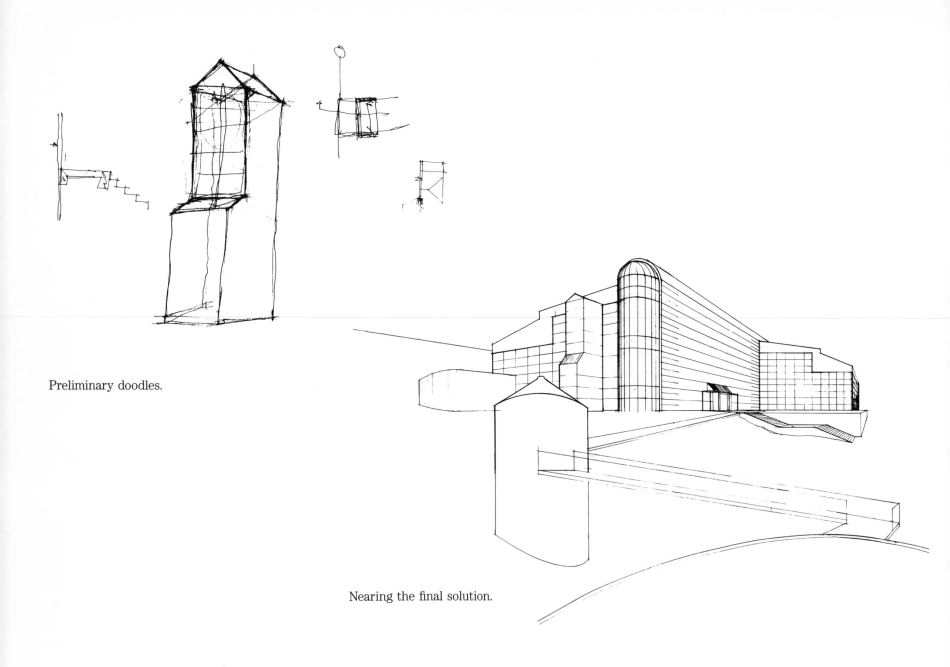

Preliminary doodles.

Nearing the final solution.

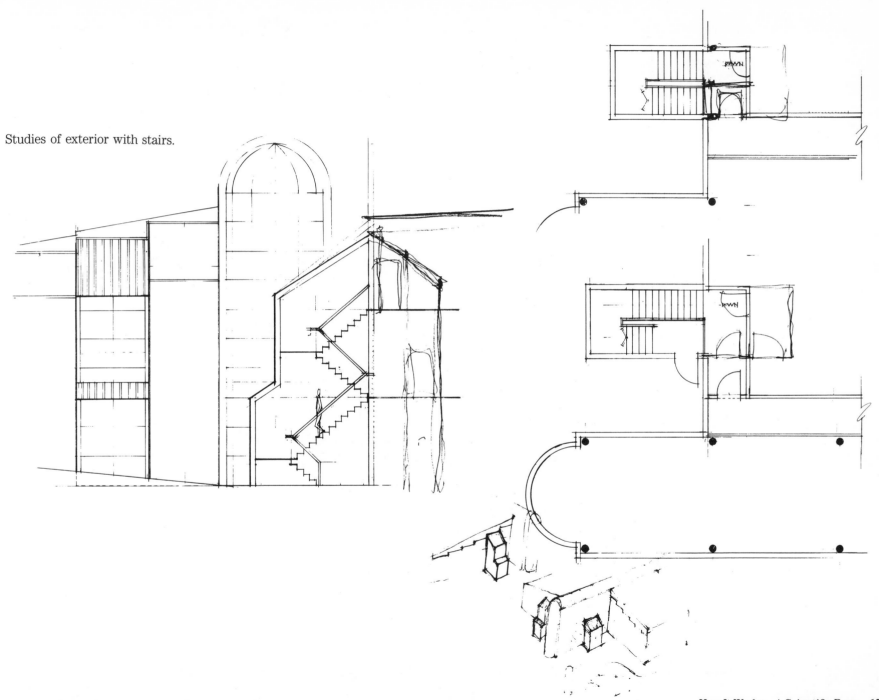

Studies of exterior with stairs.

Dreams of lofty, barnlike spaces.

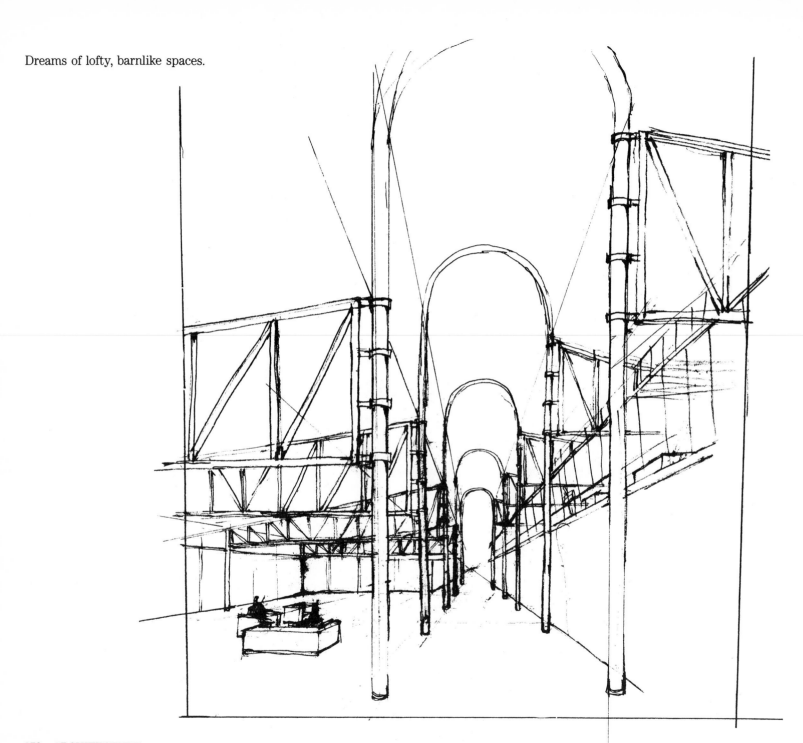

A number of things starting to happen.

Stair bracket—handrails which will be partially shop fabricated, finished at job site. Top rail welded into continuous piece on site.

Handrails and curtain walls are not related. They do different things. Why should they align? There must be a reason for aligning building elements.

Stair landings and curtain walls should align, for the curtain wall sets the window locations; floors and window mullions must align; but not the handrails.

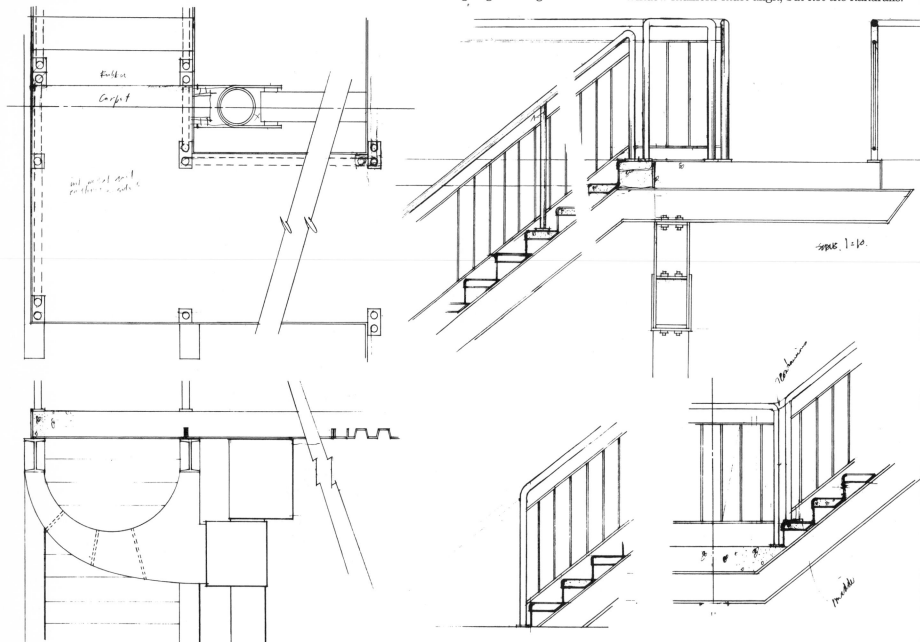

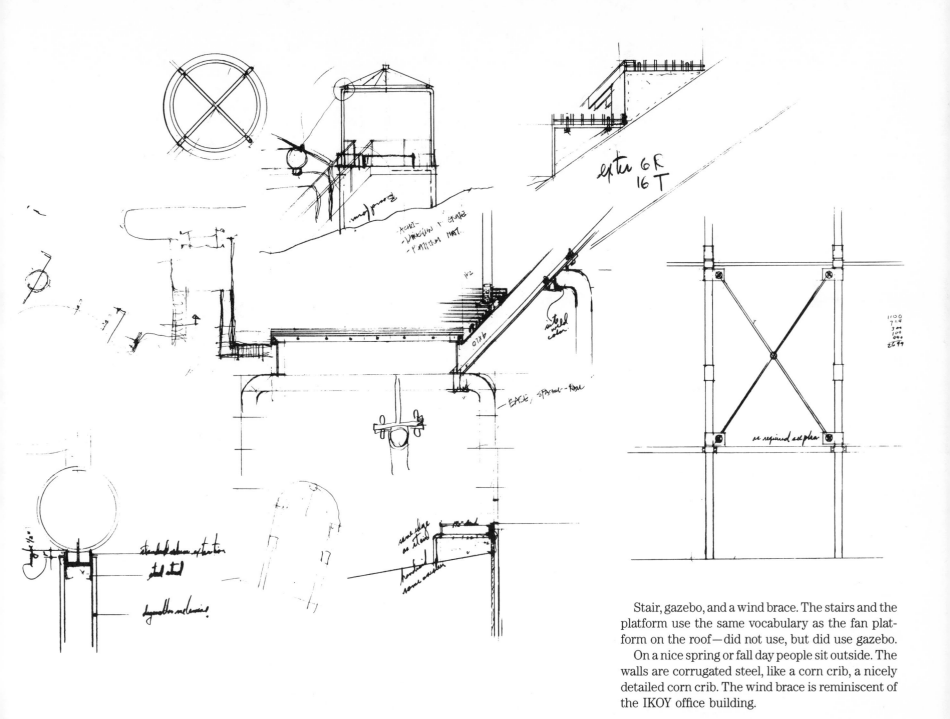

Stair, gazebo, and a wind brace. The stairs and the platform use the same vocabulary as the fan platform on the roof—did not use, but did use gazebo.

On a nice spring or fall day people sit outside. The walls are corrugated steel, like a corn crib, a nicely detailed corn crib. The wind brace is reminiscent of the IKOY office building.

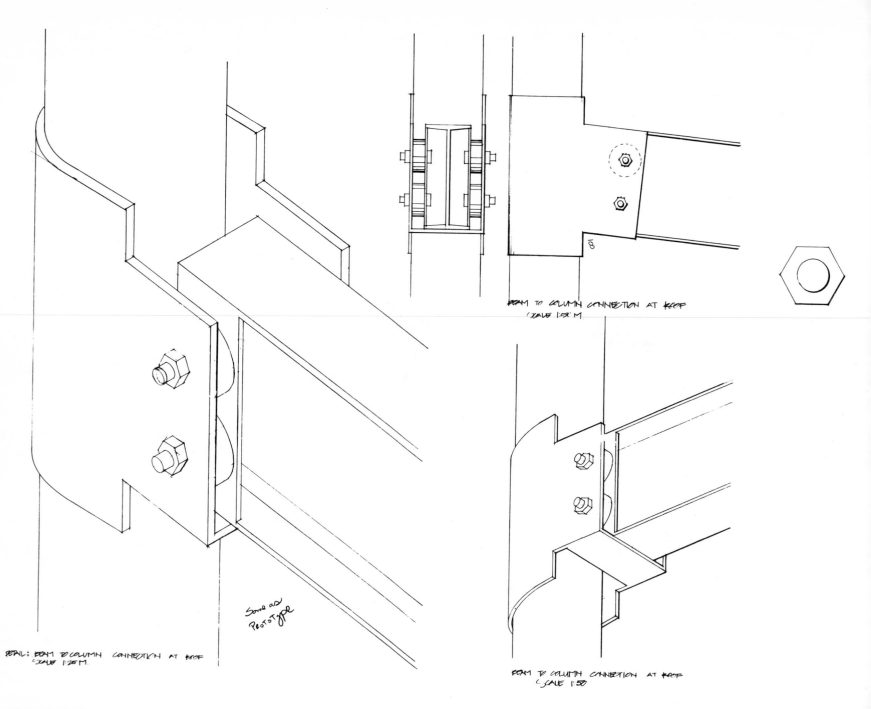

BEAM TO COLUMN CONNECTION AT ROOF
SCALE 1:20 M

Some as
ProtoType

DETAIL: BEAM TO COLUMN CONNECTION AT ROOF
SCALE 1:20 M

BEAM TO COLUMN CONNECTION AT ROOF
SCALE 1:50

Wide flange beams (WF) connected to pipe columns. The coupling device—a connection—brings together two completely dissimilar dimensions and shapes.

The pipe columns will be delivered to the site with welded clamp brackets. The wide flange beams are dropped into the seat. The large interior washers between beam end and seat are slipped in.

Bolts are inserted and tightened. This is similar to the common steel erection procedure of resting beams on seat angles prior to connection.

The connection is manufactured by running standard sheets through rollers then cutting them into standard U-shaped pieces.

The clip connection can rotate 360 degrees horizontally and the beam can tilt up or down to the desired angle. Roof beams tilt, floor beams are horizontal. The pipe columns are 11 inches in diameter, the WF beams 7 inches deep.

Stair support bracket in greater detail. It uses the same principle as the beam bracket to support stairs or a bridge. The stair support is inserted instead of the WF beam. The beam bracket drops down and the stair support bracket reaches up.

This is a special shape repeated throughout the building. It is mass produced from metal plates using a sheet metal template in the field fabricator's shop with standard tools and skills. Plates are connected by stiffeners, resulting in a geometric form without expensive casting.

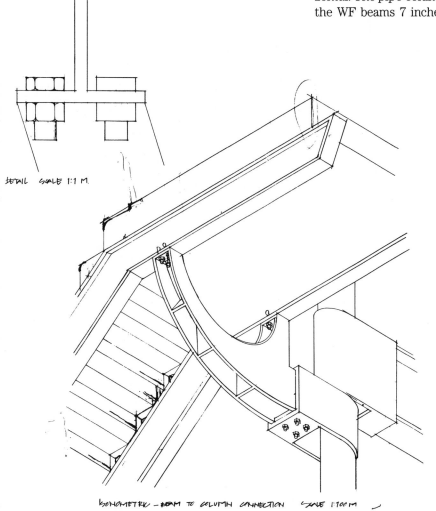

DETAIL SCALE 1:1 M.

ISOMETRIC — BEAM TO COLUMN CONNECTION    SCALE 1:100 M.

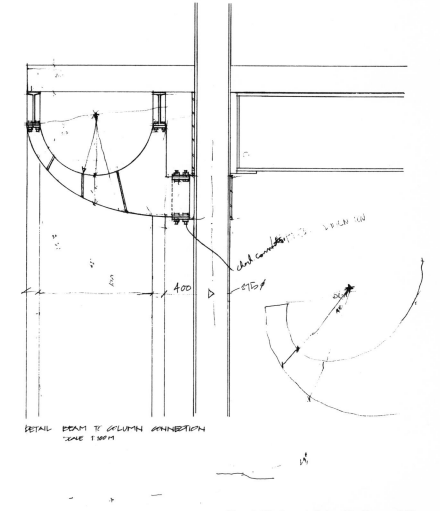

DETAIL BEAM TO COLUMN CONNECTION
SCALE 1:100 M

Earlier stair bracket at beam connection.

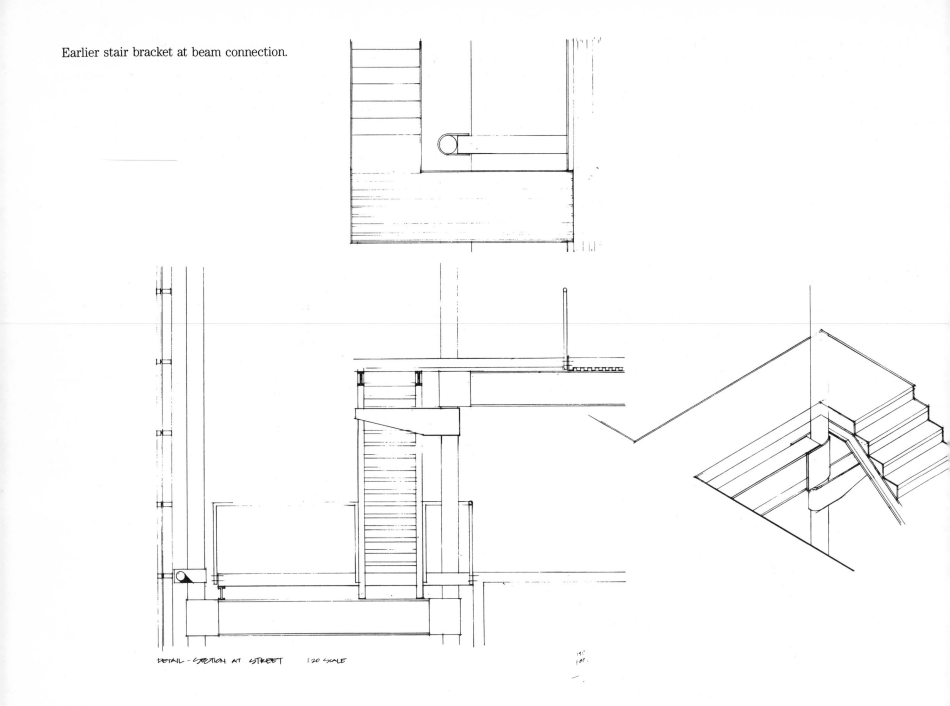

DETAIL - SECTION AT STREET    1:20 SCALE

Detail at center of office roof, showing beams tilting up and down.

The roof is part of the wall—an angled, horizontal wall. The roof is a skin, not a roof. It is stainless steel, and begins with the first cap of the foldover of the standing seam.

Oversized bolts stitch the flashing piece to the building side. The roof not only changes plane but changes material from stainless steel to aluminum.

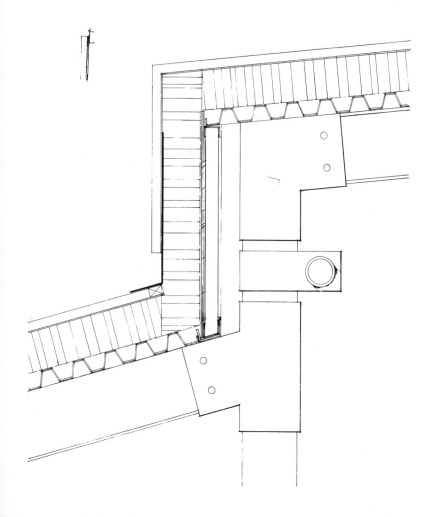

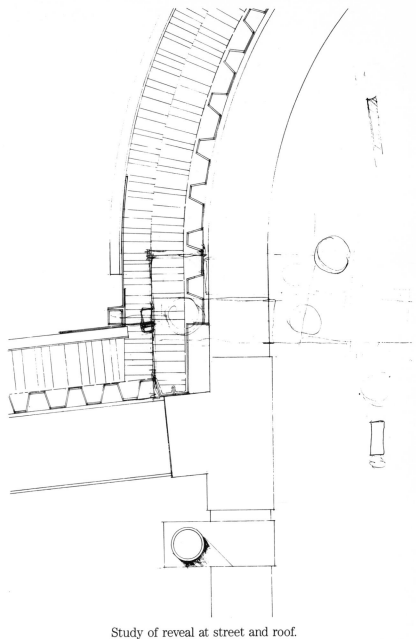

Study of reveal at street and roof.

Structure of the galleria space.

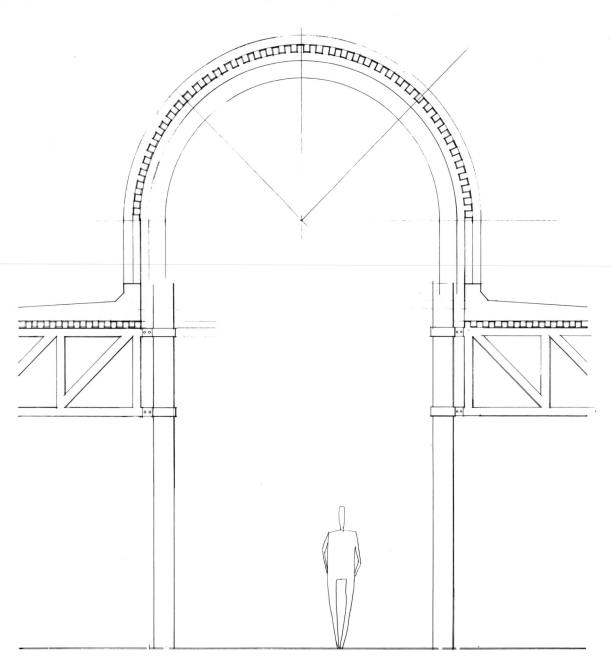

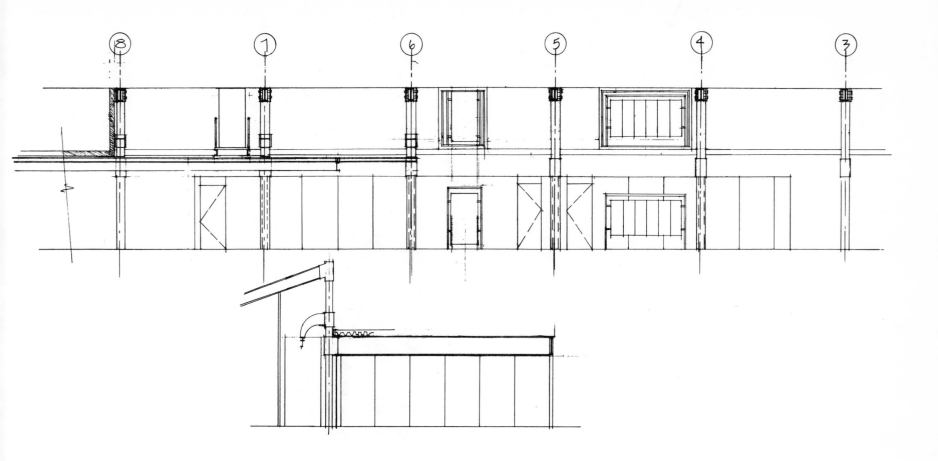

The columns appear, upside down stair bracket.

Study of potential problems in perspective.

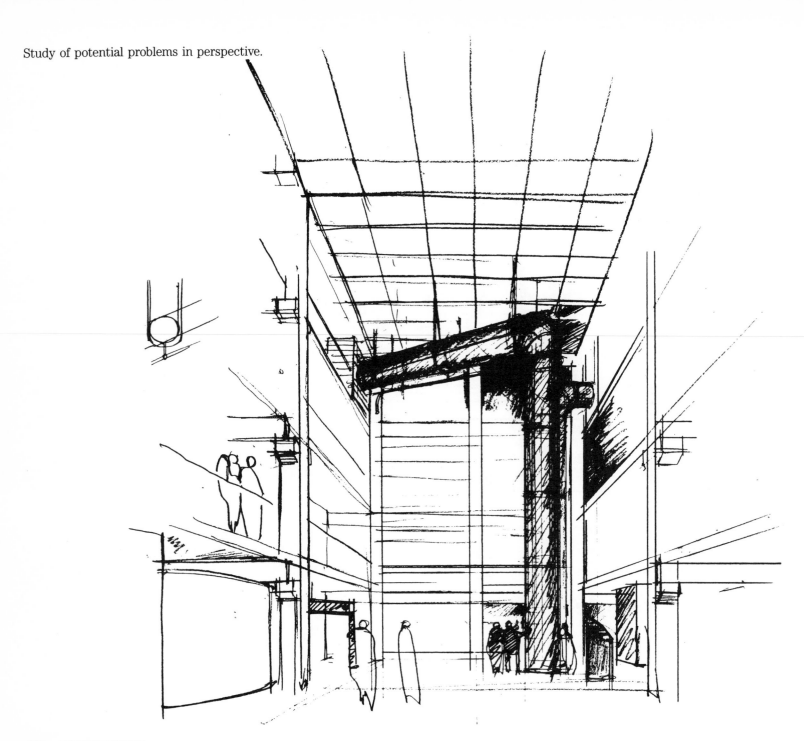

Study of potential problems in perspective.

Fume hoods connect outside on the building's roof. Welded pipe connects fume hood to motor. If seals leak, they do it outside. Inside they are difficult to repair and leaks are very dangerous. There is no assurance seals will not fail, no matter how detailed. Motors are oversized to start in cold temperatures. The roof has a special walkway for motor servicing. Motors are shielded by a perforated metal screen. Such motors rarely fail and can be maintained in good weather. Even if they do fail, that is preferable to interior leaks. The tradeoff was cold fingers or toxic fumes in the lungs.

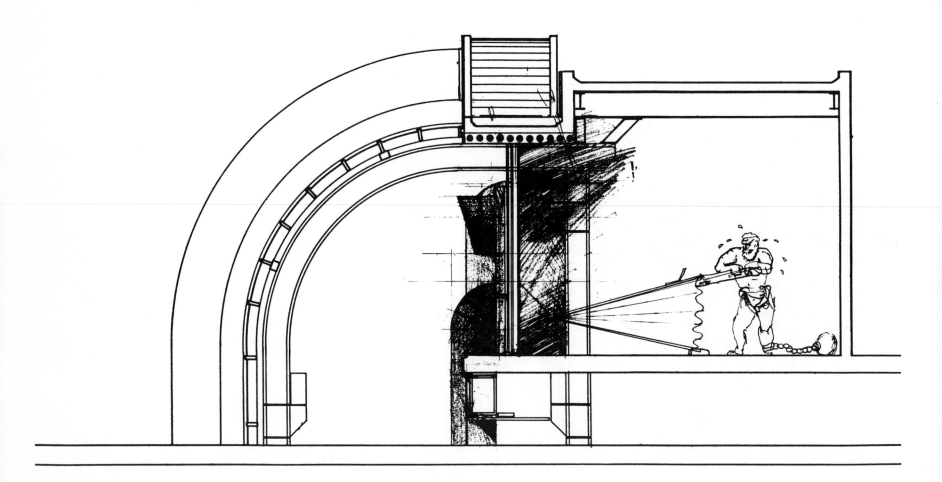

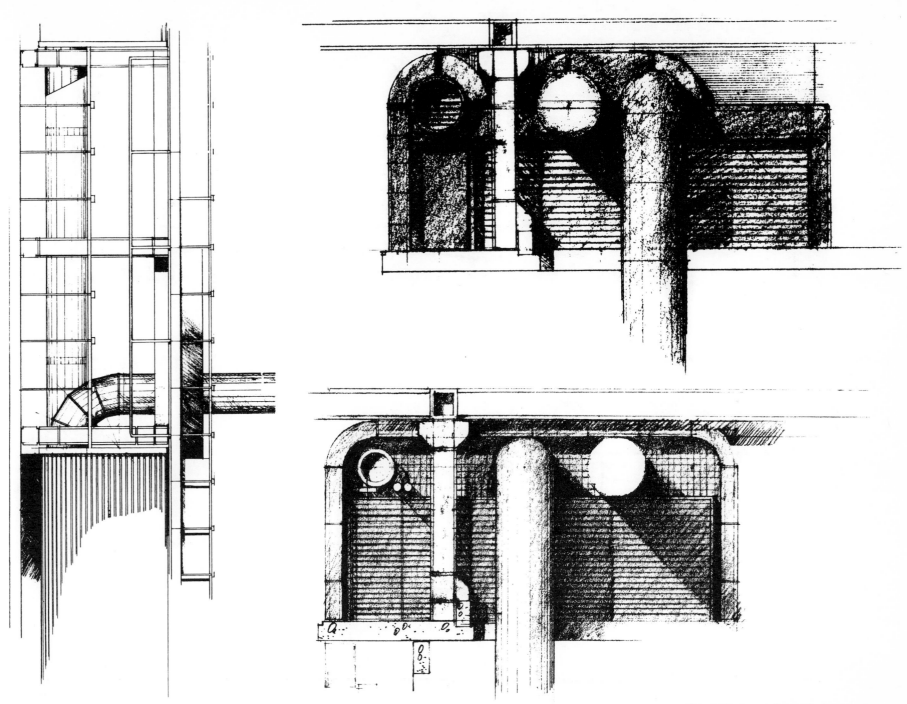

The building has 1 to 5 critical dimensions. Centerline of columns, inside of curtain wall to roof parapet. Centerline of column to inside face of frame.

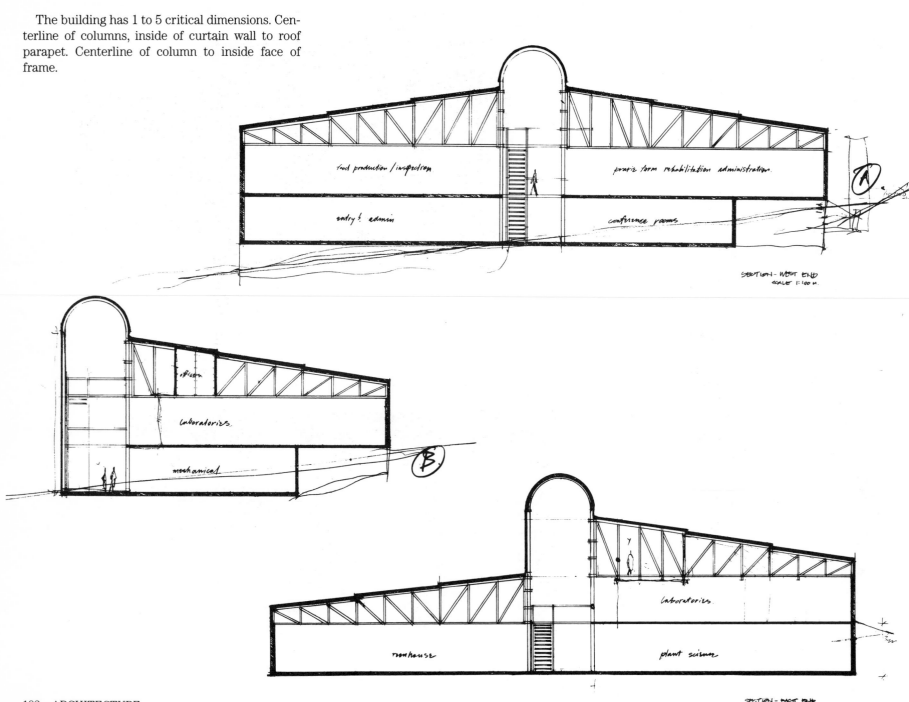

SECTION - WEST END
SCALE 1:100 M.

SECTION - EAST END
SCALE 1:100 M.

The exact dimensions of the galleria were sized by the size of a standard silo purchased from a silo manufacturer; the galleria was sized to fit its standard 14-foot diameter.

At the galleria, the silo end, the profile is switched to corrugated.

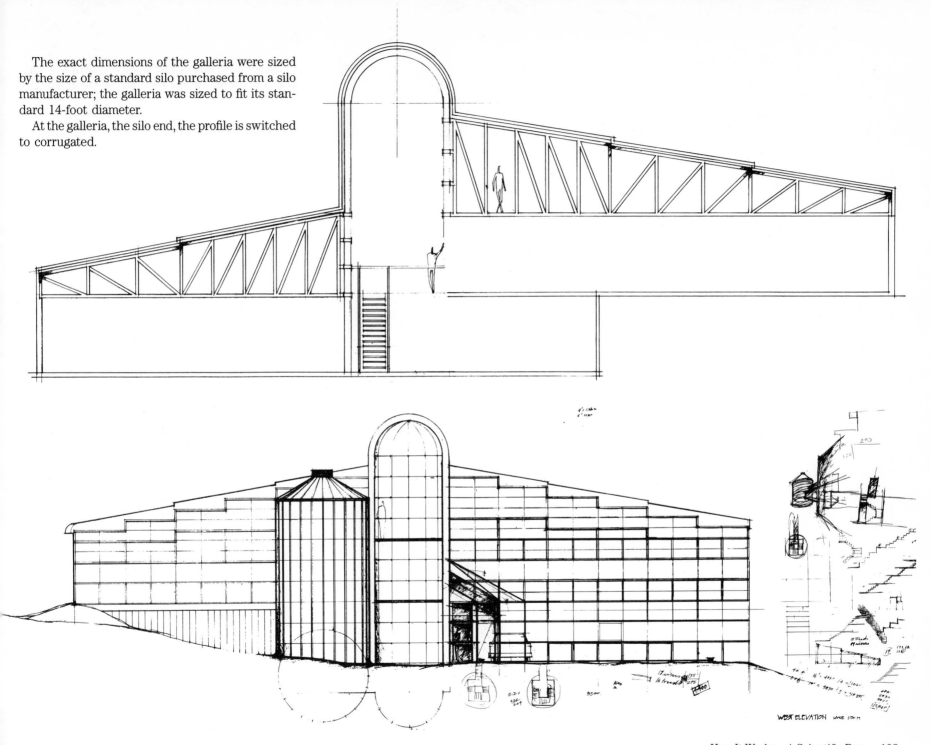

WEST ELEVATION

Putting it together.

Domes are made in a farm silo company's factory.
Half a silo was used at each end of the building

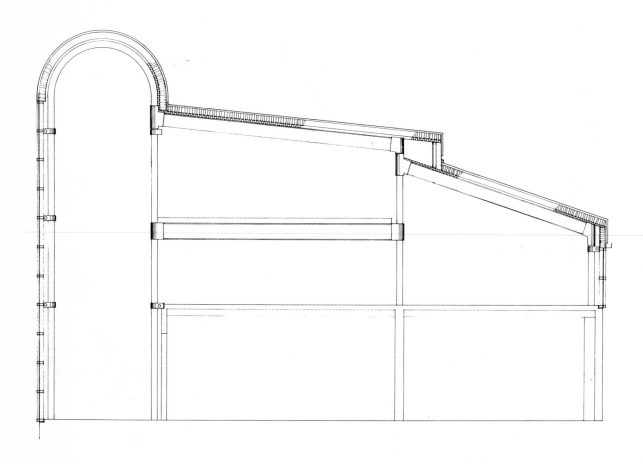

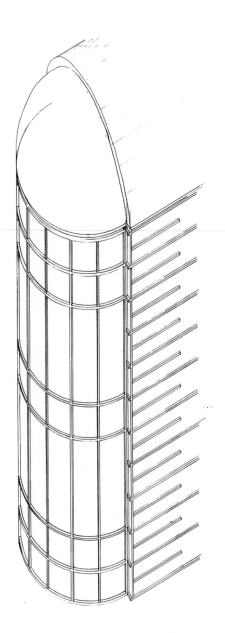

A curtain wall corner is a major problem. It is best in the Canadian climate to turn the corner with a radius. But a scientific barn would not be a scientific barn with radius corners. They had to be right angled. The solution was influenced by masonry quoining and a "negative" corner that emphasized with shadow.

A curtain wall is modular, like brick. Masons use quoins for strength and to end the wall with emphasis. Curtain walls can obviously not be quoined or rusticated. It is made up of horizontal and vertical frames. The strangeness of curtain walls is that all of the pieces do not hold in the glass. The strongest visual influence is made by exterior frame members used to protect clips, neoprene gaskets, and pressure plate screws.

A special corner piece was used to visually enunciate the end of one and the beginning of the next right angled curtain wall. The idea was inspired by masonry to visually enhance the corner, turning end and beginning.

The roofing is standing seam stainless steel. The first proposal was for standard painted, standing seam roofing because the aluminum product manufacturers claimed anodized would crack and craze if crimped.

This seemed strange, for roofers commonly put steel and aluminum rollers on back of flatbed trucks, buy coils of roofing material, and do standing seam industrial roofs on site. The architects had anodized aluminum coils put through rollers with no difficulty. They then did the same with stainless steel and it performed wonderfully. The client ended with a stainless steel roof at 50 cents less than the original painted steel.

The siding is a common material called "shadow form." The pieces slip into each other somewhat irregularly and catch the sunlight. They read like weathered barn boards. It is a material that has been in use for many years and is inexpensive, a quarter of the price of 4 x 8 metal sheets. It is an off-the-shelf material that does not "oil can" (crinkle). It is an old extrusion that has stood the market test for 40 years, stocked by all manufacturers and easily replaced.

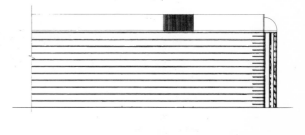

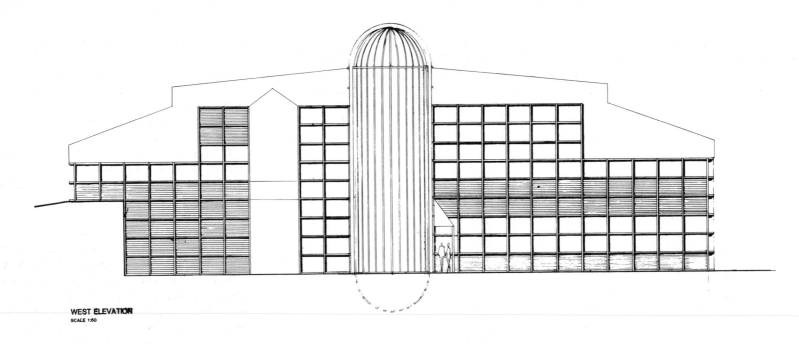

**WEST ELEVATION**
SCALE 1:50

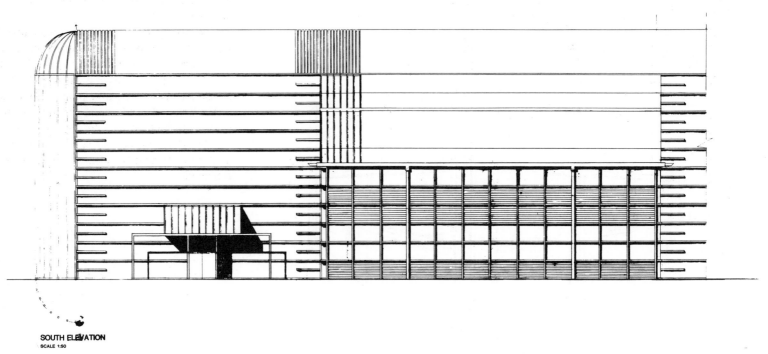

**SOUTH ELEVATION**
SCALE 1:50

196  ARCHITECTURE

The rainwater gutter off the sloping main roof must be studied at the corners for they terminate the shape. It was determined not to put it at the edge of the roof but several feet down instead. Different forms and materials coming together at the corners the gutter would cause confusion. A shed roof takes the water with external drains but flat roofs drain internally or could use the gutter to terminate the curtain wall.

There is a vertical piece of wall above the curtain wall that follows the angle of the roof. The roof sits on the wall as if it were a hat. There was no reason to run the curtain wall all the way to the top. It went as high as the windows and that was all it had to do.

The primary entry doors lead to a vestibule. The difficult problem is designing an entrance through the skin, which must be penetrated at some point, and coordinate the penetration with the control grid pattern.

The location is largely arbitrary from outside, but inside it must be purposeful as "the place you should enter."

This is not a classic building with a pediment that yells "entry" at the symmetrical center. The center of a thermodynamic skin is seldom perceptible.

A space 5 or 6 feet wide and 7 feet high is all that is needed for people and furniture to enter the building. This is not a concert hall; one, two, or three people enter at a time. Many rural barns have funny shed roofs or canopies over their doors and barns have a history of things attached to them.

Sometimes there is a door within a door, like the people door through the equipment door of a real barn, or Gaudi's door within a door of his apartments in Barcelona.

Barns have appendages, silos, storage bins, lean-to sheds, canopy covers for the hay, canopy cover for the door. All of these things and more are attached to a working barn.

Instead of doors in the thermodynamic barrier the architects designed a carefully machined little shed. It straddles the curtain wall and is in reality an air lock, a vestibule, or an air lock shed, a place to "shed" the exterior. The Canadian climate demands double doors and vestibules. This is a vestibule designed with the precision of a scientific machine.

Where farmers would have used a lean-to shed the architects used aluminum plate and stainless steel acorn fasteners. The inspiration was partially fume hoods—shed and fume hood combined.

A stylized rendition of an industrial garage door. This is a big mechanism on a real barn. The opening looks larger than it really is because the door slides to one side.

The vestibule has a sloped roof to catch the rain that pours down 35 feet of curtain wall. Without protection people entering the building would be drenched. A structural frame counteracts the water pressure. The water is diverted in a gutter sitting on pipes as fingers to channel the water into a spill path.

There are rounded tubes cut off at an angle along the curtain walls on the galleria, main floor. The radiators along the floor can only free the glass from frost for 8 feet up. The walls are 30 and 40 feet high. If air were blown up from the floor with sufficient velocity to clear the glass to its full height passers by would blow away.

Six-foot-high cutoff tubes blow air over the high part of the wall above people's heads. In the summer, cold air is blown which descends slowly.

Fan coil units are used to heat and cool the labs from cold water systems. The air of one lab is not mixed with that of another. There are chemical and radiation labs and the air can not be mixed.

The "lab block" is differentiated from the galleria architecturally by a corner. Laboratory offices are enclosed in standard curtain walls similar to those used in commercial office buildings and glazed in transparent "solex" glass. The galleria curtain wall is custom and glazed in green silver mirror glass.

The galleria faces south and the glass gives a much better energy coefficient than solex. We determined the building should not be red like the barn next door. Farm barns are invariably red in Manitoba but in southern Ontario there are light green barns enclosed in galvanized silver in two colors.

The decision was to go toward a silver green. The site is a natural brush-covered hillside and an arboretum. From the roadway the building is partially behind the arboretum. And those in the building look toward the arboretum to the view.

The trees break the scale of the building. The green silver glass will reflect the sky, the experimental grain field, and the arboretum trees. The mirror glass joins the building to the site with reflections. It will change as the sunlight and the clouds change and respond to the changing world around it.

Barns are traditionally opaque, not transparent. From the outside the mirror glass gives the appearance of a solid wall. From the inside the wall is transparent. When visitors pass through the skin they are immediately confronted by a powerful overlapping structure reminiscent of "barn." In other buildings the structure and inside is revealed through the skin. This building wanted a visually opaque wall and the Computer Research Center wanted a highly transparent skin. There those approaching looked through the screen and saw images. Here the wall reflects the wheat fields, barn, and arboretum.

The problem was that of a negative wall that joined two quite different kinds of curtain wall. Masons were the inspiration. We ended the strip of wall by introducing an extra frame to create visual quoining. The surface was ended and allowed another surface to join it. The visual impact of connection has been amplified.

# COMPUTER DRAWINGS

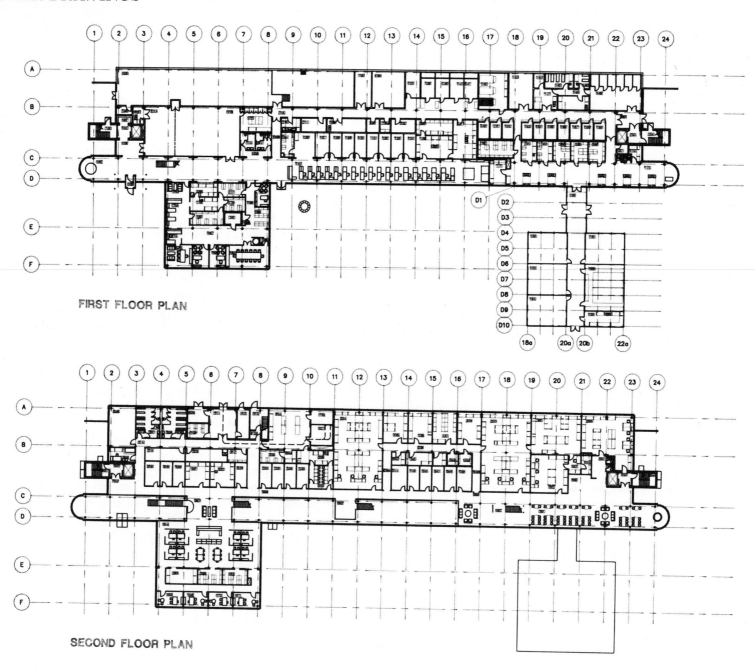

FIRST FLOOR PLAN

SECOND FLOOR PLAN

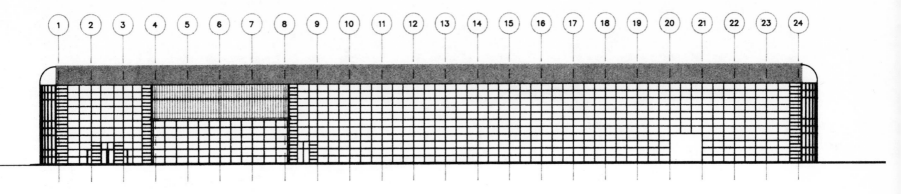

SOUTH ELEVATION

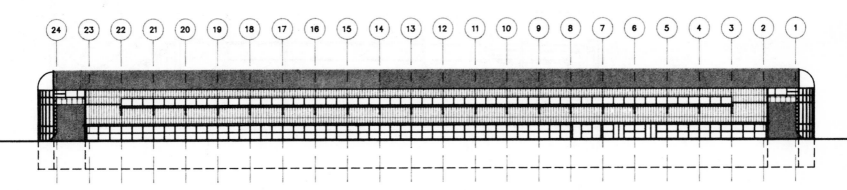

NORTH ELEVATION

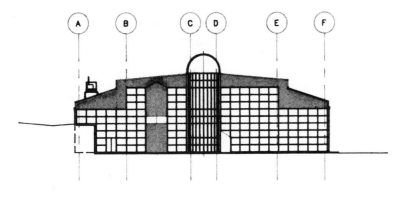

WEST ELEVATION

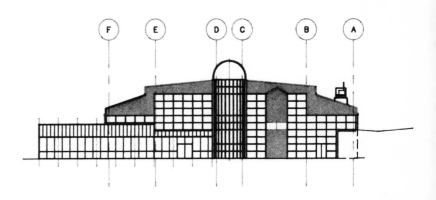

EAST ELEVATION

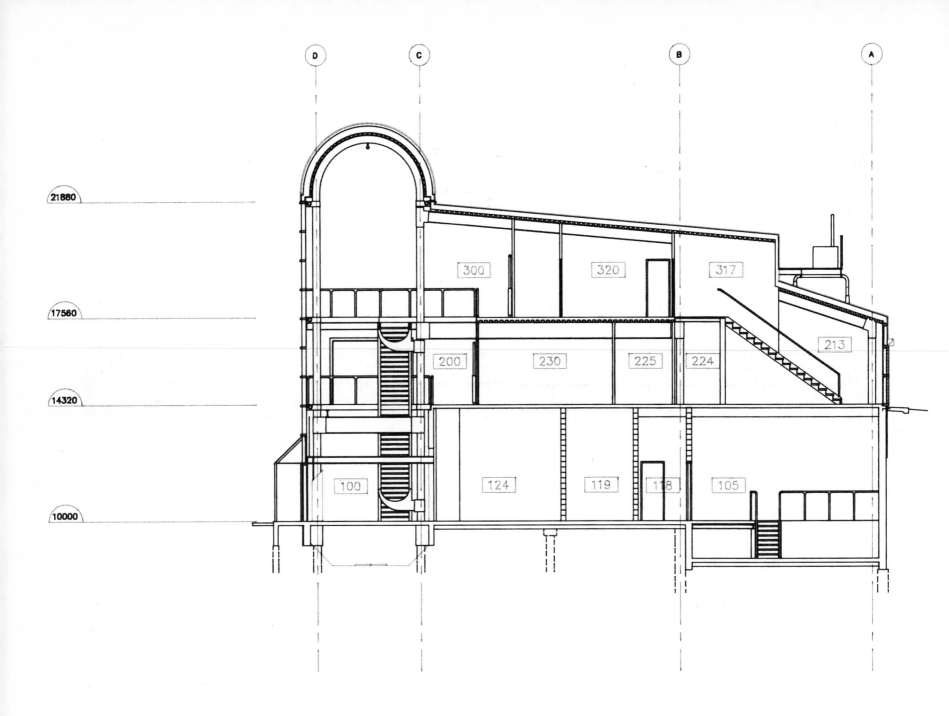

SECTION G-G

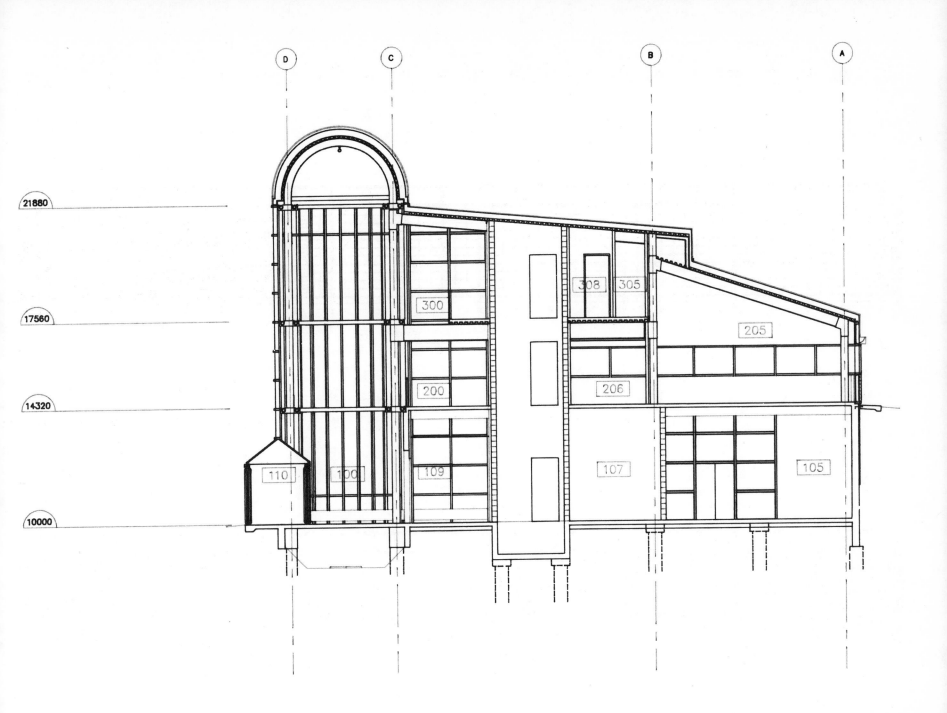

SECTION F-F

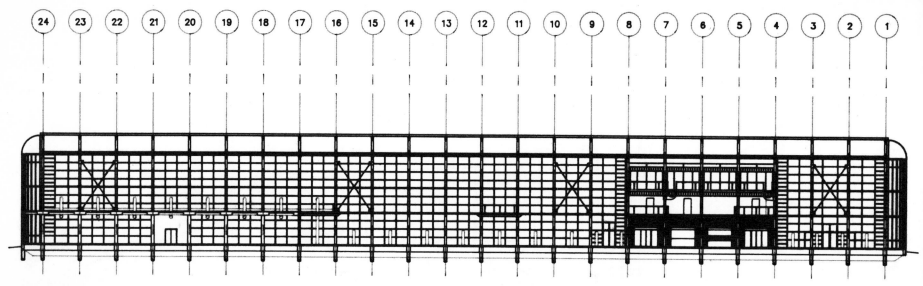

**SECTION B-B**

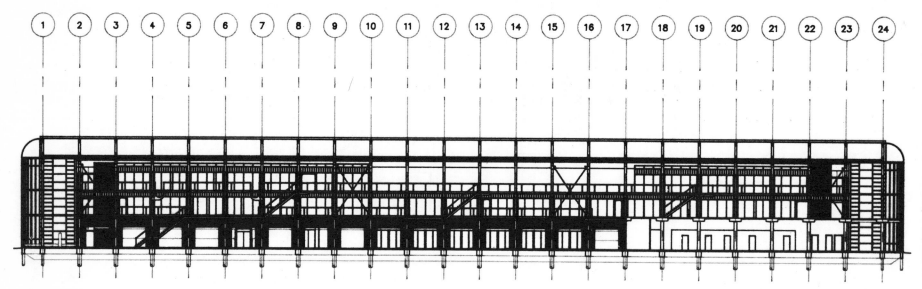

**SECTION A-A**

# Chapter 9

# On Style in Architecture

*William Loerke*

To identify style in architecture, whether of person, place, or time, is a complex enterprise, indeed, a modern one.

At the heart of architectural invention is the act of designing, the activity par excellence of the architect. In this act, the architect addresses the future, seeking the visual idea that will accommodate and express the function of his building. He or she may also be addressing the long-term future of the structure, i.e., its capacity to survive the loss of its first function and continue to provide service to the community for functions unknown at the moment of construction. The architect faces the future; the architectural critic and historian faces the past. The one tells us where we are going; the other, if he or she gets it right, tells where we have been.

The critic needs spatial distance to grasp the physical context of the building; needs some temporal distance to grasp its moment in architectural history. He or she works best at their trade when they bring to analysis a knowledge and experience sufficient to assess the architect's respect for the site, response to the social function of the building, as well as mastery of the materials of which it is built. At the conclusion of analysis, the critic often summarizes views by defining the style of the building, frequently pinning a well-known label on it. This is a modern habit, not more than 200 years old in English architectural criticism.

Stylistic labels and definitions function as short cuts to knowledge, creating more often the illusion of knowledge than supplying its substance. The contemporary widespread concern about the style or styles of individual architects, fostered by a flood of publications, has led many architects to fulfill stylistic expectations as they design their buildings.

To do this is to succumb to a current mode of architectural discourse, to blur the clear distinction between the task of the architect and that of the critic. The architect surely works best when they concentration upon the basic task is so great that the notion of style can not enter their head. The style which they will undoubtedly bring to their work should emerge as the end product of the capacity to solve substantive architectural problems posed by the site, the function of the building, and the appropriate expression of that function. To allow considerations of style to enter early in the design process is to vitiate that process. The architect who does so may be compared to the novelist who writes with one eye on Hollywood.

In recent times the distinct functions of architect and critic have become blurred. This was not always so. A survey of the notion of style from its origins will help to mark its entry into architectural discourse and give us a vantage point from which to assess its effects upon architectural design.

*Style,* both as a term and as a concept, has a history in English literary criticism going back to about 1300. But more than 400 years passed before *style* was first used in architectural discourse. According to the Oxford English Dictionary, from 1300 on *style* could denote the personal characteristics of a particular writer. The term *life-style* is documented in 1412. The style of painters and sculptors was noted and discussed from ca. 1700. But *style* with reference to architecture, *Grecian style, Gothic style,* seems not to appear before 1770. To discuss style in architecture is a phenomenon of only the past 200 years. How did we manage so long without it? Granted, a phenomenon is not born on the day we find a word for it. Granted, the historic styles we now write about were apparent to cultivated persons before 1770. Still, the fact that no one felt the need to discuss architectural style or styles for so long a period after the concept was known surely casts our present obsession with architectural styles, whether of person, period, place, or theme, into a useful and chastening historical perspective. An issue important for both the criticism and the history of architecture will come to light if we pursue the origin and growth of the term *style.*

Athens, Zeus Olympia. Olympeion B.C. 515–AD 132 Hadrian. *Photo:* Loerke.

# A HISTORY OF STYLE

The term *style* derives from the Latin *stilus*, the name for a writing instrument, pointed at one end, broad and flat at the other. It was used to write on wax tablets. The Roman incised his letters with the sharp end. When he wished to correct or improve his text, he turned the stilus around and erased the words and smoothed the wax in one stroke. To turn the stilus, "stilum vertere," meant to improve your style. The name of the instrument became a term of literary criticism. In this context, to have style was to have a fine, polished, improved style. Equally important, to have style was to have a personal style, for style derives directly from the use of an instrument held in the hand.

The term soon acquired generic meaning as it spread from writing to sketching and painting, and also to sculpture, where the principal instruments were mallet, chisel, and drill. Cicero and Quintilian, in their brief sketches of Greek art, speak of the particular styles of sculptors and painters, like Pheidias and Apelles, as well as the styles of Demosthenes and Euripides. They were also aware of the longer range of period styles: they knew that the style of early Greek sculpture (6th Cent. B.C.) differed markedly from later works (5th Cent. and Hellenistic, as we would now say). They, like Aristotle long before, made cogent comparisons between the styles of dramatists and sculptors. A sophisticated notion of style, and of styles, both of period, place, and person, was widespread in Latin culture from the time of Cicero (1st Century B.C.). What is interesting in this phenomenon for us is this: architects and their buildings, whether Greek or Roman, do not appear in this discussion. Ancient architecture in antiquity was immune to stylistic analysis.

Athens, Acropolis, Parthenon; South flank, foundation.
*Photo:* Loerke.

Vitruvius published his *Ten Books on Architecture* about 22 B.C. without once feeling the need to discuss style. Nor can we say that a notion a style was embedded in the ancient orders which he described. Vitruvius does not use the term *ordo* in describing Doric, Ionic, or Corinthian columns, capitals, and entablatures. His term is a neutral one drawn from the life sciences: *genus.* The equivalent term in the Greek treatises he quotes is *rhythmos.* Indeed, if we pursue this question of terminology into the second general treatise on architecture of western civilisation, Alberti's *Ten Books on the Matter of Building (De Re Aedificatoria,* first edition, in Latin, 1485) — we find him using *genus* as Vitruvius did. In the 16th Century, however, the treatises of Serlio and Vignola mark a sea-change in the presentation of ancient and contemporary architecture. We must note this fundamental shift in attitude to architectural design, for it laid the groundwork for the entry of style into architectural discourse.

Athens, Acropolis, Parthenon; East front, 448–432 B.C. Ictinus and Callicrates. *Photo:* Loerke.

Athens, Acropolis, Parthenon; West front, Ictinus and Callicrates. *Photo:* Loerke.

Serlio's treatise, titled *"Regole generale di Architettura, sopra le cinque maniere degli Edifici,"*
was published in segments between 1537 and 1545.
Vignola's treatise, titled *"La regola degli cinque
ordini d'architettura,"* was published in 1562.
From the titles themselves, two new ideas immediately leap to the eye: the notion of *rules* and the
notion of the *five orders*. Rules and orders radically
redefined the scope of architectural theory. They
narrowed the focus of the architectural enterprise
from the broad base laid out by Vitruvius and Alberti to an instructional manual on how to design
Doric, Tuscan, Ionic, Corinthian, or Composite facades. Vitruvius had dealt with the orders, which he
called *genera*, in a mere two of his ten books. Alberti had done so in a few sections of his seventh
book. Neither Vitruvius nor Alberti spoke of architecture as consisting of orders (let alone five), subject to rules. They offered a broad range of advice
(city planning, siting of buildings, nature of materials, etc.) to mature architects who had learned
their trade. The new treatises clearly presented
their essential and useful data on large plates, offering a broader audience quick entry into the art of
judging and designing classic facades.

The treatises of Vitruvius and Alberti offered no
basis for a stylistic treatment of architecture. In the
case of Alberti this is rather remarkable, for he had
devoted half of his treatise, the last five of his ten
books, to "delight," the third of Vitruvius' three
principles of architecture, (firmness, commodity,
and delight). In this extended treatment of beauty
and delight, where he clearly distinguished between
ornament and beauty in architecture, he found no
occasion to discuss style.

Athens, Propylea; Interior West front seen from South.
*Photo:* Loerke.

The treatises, or rather pictorial manuals, of Serlio, Vignola, and others were widely disseminated, in both Latin and vernacular languages, in the major publishing centers of Europe (Venice, Rome, Paris, Madrid, London) from the 16th Century to the present. The printing press and the engraver created a body of architectural instruction drawn from theory rather than, as in antiquity and the Middle Ages, from building practice. Vitruvius's theory, insofar as he had one, derived from his experience as an army engineer under Julius Caesar, as a civil engineer collaborating with Marcus Agrippa on the water works of Rome, and from his reading of monographs by architects on their own buildings. Renaissance treatises and manuals enabled the architect to get his theory first, his experience on site second, if at all. This reversal of direction in the formation of an architect was accelerated when the first architectural schools were formed. The ancient and medieval apprenticeship system gradually gave way to private study and the classroom.

Manuals like Freart de Chambrai's *Parallel of Ancient and Modern Architecture* (Englished in London, 1733) brought together texts of Alberti, Serlio, Vignola, Scammozi, Palladio, et al. and fed the notion that architecture consists of a variety of styles among which the student may browse, rather than a variety of experiences in the craft of building. In this context, where the verbal and the theoretical became increasingly the point of departure for architectural design, one need not wait long for two false principles: the identification of architecture with style; the identification of style as the element by which an architect is to be assessed.

Let us return to an unanswered question. If Greek critics from the Fourth Century B.C. and Roman critics from the First Century B.C. were able to

Athens, Propylea. *Photo:* Loerke.

recognize the distinctive styles of poets, dramatists, orators, painters, and sculptors, why not also the styles of architects? The first answer to this question may be that architects did not and were not expected to have a personal style. If we ask, Why not?, then the deeper answer must surely lie in the geometrical character of architectural design.

Greek temples appear to be a geometry executed in cut stone, the product of rigorous logic, minimally stated, governed by an impersonal, mathematical esthetic. Euclidean geometry itself reads like the disembodied speech of the cosmos, the language of the Prime Mover, the product of pure intelligence, not subject to sublunar moods and personal identity crises. Hence the creative advances in architectural design by Ictinus, architect of the Parthenon, or by Domitian's architect Rabirius, or by Trajan's architect, Apollodorus of Damascus, count in much the same way as new theorems of Archimedes— extensions of an impersonal mathematical language, whose authenticity rests on their appearing to come from some cosmic storehouse, unmarked by personal or idiosyncratic traits. Hence, unmarked by style.

Ancient architects, unlike ancient writers, orators, and poets, saw their personal contributions absorbed anonymously into a communal architecture of the body politic. If we now speak of style in ancient architecture, e.g., Greek as distinct from Roman, it is the style of a community, not of an individual. And the community took instinctively and seriously the inscription Socrates would place over his ideal school: Let no one unacquainted with geometry enter.

In imperial Rome, architecture emerged from a society aware of styles in literature and the arts. Why did architecture remain immune to this awareness? Public architecture, though often funded by

Athens, Acropolis Erechteion; North Porch, detail.
*Photo:* Loerke.

Western Greece, Olympia; Temple of Zeus, South flank.
*Photo:* Loerke.

Western Greece, Olympia; Temple of Zeus, fallen
columns. *Photo:* Loerke.

Western Greece, Olympia; Temple of Zeus, capital block.
*Photo:* Loerke.

individuals, was an arm of the State, serving both as its image and, very nearly, its fabric. In the Roman view, the fate of the State was guaranteed by maintaining good relations with divine powers, marked visibly by temples, vowed often at critical moments in Roman history, then consecrated and dedicated in fulfilment of that vow. Each temple was a contract with a god or an abstraction (Virtus, Honos, Fides). The contract was eternal. When the temple was damaged or destroyed, it was rebuilt on its site in order to renew the contract. The contractual nature of Roman religious buildings must be grasped if we are to gain a Roman view of Roman architecture.

More grandiose and spectacular than most temples was the Roman architecture of public display and spectacle. When all were seated in their designated places in the Colosseum or Circus, the full hierarchy of the State was visible to all. Both the structure of the State and the history of its main events became palpable in these assemblies. At once popular and commemorative, they were held annually or at longer intervals. Each order of society (senators, knights, plebs, slaves) reached its seats in the Colosseum through its own staircases, without meeting the others. When the architects had provided for the spectacle itself and for all associated functions, they had produced a design grand in its totality and carefully worked out in its details. The grandeur of Roman imperial structures functioned as the stage for civic liturgies of a Mediterranean state. For later societies, this grandeur had become a style to emulate. In ancient Rome, it was a function.

Romans did not speak of style in architecture because they knew what style was: the careful polishing of expression, literary or artistic, by a gifted writer or artist. Architecture was in a more important category: it made visible the structure of the state and its link to the cosmos.

The practice of architecture in antiquity lay firmly embedded in the ancient understanding of the city (the *polis,* the *urbs*) and its relation to the powers of the cosmos, not to mention the daily and annual track of the sun, the sanctity of a given site, as well as its proper drainage and the direction of the prevailing winds. In short, many concrete problems, theological to topographical, were posed in the decision to establish a temple, a stadium, a theater, an amphitheater, a commercial stoa or marketplace. The citizens had a grasp of these problems, sat on committees which accepted or rejected proposals. In this situation, it can come as no surprise to view ancient architecture as the surviving solutions to problems, well defined and well understood. Among these solutions, ingenuity may be prized but idiosyncracies are mistakes, to be banished rather than published and built.

The ancient architect was essentially, if not exclusively, a problem solver, an engineer as much as an architect. This comes clear in Vitruvius's Preface to his Seventh Book, where he lists more than 30 architects, engineers, or theorists among the Greeks whose published works he knew. Many wrote on *symmetria,* or proportions, like Silenos, who wrote on the proportions of Doric buildings; Philon of Byzantium, who wrote on the proportions of sacred buildings in general; or Arkesias, who published a treatise on the proportions of the Corinthian genus. Those who wrote on their own buildings seem to have had special reasons, apart from personal pride, for doing so. The architects of the great Ionic temples of Hera on Samos and Artemis at Ephesus had to site each temple in a swamp. Their monographs no doubt laid out the problems they faced and solved. Iktinos collaborated on a book on the Parthenon, famous for its subtle refinements. Satyros and Pythios, architects of the tomb of King Maussolos in Caria, southwest Turkey, published a monograph on this paradigm of all later mausolea. A third group, professional engineers, wrote on the design of machinery required to move heavy blocks from quarry to site and up into position on the building. So far as we can tell from the titles and meager quotations that survive from this lost literature, these professionals came to grips with concrete problems of design, construction, and transport. They created a substantial body of scientific, professional work.

In this literature we come upon a few remarks that show an awareness of something close to style. Philon of Byzantium (late Third Cent. B.C.) flatly stated that the oldest buildings (of the Greeks) do not exhibit correct form, which can only be achieved by experiment. We have quoted his remarks elsewhere in this book, but they bear repetition here: "Some parts of buildings, though they are of equal thickness and are straight, do not seem to be equal or straight, because our sight is misled by different distances. So by trial and error, taperings and inclinations, they make the parts of the structure apparently well shaped, that is, to agree with our vision—for this was the aim of that art." This remark is an acute recognition of the difference between an early temple without refinements, and a later one with them. Trabeate design escaped the rigorous control of geometry, when builders corrected not only for optical effects, but also to enhance the sense of organic life in their stone structures. They curved the stylobates, tilted the columns back, pitched the architraves slightly forward. These refinements were expensive and could only be sustained by a substantial budget. The Parthenon has them, but not the contemporary Doric temple of Hephaistos in the Agora. Yet Philon is probably right to note the absence of visual experiments in early temples and their presence in some later ones. In all of this, however, a builders' eye is at work, addressing a general problem, not a personal one. Hence his comment is not about style, in the ancient sense of the term.

When does an individual style begin to appear in the work of an architect? One is tempted to point to the designs of Hadrian and his architects at the Villa at Tivoli, where a highly creative and unprecedented dialogue between trabeate and arcuate forms suddenly appears. The designers at Tivoli unquestionably enlarged the vocabulary of their craft, but did so, it seems, without interjecting the personal note. The architecture described in Vitruvius' sources, and in his own comprehensive summary, lay almost exclusively in the realm of trabeate design. The post-Vitruvian Roman revolution in architecture, represented by the great arcuate structures of the empire, enlarged the scale of projects, radically altered the principles of design. When ancient trabeate forms in stone, limited in span and scale, were combined with walls and vaults of brick and concrete, vast in span and scale, a new and difficult problem was posed for Roman architects and builders. The Roman engineer-architect, a problem solver as well as a designer of geometrically proportioned ground plans and elevations, has left us his imposing solutions to these problems in the great imperial baths and elsewhere. Apollodorus of Damascus, Trajan's army engineer, designed both the bridge across the Danube that marked the start of the Dacian campaign, and the Forum and Market of Trajan that celebrated its conclusion. He wrote a monograph on the bridge, but not on the Forum, perhaps because the bridge represented a more interesting technological achievement. But in the Forum, which guaranteed his public reputation, he had translated stone trabeate forms into brick and had combined them with vaulted spaces ingeniously linked on a steep slope. This was no mean achievement, but it was a commercial one, capable of evoking admiration from the modern developer as well as the modern historian. Hence, not on a level with a grand bridge spanning a mighty river and serving the victorious legions of the emperor.

Such fame as ancient architects enjoyed came to them as successful problem solvers. If an ego was involved, it was far more likely to be that of an emperor like Nero or Domitian than their own. The

Southwestern Turkey, Temple of Apollo at Didyma. *Photo:* Loerke.

broad discipline within which they worked was the widespread knowledge of what a city was, and what a public building could do for it, both in terms of its function and of its image. This subliminal discipline continued into the post-Roman millenium, misleadingly called the Middle Ages, and established a major bond between ancient and medieval architectural practice. A further and equally fundamental bond lay in the fact that both ancient and medieval architects could gain greater interior space only by finding more ingenious ways of maintaining arches and supports in compression. Both had to organize large work crews and tons of material around ground plans pegged out on the site. Elevations could be precisely worked out by architects and foremen trained in geometry and with extensive first-hand experience in carpentry and masonry. They knew timber, wood, brick and stone. They rose to the post of master of the work from decades of hands-on experience within a defined but open-ended tradition of a craft. For unity of the whole, they relied on basic geometry and an experienced eye. Their competence as well as their new solutions to old problems could be objectively judged. Their innovations were absorbed into the prevailing architectural language much as a new word or phrase might enter the spoken vernacular, i.e., anonymously. When experts gathered to thresh out a problem of great magnitude, as they did in connection with the completion of Milan Cathedral in 1401, they argued principles, not personalities. The French stormed out of the meeting, saying, "*Ars sine scientia nihil est.*" (Craft without knowledge [without the right geometry] is nothing.) No room here for personal style.

Antiquity and the Middle Ages do not seem to offer a context in which an architect could establish a career or reputation on the basis of an individual

Didyma, Southwestern Turkey. *Photo:* Loerke.

way of designing, that is, on the basis of a personal style. When did this become possible?

It seems that this moment may be connected with one aspect, not widely appreciated, of that breakpoint between past and present known as the Italian Renaissance. If we examine the practice of architecture vis-à-vis publications of architectural theory, a startling fact emerges: the virtual absence of theoretical works and practical manuals before 1500, and the flood of such publications after 1500. In antiquity architects built first and wrote afterwards. In the Middle Ages, they built and never wrote, if we except a few unsystematic notebooks. Beginning in the 16th Century it became possible to develop a career in architecture by writing, without having built. This sea change in the history of Western architecture opened new paths to the practice of architecture, breaking the medieval link between experienced craftsman, foreman, builder, and master of the work. An expert in theory could bypass these stages. Moreover, his study of treatises and manuals could quickly offer him a range of options, complete with rules of proportions. Personal choice, somewhat detached from building experience, could be made. The matter of these treatises was a combination of ancient and modern (i.e., 16th Century) architecture, with stress laid on trabeate, columnar facades. This language of architectural design, soon called Classical, became the formal expression of the establishment, governmental and private. So established, it became a norm, against which to revolt, against which to form a personal style.

## SUMMING UP

Architects enter upon their professional careers in the midst of a prevailing architectural language. The young architect in 15th or 16th Century Italy faced options different from those offered in 17th Century France, 18th Century England, or 19th Century America. Yet for most architects in this half

millenium, most options lay within a trabeate structural system wearing Greek clothes, a Roman-Romanesque-Gothic vaulting system, or a Roman-Byzantine-Renaissance domical tradition. A burgeoning number of books and journals kept architects abreast of variations within these systems, as well as with a wide range of architectures outside the European tradition: native and vernacular architectures, Near Eastern and Far Eastern systems of construction and design. To this range of regional and historical stylistic options was added a choice of new materials. These gave the architect structural options unknown to any of his predecessors. Large sheets of glass enabled him to lighten and brighten his structure. Steel and reinforced concrete concrete enabled him to invert the ancient ratio between compression and tension, to invert the ratio of weight to support; even to annihilate that ancient distinction in the geodesic dome.

In this fluid, rapidly changing environment of architectural theory, design, and construction, to be conservative meant to stay within the appearance, at least, of the canon, which generally meant classic trabeate forms; to be avant garde meant to be daring in the use of new materials and exotic forms, or startling in abruptly juxtaposing well known historic forms. It is understandable that many architects, faced with this kaleidoscopic panorama of seemingly infinite possibilities, came to their design table more aware of their kit of parts than willing to solve from scratch a fresh problem.

Amid the nearly limitless options offered the modern architect, we can appreciate the discipline imposed in the past on the architectural imagination by limited materials. This discipline, an unquestioned necessity from antiquity to the 19th Century, had been the mother of many inventions, but now has become one of many options. Why submit to something like it now? What, indeed, would be the modern equivalent of that discipline? The Gothic architect, like Palladio and Borromini, was an ex-stonecutter. With modern materials, how

can the ancient connection between a building craft and architectural design be reestablished? Should two years in a steel plant, glass factory, or lumber mill be prerequisite to entry into an architectural school? One of Mies van der Rohe's early students at Chicago recalled his first interview with the master: "What do you know about bricks?" — "I can draw a brick wall." — "Go out and learn about bricks; when you know something, come back and we'll talk." That direct approach to architecture through materials, once the norm, has been largely supplanted by the drafting table, bumwad, and miniature model making. Something important has been lost. With it has been lost an important link between materials, function and design. That linkage defines the root of architecture; when it can be recognized in a building, the concept "style" becomes secondary, if not irrelevant. That linkage, we believe, characterizes a small number of buildings, including those of Keenberg.

Perhaps the best we can do is to restore something of that craft experience in our schools of architecture. Not out of nostalgia, but to introduce into the process of design an architectural logic rooted in the direct experience of structure and materials, and of sufficient rigor to distinguish professional progress from sterile innovation. An architect so trained might reject spectacular statements which solve no problems. He might gain sufficient strength of will, focus of mind, and awareness of fundamental principles to believe that respect for the site, a grasp of the function of his building in its broadest sense, and a design which marries appropriate materials and technologies to this site and function will inevitably lead to a significant architectural statement.

Behind the ancient meaning of the Greco-Latin term *architekton* or *architectus* (master builder) lies in Greek the image of woodworker-joiner (*tekton*) and in Latin the image of a roof (*tectum*). Perhaps now is the time to remind the architect of the ancient roots of his and her profession, i.e., that

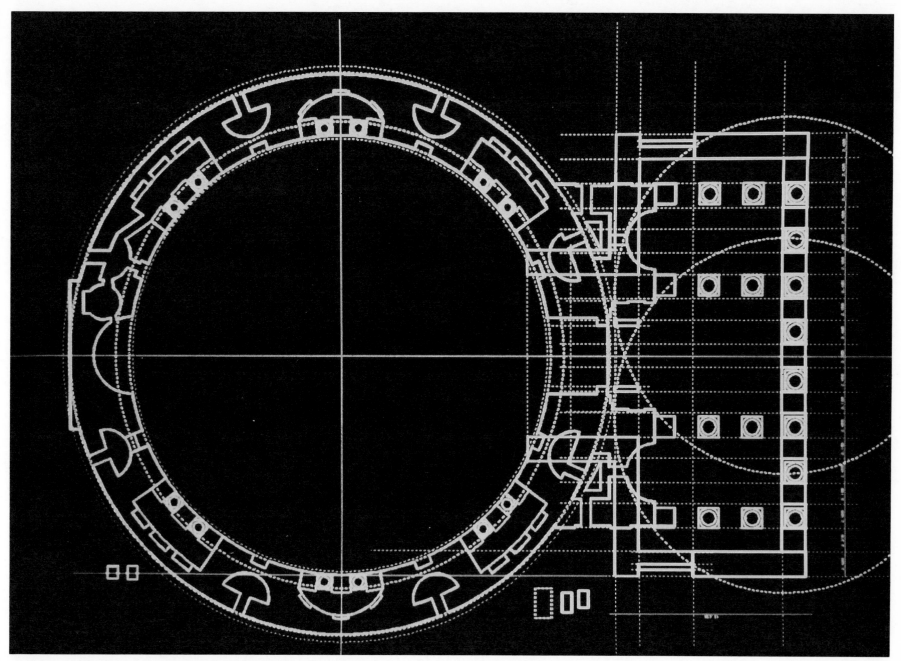

Parthenon plan: Computer graphics by Steve Sachs and William Loerke.

he and she stands or falls on how well they design, erects, and supports a roof, and for what purpose. This is a deed that can be objectively judged by impersonal, i.e., nonstylistic standards.

The study of ancient and medieval architecture shows that a style, sometimes even a personal style, can sooner or later be identified in the work of an architect who concentrates on first principles to the exclusion of stylistic concerns. But modern time runs differently from ancient or medieval. What those architects took as a matter of course, satisfaction in their work rather than in their public relations, now requires an excruciating exercise of patience. Prior to the printing press, it was chiefly the completed work which spread the architect's fame, the fame of a master craftsman as well as of a creative designer. Their own character stood revealed in the character of their work. This is something different from the ego of an architect revealed in the idiosyncracies of style.

We can sympathize with Manet's wish that he could read while alive the tributes to his painting that would appear upon his death. Yet Manet kept his eye on nature and his canvas, not on the journals and the critics. Brunelleschi kept his eye on that dome while Florentine politics swirled around him. Fired and rehired several times in those twenty years and more, he was only granted the title architect when the town council resolved that the term Architector be inscribed on his tombstone. The modern architect will have good company while waiting for someone to identify his or her mark, his or her style. Meanwhile could they not be nourished by professional satisfaction in having fulfilled and expressed in a direct manner an authentic aim of their society. While the stylistic debate goes on, the structure will continue to serve its people, and remind them of who built it.

# Chapter 10

# Tomorrow's Buildings?

Design alters a system to create the effect the designer wants. There are always effects the designer does not want, for the entire system is not under the designer's control. Unwanted effects cause bridges to collapse, ships to sink and buildings to fall down.

Building systems give an illustration of permanence. But all buildings will eventually fall as all people will eventually die. Designers can not create an everlasting structure or an immortal person. The purpose of design is to delay collapse and death for a decent interval.

The length of a decent interval has changed over time. Pyramids have lasted 5,000 years and the people that built them were lucky if they lived for 25. Today's average building will probably last 50 years and an average person 70.

A definition of modern architecture might be: buildings that do not last as long as the people that build them.

Designers do not tell their clients the buildings they design will become obsolete and inevitably collapse. The secret is well kept, so well kept, in fact, that designers often do not admit it to themselves.

When designers do think of this grim truth they must admit that the best they can do is alter systems to achieve decent intervals. The task of design is simply to understand as much of the entire context in which buildings are designed and built as humanly possible. Style is a minor issue, if designers wish to pursue it.

Designers and builders seek methods of thinking which will encompass as much of the system as they can conceive. This is why Vitruvius sought an ordering system, Alberti wrote books on architecture, Le Corbusier invented the "Modulor," and architects today search so hard for "strategies" and "action plans" to comprehend the complexities of systems and minimize their unwanted affects so that they

can achieve decent intervals of building use and human life.

As building usefulness spans shorter intervals and people live longer the elements factored into the design system change. The challenge of making decisions for an average person in a designed space is overwhelming. The "average" person is no longer average. The deaf, blind, young, aged, handicapped, republican, faculty member, and those with allergies must be accommodated, by law.

The occupants of "smart" buildings are "smarter." They have learned to access information in peculiar ways. The authority of decision-makers is questioned. Knowledge is power and today it is dispersed everywhere. The world is therefore less predictable and controllable. Those who use buildings demand that buildings respond to changes in the human condition as they always have in the past.

Today's buildings with indoor plumbing, electric lights, and air conditioning are not necessarily healthy buildings. Buildings with intelligent technologies are not necessarily intelligent, says professor Walter Kroner of Rensselaer Polytechnic Institute. Healthy and intelligent buildings may be significantly different in form, quality, meaning and performance than those we build today.

There has not been enough time to fully explore the potentials of new technologies or to invent an ordering system that will apply to circumstances we do not yet understand. New technologies are simply "inserted" into historic architectural containers. The visible architecture that results does not yet enrich culture, supply meaning or purpose.

A century of technical change.

Humans change unpredictably by the day, hour, and minute depending on age, sex, clothing, activity, dietary pattern, health, political preference, mood, and whim. Only the individual knows what constitutes health, well-being, and comfort for himself or herself from moment to moment. Only you and I are the true and best judge of it. As Walt Kelly's cartoon character Pogo Possum once said, "I is an expert on me." The design challenge today is to provide the architectural means for humans to respond to what their body senses and their mind tells them is appropriate.

Drawings after "Water Mill and Hammer" by Paul Klee.

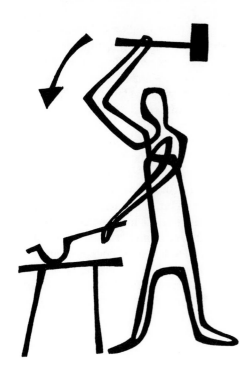

Turn of the century handcraft.

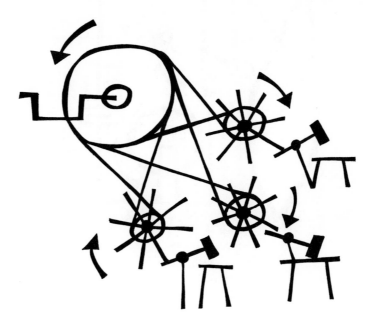

1910 to 1930. Mechanization takes a stand.

Every new technical idea offers the opportunity to rethink the fundamentals of architectural and urban design theory. Designers can go far beyond inserting intelligent systems into existing dumb buildings and creating new styles every 15 years to clothe them. The assumptions of the ordering principles of the past must be examined.

Advanced electric appliances, photocopiers, automatic bank tellers, telephone answering and recording devices, word-processors, smart buildings that operate elevators, security, monitor energy consumption and control air flow—all these things interact with their users in a different way than inanimate objects, says Ezio Manzini, Italian designer and educator [1].

There are no points of reference for judgment based on traditional cannons of beauty. The components that make the object "intelligent" are invisible. If we see a microchip, it may be working furiously or sitting on its tail. We have no way of knowing.

Manzini sees function as flexible, therefore impossible to categorize in traditional ways. A personal computer runs a computer game, causes a "run" on the stock market, or lists silk stockings purchased in a department store with a shift of software.

1930 to 1940. Idling.

The number of intelligent and communicative objects increases, from calculator keyboards to talking cameras. There is no line of demarcation between utility or functionality and amusement. The form of the electronic game, talking camera, or heartbeat recorder is no indication of the seriousness of its purpose, Manzini warns.

Computerized work systems demand the same attention as computer games. The technology of sensors, actuators, displays, and digital and analog controls achieve its aims invisibly. Form, color, shape, or style is no indication of use.

The degree of automation has recently arisen as a design question. Should washing machines talk? Should we press a button or a sensitized membrane to do the laundry? These may become critical questions as "intelligence" and "smartness" proliferate. They are critical today in the cockpit of an airplane, in the control panel of a skyscraper or of a nuclear reactor, in a laboratory fume hood, and even in a fast-moving automobile.

1940 to 1945. Boom....

1945 to 1950...and after.

1950 to 1960. Tooling up.

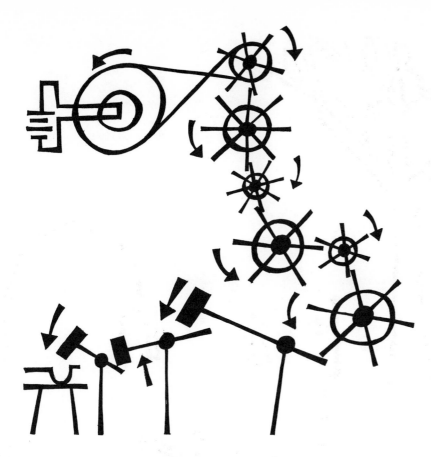

1960 to 1970. Full throttle.

1970 to 1980. Smart machines.

1980 to ?. Smart Buildings.

The common denominator of interactive objects is *time*. Sitting is an interaction between chair and sitter programmed by physical shape of chair seat and human back side. Form establishes a program of passive use. Passivity is a given characteristic, says Manzini.

A microchip can sit anywhere depending on the quality of its interaction. The behavior of the smart thing is modified by external variables. Light sensors turn lights on and off when they detect movement, sprinkler heads flood the room with water or gas when temperatures rise, or when they inhale smoke. They are not passive. Object and environment react with each other.

Design during the last years of the 20th Century and the beginning of the 21st Century is not an easy task. It is more complex than ever before, but then no one ever promised Appolodorus, Vitruvius, Brunelleschi, Le Corbusier, Utzon, or today's designers a rose garden.

The designers of fine buildings had plans of action, they found the building's attitude, placed it in time, and created its value. The problems at hand were too serious to think of in terms of style. They left that to future historians. There were perhaps designers that simply expressed themselves like poets, painters and writers, but it is difficult to describe them, for they left so little to remember.

## REFERENCE

1. Ezio Manzini, "Interactivity," in Ottagano, *Design in the Information Environment;* p. 74 Whitney, Kent, and Knopf, New York, 1985.

Socrates—word of mouth.

Hummurabi—word of hand.

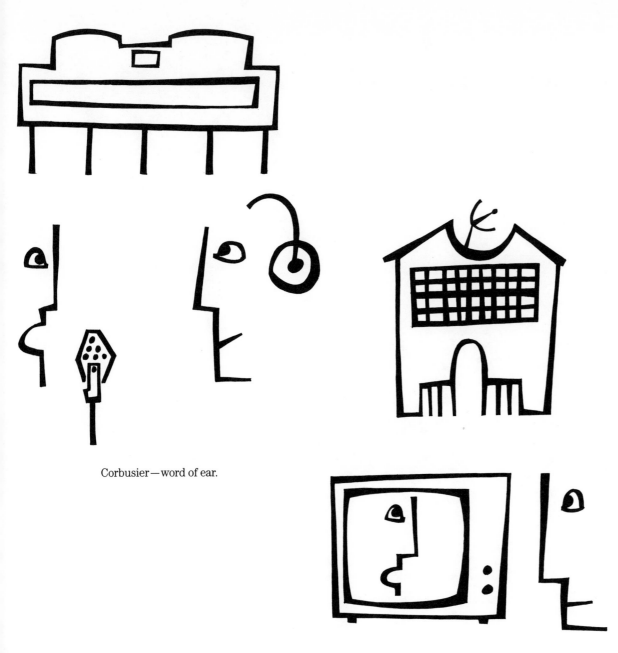

Corbusier—word of ear.

Today—word of eye.

Tommorrow—the taught teach.

# Architectural Glossary

**Abacus** the flat top of the Doric capital of a column, supporting an entablature, square without chamfer or moulding.

**Acanthus** a plant whose leaves, conventionally treated, have been used in the decoration of Greek, Roman, and Renaissance Corinthian capitals from mid 5th Century B.C. to the present.

**Acropolis** the highest part or citadel of a fortified Greek city. The most famous example is the Acropolis of Athens, on which the Parthenon stands.

**Act of Building** the visualization every aspect of the building in material and time. Every design decision is directed by a regulating idea which may have many names: scheme, parti, conceptual model. The regulating idea assimilates the client's needs, manner of building, relation of the building to the society, industries, technologies, the builders, and other buildings.

**Aesthetics** the appreciation of the beautiful in accordance with the principles of good taste. Architecture, painting, and sculpture are visual arts that appeal to the eye as music appeals to the ear. But architecture differs from the other fine arts in that vision is only one of the senses influenced. Buildings are experienced through sight, sound, touch, and smell. Its sensual limits overlap; we therefore explain it in terms of "taste."

**Agitation** (architectural expression) disturbance. Resistance to loads and external forces can be achieved by exposed or hidden structures. Each stimulates a different perceptual reaction that influences the building's expression.

How a building carries its load stimulates reactions in the observer. A Greek temple exhibits calm strength in repose; one feels awed and secure. A Gothic cathedral exhibits a skeleton held together by tendons; one feels awed and aroused.

It is difficult to feel tranquil in a space where walls or roof appear on the verge of collapse, even though in reality they are securely fastened by hidden structure. Omitted keystones, apparent gravity defying structures, and strangely tilted columns arouse feelings of uncertainty.

**Agora** a space for public assembly in a Greek city. The Roman forum is the equivalent. This city space was usually surrounded with public buildings and colonnades, sometimes planted with trees. It was a place of open air assembly, markets, and sacred spaces.

**Apse** the semicircular or polygonal termination of the cella of a Roman temple, the hall of a Roman basilica, or the nave of a church.

**Arcade** a range of arches supported on piers or columns, attached to or detached from the wall. A covered walk between two such ranges or between an arcade on one side and a solid wall on the other.

In modern usage the covered walk between ranges of shops as in a shopping mall.

**Arch** curved, self-supporting structure composed of bricks or stone, capable of carrying a superimposed load over an opening. The structure of wedge-shaped blocks transmits weight to its flanking supports over an opening arranged to hold together when supported only from the sides.

**Architect (Renaissance)** designer of buildings who prepares plans and superintends construction; designer of complex structures; the Creator — Renaissance humanists considered architecture the Queen of the Arts. It was practiced by gentlemen and the nobility. Scholars considered the mathematical problems involved in the aesthetics of proportion and the physics of building structures to be fitting subjects for philosophers.

Great Renaissance architects may have begun as carpenters, masons, painters, or goldsmiths. But they could not aspire to the proud title of architect until their work had been recognized as architecture.

During his lifetime, Brunelleschi was not referred to by the title "architect." After his death, the title "Architector" was inscribed on his tombstone.

The often quoted definition by Sir Henry Wotton, an amateur critic quoting Vitruvius in his book, *The Elements of Architecture,* 1624 stated that it must fulfill three conditions, "Commoditie, Firmenes, and Delight," meaning that to constitute architecture, a building must not only be conveniently planned for its purpose (commodity), but also be soundly built of good materials (firmness) and give pleasure to the eye (delight).

**Architecture** (short version) the art or science of building. (legal version) Architecture is what registered architects do, and that is determined by state and federal laws under which the architect receives his or her license to practice.

**Architrave** the beam or lowest division of the entablature, which extends from column to column.

**Ashlar** masonry formed of accurately squared stones with a smooth face, laid in regular courses with fine joints.

**Assemble** gather together, place in order, fit parts together. The test of a successful building assembly is in how easily and quickly it can be taken apart. A contemporary building can be compared to a sailing ship. It is a complex, expensive, product floating in a fluid market. It must constantly shift its cargo to remain afloat economically in the shifting tides of technical change.

Modern building assemblies must have a minimum number of pieces. Materials are dry, light, large, bolted sections erected by man-guided machines such as cranes.

**Assembler** one who assembles. Fitting and attaching building elements is the most expensive operation in the erection of a modern building. The cost of on-site labor is balanced against the cost of factory manufacture and on-site labor eliminated wherever possible.

The crucial link in the chain from manufacture to finished building is the assembler's understanding of the task of putting the building together. Clarity of assembly speeds erection, improves quality, reduces costs, increases profits.

**Atlantes** carved, over-life-size male figures serving as pillars; also called *Telamones.*

**Attitude** the stance or bearing of a building. Its total effect upon an observer. This includes, materials, spaces, color, solids, linkages, entries, all directed to a single overall impression.

**Baldaquin** or **Baldachin**—an isolated canopied structure over an altar.

**Barrel Vault** a continuous semicircular arch or tunnel of brick, stone, or concrete, used from early times in Roman and Romanesque architecture (see **Vault**).

**Basilica** a public hall for the administration of justice and the transaction of business in a Roman city. It usually adjoined the Forum or market place. An early Christian church that resembles a Roman basilica.

**Beam** one of the principle horizontal supporting members of a building. Originally, a tree trunk or log which was squared. Any horizontal structural member of any material.

**Bid** an offer made for a stated price. A reasonable proposal when submitted that becomes unreasonable when accepted.

**Blackguard** a rude or unscrupulous person; to talk about or address in abrasive terms. One who criticizes the architect's design; distinguished from the connoisseur, who praises it.

**Bracket** a support projecting from a wall or column. In classical architecture it is usually called an *ancon,* a *console,* or a *modillion,* in medieval building a *corbel,* and in modern construction a *cantilever.*

**Brunelleschi,** Filippo (1377–1446) Italian architect and sculptor. Began his working life as a goldsmith's apprentice. Designed the dome for the cathedral Santa Maria del Fiore in Florence. Other buildings designed by him include the churches of San Lorenzo and Santo Spirito, the Pazzi chapel, the Ospedale degli Innocenti, and the central section of the Pitti Palace, all in Florence.

**Budget** that which controls the limits within which the architect–designer–builder must choose—never cheaply, hopefully ingeniously.

**Builder** a person who builds. A master builder or building contractor, who employs all trades or categories of building craftsmen, including steel workers, pipefitters, assemblers, masons, bricklayers, plasterers, plumbers, and painters and for important building contracts works under the direction of an architect. The building contractor did not make his appearance until the late 18th Century; previously each craft worked under its own master.

**Building Code** the best that can be expected from the worst architect or engineer or the worst one can expect from the best architect or engineer.

**Building Constants** what S. Geidion called "constituent facts" that won't go away, such as the facts of climate, weight and support, materials, work, workmanship.

**Building Staff** body of persons carrying on work under a manager. Almost all building complexes today employ operational directors and maintenance staffs. These are often skilled engineers, designers, and facilities managers. They constantly inventory, manage, move, and control the building.

Traditionally buildings were attended by janitors and superintendents.

Building staffs exert considerable influence on building design. They exercise veto powers from preliminary design through final construction documents.

**Buttress** a vertical mass of masonry or brickwork, projecting at intervals from the external face of a wall, to resist the outward thrust of a vault or a roof-truss, or to stiffen the wall.

**Camber** the slight curved rise given to a beam of wide span or to the underside of a truss or "flat arch" to avoid sagging or the appearance of sagging.

**Cantilever** a beam projecting like a bracket from a wall, held down at one end either by the weight of the wall or some other means.

**Capital** the moulded or carved top of a column serving to concentrate the loads on the shaft from the beam or architrave above. The critical block between vertical support and horizontal weight.

**Cavetto** a concave moulding, approximately a quadrant in section.

**Cella** the central room of a Roman temple, excluding any portico or surrounding colonnades.

**Cheapness** low value, price, or charge. If a structural member is to be exposed it can serve two functions, that of support and as a visually meaningful element. If the cheapest, crudest structure is selected it may not be comprehensible. The cost of covering it and the time that it takes to do so is often more expensive than the few dollars paid for an element of higher cost and greater communicative value.

**Cladding** an old English term for clothing applied in modern architecture to a thin external covering of various materials over a hidden structure of other materials such as steel frames or reinforced concrete.

**Cloister** a covered walk or arcade in a monastery or college.

**Code (Building)** a systematic statement of a body of law, a system of principles and moral rules. Building codes are regulations, not laws. Regulations are guidelines. Almost all state, as a fundamental principle, that approved equivalents are acceptable. If requirements are met substitutions are possible.

For example, sprinkler systems, whether required or not, give added freedom in the stipulation of interior furnishings, finishes, carpeting, and materials that far outweighs the cost of the sprinklers. The possibility of exceeding code requirements for beneficial tradeoffs cannot be ignored.

**Coffering** a series of deep panels sunk in the surface of a ceiling, vault, or dome.

**Colonnade** a row of columns supporting an entablature.

**Colonnette** a small column.

**Column** a principal vertical supporting member of a building; a cylindrical and slightly tapered pillar, serving as a support to some portion of a building; a similar pillar standing isolated as a monument, such as Trajan's Column at Rome.

The column explains why the building stands. It defines and modulates space. It can generate rhythm and order. It explains the size of the building and its height by the particular size of its parts. Medieval masons could extrapolate the height of a cathedral by the thickness of its masonry walls and columns shown in plan.

**Column Bay** that part of the building, usually square or rectangular, defined by the column spacing. The column spacing establishes the flexibility of the design.

**Complex Products** consisting of complicated parts and multiple functions. Buildings are complex products, more complicated than irons, pencils, or toasters. Each is a unique, large, static object.

They are only seen as total compositions on the designer's drawing board. If they are to be comprehended they must be designed so that each element of utility will be reminiscent of itself and be seen to act in concert with the other interrelated elements.

**Comprehension** grasping with the intellect. A viewer's appreciation of a building is directly proportioned to his or her understanding of it.

**Consultant** (a) One who officially approves the architect's decisions. A second opinion the architect solicits to reinforce the client's confidence in the first. (b) One retained to do what the other can not. The client pays for both.

**Context** the act, process or manner of weaving parts into a whole; a structure so formed. The choice of materials during the act of building must respect place, time, and cost. The context may be interpreted as the product of the spirit of the times rather than matching building parts and materials in harmony with adjoining buildings.

**Corbusier** (Le Corbusier) pseudonym of Charles Edouard Jeanneret (1887–1965) Swiss architect who lived and worked mainly in France. He said, "A house is a machine for living," before machines that could build houses like machines for living were invented.

**Corner** place where converging sides or edges meet. The vertical and horizontal corners of the building skin are visually and thermally critical. A radius at vertical corners emphasizes the skin's continuity. Radius corners are also more economical to detail than corners at right angles and provide better thermal continuity.

The corner is a crossroad, junction, intersection, positive and negative (outside, inside). A corner is a sensitive juncture in the decision process, a turning point in the building.

**Cornice** a projecting horizontal feature, usually moulded, which crowns an external facade or occurs internally at the junction of a wall and a ceiling. In classical architecture it is the topmost member of the entablature.

**Corporate Image** an artificial imitation of the external form of a fictitious person created by charter, prescription, or act of the legislature. As an image—a form pretending to be a corporation logo.

The corporate image seeks to create an illusion of wealth and power, which is a difficult stylistic problem. The great diversity of images demonstrates the extent of the problem. The corporate image is not specific to any corporation. The one commonality is an impression of expensive materials and conspicuous consumption.

**Cost** the amount or equivalent paid or charged for something; the outlay or expenditure of effort or sacrifice made to achieve an object. Cost tempers all design decisions and choices.

**Cost Control** the power of directing the outlay of expenditures. If architects cannot create an aesthetic object within the cost control constraints of their client they should not term themselves architects.

**Course** a continuous layer of bricks or stones of equal thickness in a wall.

**Crenellation** notched or indented battlements. In feudal England licenses were issued "to crenellate," that is, fortify one's house.

**Crown** the highest point of a semicircular arch or vault which corresponds to the apex of a pointed arch.

**Curtain Wall** in medieval military architecture a length of wall between two towers or bastions. In a modern steel or reinforced concrete framed buildings it is a thin wall bearing no load, between or often in front of main structural members.

**Cyborg** (cybernetic + organism) a human being linked to one or more mechanical devices upon which some of his or her vital physiological functions depend. Architecture has moved from "a machine for living" to cyborgs in the atria. Before 1850, buildings were little more than structures enclosing space(s). Plumbing was minimal and there were no electrical or mechanical systems. Buildings simply sheltered. Some were small and modest, like houses. Others were grand, like churches. But despite impressive bulk even the grandest served simply to cover.

If there were machines in the building the building simply protected them from rain. But today's buildings are machines that shelter. Modern buildings have become complex cybernetic life support instruments.

The change from static to kinetic building systems in which human life in buildings is dependent on mechanical life support systems is the unique architectural development of our time.

**Cyma Recta** in classical architecture, a moulding which is concave above and convex below. Also called an *ogee moulding*.

**Cyma Reversa** in classical architecture a moulding which is the converse of the Cyma Recta, that is, convex above and concave below.

**Cymatium** in classical architecture, the crowning member of a cornice, usually in the form of a cyma recta or cyma reversa.

**Dado** the lower part of a wall to a height of 3 or more feet above floor level. Usually capped with a moulding which can be the chair or dado rail. In classical architecture, the plain part of a pedestal between its base and its cornice.

**Decastyle** in classical architecture, a portico having ten columns in a row.

**Dentil** a small block used in rows, resembling a

row of teeth, in the cornices of Greek and Roman buildings for ornamental purposes.

**Design** the architect's graphical direction of an action. A set of strategies to direct the choices required to make a product, complex or simple, that will have commodity, firmness, and delight.

**Dialogue** conversation; exchange of proposals. Clients and users of buildings describe buildings in terms of other buildings. Their comments must be interpreted by the architect.

**Disconnection** breaking apart. Disconnection determines connection selection. The more easily connected the easier to disconnect. The test of an adjustable assembly is an ability to come apart.

**Distyle** in Greek architecture, a portico having two columns.

**Dome** a convex roof of approximately hemispheric form, erected over a square, octagonal, or circular space in a building. A *saucer dome* has a flat curve, less than a hemisphere. Domes may be constructed wholly or partially of stone, brick, concrete, reinforced concrete, hollow tiles, steel, wood, or aluminum framing and may be covered externally with lead, copper, or other materials.

**Door** a movable barrier closing the entrance to a building or a room. It may be hinged at the side, or pivoted at top and bottom, or made to slide. It may be secured by locks, latches, or bolts. Doors are made of wood, steel, glass, and in ancient tombs were made of stone, and the doors of the Pantheon in Rome were made of bronze.

**Dormer** a vertical window projecting from the sloping roof of a house, having vertical sides and a flat or sloping roof.

**Eaves** the plural of *eave,* but the singular is seldom used. The eave is the lower edge of a sloping roof, overhanging the face of the wall. There is normally a gutter fixed to the eaves to carry water off the roof to the downspout which takes it down and away from the building.

**Echinus** in classical architecture, a covered or ovolo moulding beneath the abacus of a Doric capital.

**Egg and Dart Moulding** in classical architecture, an ornament carved on an ovolo moulding and consisting of alternate eggs and arrowheads.

**Electrical** related to or operated by electricity. The building's electrical systems perform two major purposes: to provide power and to light. The source is usually the city or electric utility, which supplies power through transformers.

**Emphasis** that which makes greater, expands, in amount, importance, intensity. Each component, connection, fastening of the building must look like it is doing what it does more than it does when it is doing what it does normally.

**Engaged Column** a column which is partially built into a wall, usually for half of its diameter.

**Enneastyle** in classical architecture, a portico which has nine columns in a row.

**Enrichment** the decoration of surfaces and architectural features with carved, modelled, or painted ornament.

**Entablature** a member laid flat upon a table or other support. In classical architecture, the arrangement of three horizontal members, architrave, frieze, and cornice, above the supporting columns in any of the classical orders.

**Energy Conservation** the saving of natural power vigorously exerted. Mechanical plants are best separated from the mass or balance of the building. Large equipment can thus be easily removed and newer equipment plugged in. These changes should take minimal time, preferably less than a day. This allows a rapid upgrading of heating and cooling equipment. At the present state of improvement the owner will recoup the cost of new equipment through saved energy expenses in two or three years.

"Passive solar energy" is in fact active. Water is heated and stored; a secondary system must be installed at considerable capital cost. Both passive and active solar heating systems are costly additions to normal heating and cooling. For example, concrete walls for thermal mass instead of steel studs and dry wall will add extra cost to the building. Walls in front of windows, a popular means of collecting solar heat, are questionable, as are huge water cylinders or an entire basement filled with six feet of water in which the owner cannot swim. If building materials are properly selected active mass thermal storage can be achieved at no additional cost without the above listed inconveniences.

**Engineer (Renaissance)** a designer and builder of engines. During the Renaissance and Middle Ages, architecture included all of what we now term engineering. The word *ingeniarius* appeared in the late Middle Ages and was applied to the makers of *ingenia,* ingenious devices, usually military. The two terms were interchangeable, and those engaged in design and building were awarded either title. A man might specialize in a branch of architecture, as millwright, "conductorr of waters", or a master of ordinance and fortification. But all ingeniarii were ready to design and build conventional buildings.

**Err** make a mistake; sin. At least five million pieces are needed to create a modest modern building. The architect must put each in its proper place, a heroic effort that is liable to heroic failure. No building is perfect nor are its architects. Perfection is a religious, not an architectural term.

**Entasis** in classical architecture, the almost imperceptible and subtle convex tapering of a column to correct the optical illusion of concavity created by simple tapering.

**Fabric** something made by a craftsman; a building. More precisely, the structure of a building.

**Facing** the materials used for the external face of a wall when the core of the wall is of other material.

**Factory** building and equipment for manufacturing. The benefits of producing building elements in the factory, rather than on site, are speed and cost. On-site assembly requires from one-third to one-half more time than factory work. Factory labor is cheaper and more efficient, and the men and women work under controlled conditions. On-site the workmen work in the extremes of temperature without benefit of factory machinery.

**Factory Potential** industrial production possibilities. The architect makes an investigation to determine how factory procedures and on site building practices can be improved to produce better, more usable products without additional cost.

**Fashion** the prevailing style. Fashionable buildings resemble each other. The originality of each designer is judged by how well he or she interprets the prevailing building fashion. In this way art stays fashionable and fashion becomes art.

**Fenestration** the arrangement of windows in a building facade. Facades and thermodynamic barriers create different fenestration patterns. Facades are designed to create a pleasing street pattern with emphasis on the building's exterior. A ther-

modynamic barrier is designed to assure the comfort of the building's occupants by random facade penetrations as interior light is required.

**Fitments** all forms of furnishings and finishes and hardware, such as miscellaneous metal handrails, exit lights, posts, doors, nonstructural partitions.

**Finial** an ornamental feature placed on top of a pinnacle or at the base and apex of a gable.

**Flemish Bond** a brickwork bond in which headers and stretchers are laid alternately in every course.

**Floor** the undersurface inside a room or a storey of a house. In England the "first floor" is not the lowest above ground level; that is the "ground floor," and the "first floor" is the next storey above it.

**Fluting** the making of shallow and narrow concave grooves or flutes on columns or pilasters.

**Flying Buttress** a stone buttress in Gothic architecture in the shape of an arched prop that supports at one end the main wall of the building and at the other springs from a pier. Its purpose is to counter the thrust of the arches in the building and channel them to the ground through the pier.

**Fontana, Domenico** (1543–1607) Italian architect. Chief architect of Pope Sixtus. Made important extensions to the Vatican, Lateran, and Quirinal palaces. He erected the huge Egyptian obelisk in the Piazza di San Pietro in 1586 and wrote a book about the accomplishment. In 1590 he proposed to turn the Colosseum in Rome into a factory. The idea was rejected by Pope Sixtus, who dismissed him as architect. Fontana went to Naples and began building a royal palace in 1600.

**Footings** the projecting courses of brick or stone

at the base of a wall arranged to distribute the weight over a greater area of soil.

**Form Follows Function** a truism that forces architects to find functions for preconceived forms.

**Fornix** in Latin, an arch or arched basement. During Roman times, it was the custom of prostitutes to ply their trade in underground vaults which had overhead an arch or fornix, which mutely watched the girls performing. With a shift of sense, from fornix first came the name for a brothel (I'll meet you at the fornix), then a verb meaning "to frequent a brothel" (fornicari), and then the name of the pudendous activity conducted there—fornication. (Freeman, *The Story Behind the Word*, ISI Press, Philadelphia, 1985, p. 138.)

**Forum** a central open public space surrounded by public buildings, often with colonnades in Roman cities.

**Fragmentation** breaking into fragments. A building is composed of groups of parts or components. The components of a modern building can be designated as:

1. Structure—that which takes loads.
2. Mechanical—heating, cooling, ventilation, and humidification.
3. Electrical—transformers, power step-down switch gear, distribution, lighting, and controls.
4. Plumbing—clean water in, dirty water out. The systems of piping and venting and fixtures connected to the piping.
5. Skin—the thermodynamic enclosure, the external walls and roof. The envelope is defined by the current program.
6. Fitments—the interior, non-load-bearing partitions, both horizontal and vertical. The furniture, cabinets, and equipment, rails, stairs.

This could be another fragment, but is here because all can be movable without effect to other fragments.

**Frieze** in classical architecture, the middle member of the entablature in one of the orders. In a panelled room the frieze is the space between the top of the panelling and the cornice or ceiling.

**Function** an activity proper to a person or institution; an act or activity by which a thing fulfills its purpose.

**Function Zone** a subdivision of activity regions. Function zones have a high transformation capability, such as rooms that are linked as a department or operate as laboratories or offices. The designer searches for similar movement zones connecting function zones for entry and exit to and from common spaces.

**Gable** the vertical triangular portion of wall at the end of a ridged roof, from the eaves level to the apex.

**Gargoyle** in medieval buildings a stone spout, delivering water downward and outward from a parapet gutter. The end of the gargoyle was often carved to represent a grotesque head or beast.

**Girder** a primary load-carrying beam of timber, steel, reinforced concrete.

**Glass** a substance, usually transparent, hard, and brittle. Glass is a poor thermodynamic barrier but a wonderful air barrier. A transparent building skin allows light in and people to view out. It can also provide tremendous heat gain on winter days when the building is fully occupied. At night the heat passes back outside but the people have gone home. Glass can cause a major heat load problem in summer. The ideal solution is a white opaque box for summer and a black opaque box for winter. Build-ings cannot be colored seasonally, so glass is used to mitigate between these two extremes. The designer balances environmental quality and the humanity of the work space. Energy costs should not always win.

**Gravity** the attractive force by which bodies tend to move to the center of the earth; staidness. Humankind's struggle to develop buildings has been a struggle against one powerful enemy, gravity. All things, as Talbot Hamlin pointed out, left to themselves fall to the ground unless supported. Humans build hollow spaces in which to live, worship, or meet protected from rain and cold. Support of the closing elements of the hollow space has always been a major challenge. The various solutions to this problem have given rise to the most characteristic architectural forms.

**Groin** in vaulting, the line of intersection of two vaults.

**Hadrian** Roman emperor (A.D. 117–138) who was an amateur architect. He was incensed by the sarcastic criticism of his official architect, Apollodorus. He first banished him then had him executed.

**Historic Restoration** bringing back to an original state. Historic restoration is a specific recycling activity. It simply takes out the excrescences that have been added to a building over the years, refurbishes, then installs dignified mechanical and electrical equipment as unobtrusively as possible.

Because of a love of history people are willing to conduct 20th Century lives in refurbished antiquated buildings.

**Hollow Core** concrete plank, a post-tensioned concrete spanning member, 6, 8, 12 or 15 inches deep with large openings running through its long direction. A 12-inch hollow core plank can be designed to span up to 50 feet and can be used in spans as limited as 35 or less.

An efficient combination of mechanical ducts and heat distribution is achieved in 12″ or greater plank by using the cores of hollow floor planks as air delivery and return systems. Concrete has the unique ability to absorb heat quickly in its first 1½ to 4 inches of depth and no surface is more than two inches away from the core. Hollow core planks are efficient active mass thermal storage device.

**Haunch** the lower part of an arch.

**Hellenic Architecture** Greek architecture from about 700 B.C. to about 323 B.C., which was the date of the death of Alexander the Great.

**Hellenistic Architecture** the architecture that prevailed from Alexander the Great's death onwards. Also termed the *Graeco-Roman* period.

**Heptastyle** a classical portico having seven columns in a row.

**Hexastyle** a classical portico having six columns in a row.

**Hip** the salient angle formed by the intersection of two sloping roof surfaces.

**Honnecourt, Villard** a French architect whose famous sketchbook is preserved in the Biblioteque Nationale, Paris and is believed to have designed the choir of St Quentin Cathedral consecrated in 1257.

**Hypocaust** a place heated from below. In Roman buildings, a system of hot-air heating from a furnace below ground level.

**Hypostyle Hall** in ancient temples a large hall

with its roof resting on columns, such as the Temple of Ammon at Karnak in Egypt.

**Illuminating Engineer** an engineer who deals with light. Light must define and explain structure, floor, walls, roof, and all the building's surfaces. It must do this to reinforce a chosen architectural attitude, just as light establishes character and mood in theater. The general illumination of the building parts is not enough. Light must not only illuminate with character, it must do it safely.

**Illusion** deception; delusion; misapprehension of the true state of affairs. The community either understands a building or it does not. They determine if it is artful or not. The worth of the building is determined by the people who use it and live around it, none of whom are architectural critics or art historians or read the work of critics or historians.

**Image** a solid fantasy. Sometimes people cannot see or understand what they are looking at, so it is necessary for the architect to create an image of it which, although unreal, describes what is real.

**Industrial Design** skill and guile related to industry. Architects in an industrial society must understand and work with machines and the industrial systems that use and their products if images suitable to the age and understandable to the people of the time are to be fashioned.

**Intelligent Building** a building that is fully rented.

**Intent** purpose. When we speak of the intent of a building as structure it is to mark out and clarify the limits of space. If the building's structure is comprehensible, it will define forces and express building space.

For example, if the designer is to express the building's attitude, a steel truss must not only per-

form its structural function but express an intent beyond building support. It must have an "attitude," an intent.

**Intrados** the inner curve or underside or soffit of an arch.

**Isodorus of Miletus** (Sixth Century A.D.) the architect, jointly with Anthemius of Tralles, of the church of Saint Sophia at Constantinople (A.D. 532–7).

**Jeanneret,** Charles Edouard; Le Corbusier.

**Joinery** the lighter woodwork of a building, as distinguished from carpentry, which is the heavier, structural woodwork. Joinery includes windows, doors, staircases, skirtings, panelling, cupboards, and the like. Most of this work is often done in the factory and called *millwork*.

**Joist** a synonym for beam. It is generally the member that supports the floor or roof. The size of a steel joist is determined by its depth in relation to its span. The same depth can vary from light to medium to heavy steel members. Light joists are generally used. Where floor loading is heavier the builder switches to heavier joists.

**Keenberg** He always wanted to be in a glossary.

**Keystone** the wedge-shaped central voussoir of an arch.

**Kinetics** the science of motion; the sense of constant building movement; the realization that buildings are not static.

**King-Post Truss** a truss having an upright king-post from the tie-beam to the ridge.

**Le Corbusier** see **Corbusier.**

**Lighting** illumination; an artificial supply of light or the appearance of providing it. The function of a lighting fixture is to give light. The architectural question is the purpose the light serves. Is it for walking in a corridor? for a classroom? working on computers? lighting the track in a field house or a street?

Light must be more than light and the choice of lamps, their placement and number, generates a building attitude.

**Lintel** a piece of stone, timber, steel, or concrete laid horizontally across a doorway or window opening to carry superimposed loads.

**Loggia** a covered gallery, verandah, or portico open on at least one side. A porch in the U.S.

**Louver** a ventilator, usually in the form of a turret, fixed on the roof-ridge of a medieval hall or of a church or an opening in a wall or window frame. In either case it is fitted with inclined slats to allow the passage of air and the exit of smoke without admitting rain or wind.

**Machicolation** in medieval military architecture, a series of openings in a stone parapet, through which missiles or boiling liquid could be dropped on the heads of assailants beneath. Introduced to western Europe from the East, after the crusades.

**Maintenance** (mechanical systems) maintaining or being maintained. Mechanical systems and operable valves in a modern building are constantly maintained and adjusted. Successful architectural designs make them accessible without disruption to other activities.

Equipment is better tended by building operating staffs when it is easily accessible. When ceilings must be removed or people must go outside in cold or hot weather, the equipment is not as well maintained. The building's mechanical equipment is like an automobile. It requires lubrication, tuning, and replacement of parts.

**Machine Craft** skill in managing the assemblage of parts that transmit forces, motion, and energy in a predetermined manner. Modern architectural designers must understand machines and factory process. The designer crafts through directing machines and/or their operators. The art in machine craft comes from the designer's direction, not the operator's hands.

Machines can do what people cannot, or can do in minutes what people do in months. Handcraft has largely disappeared from the construction site. Workmen are assemblers. Industrial products are complex and dominate the building site. Architects are therefore industrial designers.

Machines are operated by machine operators who are skilled caretakers of the machine's functions. There are machines operated by computers programmed by systems engineers, and even more complex machines (robots) that are operated by self-programming computers.

Certain skills are peculiar to people and some peculiar to machines. If the machine is forced to perform awkwardly the forms will be ugly and costly.

**Management** the act of supervising. Controlling cost, time, and especially the client. The objective of management is power.

**Mass Production** dense aggregation of objects produced in large quantities. A continuing goal of architects and designers is to mass produce houses like automobiles. This goal has eluded them since the idea was first introduced by Walter Gropius in 1913.

**Materials** the elements, constituents, or substances of which something can be made.

**Mechanical Systems** the systems of parts and motors that service environmental conditions. There are two major divisions: one is plumbing and the other is heating, cooling, ventilating, and humidification. This part of the building moves in constant response to human functions and human comfort.

**Megaron** In classical literature the megaron has several related meanings, and in modern works on architecture it is used for a particular type of building. This was essentially an oblong room or hall, deeper than it was wide, with an entrance on one of the short sides, usually a porch formed by continuations of the walls of the long sides.

**Membrane** a pliable, sheetlike connective tissue. The building is covered by a thermodynamic wrapping including walls, floors, and roof.

**Metope** a square space between the triglyphs on the frieze of the Greek Doric order.

**Movement** change of place or position. Buildings are alive with active parts pushing air and power. Movement tells time. Electricity flashes by in milliseconds, the building stone may take centuries to corrode. Electrical switch boxes with lights going on and off are small power festivals letting passers by know these are the poles and sub-hubs of power. The sight of electrical "stuff" coming through step-down transformers is a significant building event. Architecture is an inert stage for great activity of people and machines.

**Mouldings** ornamental and continuous lines of grooving or projections, worked respectively below or above a plane surface. In each historical phase or period of architecture the mouldings are distinctive in design and rigorously defined by practice and

rule. It is possible to estimate the approximate date of a building from its mouldings. Greek mouldings, concave or convex, are formed from conic sections. Roman mouldings are segments of a circle.

**Movement Zone** change of place or position. The movement zone is the zone of distribution of people mechanical and electrical services.

**Naos** the sanctuary of a Greek temple.

**Narthex** a large porch or vestibule across the entrance end of a basilican church. Access to the narthex was permitted to women and noncommunicants.

**Nave** the body of a church, often with aisles.

**Obelisk** a tall, tapering shaft, square on plan, generally monolithic and of granite, often used in pairs at the entrance to ancient Egyptian temples. The tallest in Egypt are about 100 feet. Many were brought to Europe and re-erected. Of these the most famous are in St. Peter's Piazza, Rome (83 feet high).

**Obsolete** disused, discarded, antiquated. Rapid change is a normal condition of the 20th Century. Social patterns, technical developments, economic growth or decline that in the past required three or four hundred years to coalesce today complete full cycles in twenty years. If buildings cannot accommodate this pattern of change they must be discarded. Modern buildings of the 1950s are now obsolete. The cost of adjusting them to contemporary work and social patterns exceeds the cost of new construction. Systems, components, or elements designed to plug in and out, bolt on and off allow obsolete arrangements or parts to be replaced without discarding the entire structure.

**Octastyle** in classical architecture, a portico which has eight columns in a row.

**Orders of Architecture** the term *orders* used today in reference to Greek, Roman, and Renaissance architecture appears to have been first introduced into English about 1563, when the manual on architecture by Vitruvius came into general use, in a translation from the Latin. Vitruvius used the words "dorico genere," not "dorico ordine," to describe the Doric order.

In brief, his system provides rules for architectural design based upon the proportions of three standard types of columns, together with their bases, capitals, and the entablature, which is the horizontal beams they support. These three types of columns are the Doric, Ionic, and Corinthian orders, named respectively after the three regions of Greece, Doris, Ionia, Corinthos, in which they originated.

The Doric order is the oldest and sturdiest of the three. Its fluted columns have a capital consisting of a flat abacus resting upon an echinus moulding. The entablature consists of three members: architrave, frieze, and cornice. The architrave is the lowest, the frieze is divided into square panels (metopes) by grooved triglyphs, representing in stone the ends of beams in primitive timber construction.

The Ionic order has a slender columns and a capital with spiral volutes beneath its abacus.

The Corinthian column, more slender still, has a capital decorated with carved leaves of acanthus. It was seldom used by the Greeks.

The Romans borrowed all three orders and made modifications in their design. They specially favored the Corinthian. They also introduced two additional types: the Tuscan order, a simplified order of the Doric, and the Composite order, a combination of Ionic and Corinthian.

The Roman types were revived during the Renaissance and later included in pattern-books of the orders which were printed in quantity in western Europe and later the U.S.

**Pantheon** a temple dedicated to all the gods; more specifically, the famous temple in Rome so dedicated, and built about 25 B.C.

**Parthenon** the famous temple at Athens dedicated to the goddess Athena Parthenos and built about 490 B.C. from the designs of the architects Ictinus and Callicrates. It measures about 100 × 230 feet and is regarded as the finest temple of the Greek Doric order.

**Pediment** in classical architecture, the triangular end or gable of a building with a low-pitched roof, which was sometimes filled with sculpture.

**Pentastyle** a Greek temple with a portico having five columns in a row.

**Peristyle** a row of columns around a building or a courtyard.

**Permanence** directly proportional to the building's ability to change economically. Research indicates an average building 40 years old has had alterations made to it amounting to three times its original cost. Based on the present rate of change projected 40 years into the future, these figures may well exceed ten times the building's cost today.

**Pier** in architecture an independent solid mass of stone, brick, or concrete which supports a vertical load or the thrust of an arch.

**Pilaster** a flat column against the face of a wall, usually engaged, that is, built into the wall, projecting from the wall a distance not exceeding one third of its surface breadth. A Greek pilaster is called an *anta*.

**Pile** pointed stake or post; heavy beam driven vertically into ground for support; large quantity.

**Pillar** a slender, vertical structural member bearing a load. A wooden pillar is generally called a *post*. A pillar may be square, oblong, polygonal, or circular in section. The *column* is always circular.

**Pinnacle** a small ornamental feature terminating either in pyramidal or conic form on the top of a Gothic buttress. Also serves a structural purpose by counteracting the outward thrust of a vault or roof-truss.

**Pirate** nautical architect.

**Plinth** the square or moulded projecting member at the base of a wall or column.

**Plumbing** the apparatus concerned with the distribution of water in buildings: clean water in under pressure, dirty water out by gravity.

**Podium** in classical architecture, either the square member forming the lowest stage of a column pedestal or a continuous base or platform under a building.

**Portico** a roofed space, open on one side at least, and enclosed by a range of columns which also support the roof. A portico may stand free, but usually forms part of a building.

**Post** a stout and long piece of timber, usually square or cylindrical in section, erected in a vertical position to support some part of the substructure of a building.

**Pozzolana** a volcanic ash found near Rome possessing special qualities which largely accounted for the excellence of Roman mortar and concrete.

One of these was its ability to combine with lime and create a hydraulic cement.

**Precast Concrete** concrete that is cast in the form of a structural element before being placed in the building. Although the material is concrete its site connections are similar to steel, as are its erection characteristics. Precast concrete must be supported by beams. Steel and precast concrete are dry, and both can be made in large elemental pieces at the factory; they lend themselves to high speed site erection with cranes and few connections.

**Prestressed and Post-Tensioned Concrete-** concrete precompressed in the zone where tensile stresses occur under load. Consequently, cracking of the concrete due to tension is avoided. The usual technique is to tension tendons of high-tensile steel in the concrete. Prestressing is classified as pre-tensioned or post-tensioned depending on whether the tendons were tensioned before or after the concrete has hardened.

**Professional Prerogative** exclusive right or privilege; the right of the professional to be wrong.

**Program** descriptive notice of a series of events. Buildings are not designed as auto/diesel shops or research laboratories. They are designed as buildings capable of accommodating these functions. The design concept is of a building that can perform a general function, and specific aspects of the building are modified to accommodate the particular demands of the user's functional program.

**Pronaos** in a Greek or Roman temple, a vestibule in front of the doorway to the sanctuary (the *naos*), enclosed by side walls and with columns in front.

**Propylaea** a structure erected in front of an entrance gateway; the specific name of such a structure on the Acropolis at Athens, built 437–432 B.C.

**Proportion** the relation of one part to another or to the whole. Architectural proportions convert engineering calculations to the visual proportions of architecture. The architectural element must feel visually correct, for the physical proportion established mathematically may appear to be incorrect.

**Purpose** a utility or end to be attained; the product intended.

**Pylon** originally a gate tower, then more specifically one of the tall tapered towers flanking the entrance to an ancient Egyptian temple.

**Quadra** in classical architecture, the plinth of a podium.

**Quadriga** a chariot drawn by four horses abreast.

**Quality** a degree of excellence. Quality is controlled by design intent, not cost. It is, however, a uniform judgment. A brick veneer over shoddy construction lacks quality. Cost determines the range of material. The best material for the price is useless without the best method of application for the price.

**Quirk** a sharp-edged groove or hollow moulding between two other mouldings.

**Quoin** the large corner stones used at the angle, often of dressed stone when the rest of the wall is of rubble masonry. In brick walls strength is added to the wall by inserting stones at the angles.

**Recycle** convert to a previous stage, especially converting waste to usable material. Buildings are modified and recycled quickly and economically to hold their a position at the leading edge of technology and service.

Recycling takes existing warehouses of no particular historic value and changes them into apartment blocks and office spaces.

Human adaptability allows cities to maintain their historic memorabilia yet provide reasonable functional space for new uses. Most of the buildings recycled were never designed to be recycled. Different functional uses were not anticipated. Their designers could not have foreseen sophisticated communication equipment, energy conservation, and HVAC systems.

**Reeding** the decoration of a surface by a series of parallel convex mouldings of equal width; the opposite of fluting.

**Registration** (architectural) the act of registering. The term *architect* is derived from *architekton*, chief craftsman, which in Latin became *architectus*. In modern practice, an architect is a person qualified to design buildings and to supervise their erection. In Greek and Roman times the architect's status was fully recognized. His duties were described in detail by Vitruvius. During the Middle Ages the title was seldom used; architects were described as *master* in English, *magister* in Latin, *maestro* in Italian and Spanish, *maistre* in Old French, and *baumeister* in German.

The status of the architect came to be more precisely defined during the 17th and 18th Centuries, and in 1834 the foundation of the Royal Institute of British Architects established a recognized standard of qualification. The American Institute of Architects was organized toward the latter part of the 1830s but did not become active until the 1880s. Architects were registered in England in 1838. Registration varies in North America, with different states having different requirements.

**Reveal** the side of a doorway or window opening, insofar as it is revealed, that is, not covered by the door frame or window frame.

**Ridge** of a roof, either the line of intersection produced by the two sides of a sloping or pitched roof, or the piece of timber known as the *ridge-piece* along the line of the ridge.

**Romano,** Giulio (1499–1546) painter and architect. Drained the marshes at Mantua, restored the medieval cathedral, embellished the medieval castle, and began building his masterpiece, the Palazzo del Te, in 1524.

**Roof** upper covering of house or building or room.

**Skin** the external limiting layer. The skin is the building's thermodynamic layer, enclosing it with walls and roof. These edges are defined by the original building program. The skin is not permanent. It must be designed to expand as pressures for more space build within the building and to contract as these pressures lessen. Therefore the materials of the skin must be selected carefully so that additions do not appear to be additions and contractions do not seem amputations.

**Smoke** visible, volatile products of burning. Smoke detection and ionizing systems are critical for safety. They get people out of the building before a fire becomes life threatening.

**Specification** detailed description of construction, workmanship, and materials. A carefully worded document describing the designer's minimum expectations and the contractor's maximum intentions.

**Steel** a commercial iron that contains carbon. Steel offers the architect choices, first of shapes, second of assembling shapes to make beams, trusses, columns, and connections.

**Structure** the manner in which a building or organism or other complete whole is constructed. Architectural structure takes the loads, defines and modulates space, and through size creates the correct scale, grain, and texture as it provides visual comprehension of the building's size, permanence, and value. Structure is more than the capability to support and span as defined by the building codes. The building may use primary, secondary, and tracery structure. That is, there may be structures within structures. The structural material will determine the speed of erection, the type of connection, the cost of transportation, and the varying degrees of texture that can be developed.

Engineering structure is to stand and withstand all the forces anticipated by the building code in any given region.

**Style** manner of doing. The style and taste of each time is different but the underlying principles of design remain the same whether the building is constructed of mortar and stone or is a steel framed auto/diesel shop. The fascination of architecture is in how each age finds ways to shape materials into buildings that express the unique temper of its times.

**Stylobate** a continuous basement or platform beneath a row of columns. Usually it is composed of three steps, in which case only the top step is the stylobate and the three together constitute a *crepidoma.*

**Tablinum** in ancient Greek and Roman houses, a room having one side open to the atrium, or central courtyard.

**Technology** the continually changing system by which a society provides its members with those things needed or desired. Technology plays a more important role in architecture than it does in any other art. Architecture is to a large extent domi-nated by laws independent of the designer's personality. It is so extremely complex and varying that specialists must be employed by the architect for many of its various aspects.

**Temenos** a sacred enclosure or precinct surrounding a temple.

**Terra-Cotta** burned earth; a hard, burnt-clay product used for wall-facings and architectural details. Glazed it is called *Faience.* Terra-cotta was largely used by the Etruscans.

**Tetrastyle** in classical architecture a portico having four columns in a row.

**Thermae** a public bathing establishment erected by the later Roman emperors, especially in Rome.

**Thrust** the downward and outward pressure or force exerted by a dome, vault, arch, roof-truss, or other structural member upon its supporting walls or piers. It was counteracted in medieval buildings by buttresses.

**Time** the measured or measurable period during which an action, process, or condition exists or continues. Timelessness in architecture is a paradox. It can only be measured in a building's ability to transform itself. The ability to change is the governing factor, for timelessness is not determined by how long a building stands but by how long it remains useful.

**Tools** mechanical instrument for working on something. Assembly should be designed for simple tools and obvious connections so assemblers can readily comprehend the logic of the work. Workmen who understand their tasks build well.

**Torus** a large convex moulding.

**Trabeated** a term applied to Greek architecture to contrast it with the arcuated buildings of Roman, Romanesque, and Gothic builders. Egyptian architecture is also trabeated.

**Transparency** transmitting rays of light so that bodies behind can be distinctly seen. When part of the building facade is transparent, then that part of the building behind the windows must be designed as part of the facade. Transparency is used to expose the structure, which should be as comprehensible from the exterior as it is from the interior. It is used to display mechanical parts and the configuration of building spaces within.

**Transformation** change of form. Flexibility, modification, change of function, change of use, change of technology, using plug-in and plug-out, expansion and contraction.

**Triglyph** in the frieze of the Greek Doric order, a slightly projecting block having three grooves or channels on its face.

**Trophy** originally, in classical times, a monument celebrating a military victory and displaying captured arms or spoils. This later became a carved festoon or swag incorporating martial or triumphal symbols or tokens. An architectural medal for fellowship or excellence.

**Utility** usefulness. The architect works with form, mass, and color, as does the sculptor and painter. But the architect solves practical problems and architecture is therefore a functional art. Utility forms part of our judgment of it. The function of buildings is to bring utility and pleasing sensual order to human surroundings.

**Vault** a continuous arch of brick, stone, or concrete, forming a self-supporting structure over a building or a part of it. The principle of the vault was known in Babylonia and Egypt but was rapidly developed to a much greater degree of efficiency by the Romans.

**Vestibule** an entrance hall, antechamber, or lobby.

**Vitruvius** (Marcus Vitruvius Pollio—First Century B.C.) a Roman architect in government service during the reign of the Emperor Augustus. He dedicated his books on architecture and building construction, *De Re Architectura,* to Augustus.

**Volute** the spiral scroll which forms the distinctive feature in the capital of the Ionic order.

**Voussoir** one of the stones forming part of an arch. Being wedge shaped they transfer stresses around the arch and make it self-supporting.

**Wide Flange Beam** common rolled steel section descended from railroad track manufacture. An early nostalgic reminder of the uniqueness of machine craft.

**Window** opening in a wall or roof of a building. Window shopping—looking for pleasure. Window dressing—adroit presentation, superficial.

**Workforce** person or group who exerts strength or faculties to do or perform a task. Today's architect inherits a workforce prepared for well over two centuries. Today's worker, the assembler, is a product of the systematic "rationalization" of labor, dividing manufacture into discreet tasks.

The division of labor replaces craft skills with the performance of a single task. It works against the generalized distribution of knowledge of the production process among all participants. The division of labor creates two extremes: at one is those whose time is infinitely valuable (the designer), and at the other those whose time is worth almost nothing.

at the other those whose time is worth almost nothing.

**Wrench** instrument made to turn nuts and bolts. The wrench is a tool of the assembler of industrial products, as hammer and nail, brick and mortar, iron and rivet were the symbols of pre-industrial handcraft societies. The wrench fastens and unfastens and is the enemy of permanence. To wrench is to change.

**Wainscot** interior wood panelling.

**Wattle and Daub** a primitive vertical covering formed of interlacing twigs or branches called *wattles,* roughly plastered with clay, termed *daub.*

**Wotton, Sir Henry** diplomat and author of a much quoted little book termed *The Elements of Architecture* (1624).

**Xystus** in classical architecture, an enclosure or colonnade or portico used for athletic exercises and recreation.

**Zone** area enclosed. There are three kinds of zone. Functional zones are the spaces where the building functions are performed. The movement zone is single- or multistoried, defined by a fixed structural grid. If the building is more than one story, the movement zone will vary from two to four stories in height, with a three-dimensional movement of people, goods, and mechanical and electrical services. There are sometimes special zones, required spaces that cannot be properly accommodated within the framework of functional spaces—for example, swimming pools, theaters, hockey arenas.

**Zophorus** in classical architecture, a frieze decorated with sculptured animal forms.

# Index